Laurie Woolever is a writer, editor, public speaker and former cook. For nearly a decade, she worked with the late author, TV host and producer Anthony Bourdain. She has written for the *New York Times*, *Vogue*, *GQ*, *Food & Wine*, *Bloomberg* and others, edited Anthony Bourdain's *Les Halles Cookbook* (2004), and then spent several years as an editor at *Art Culinaire* and *Wine Spectator*. She also co-authored *Appetites: A Cookbook* with Anthony Bourdain, *World Travel: An Irreverent Guide*, and wrote *Bourdain: The Definitive Oral Biography*, all *New York Times* bestsellers.

Care and Feeding

A Memoir

Laurie Woolever

affirm press

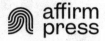

First published in Australia in 2025 by Affirm Press,
a Simon & Schuster (Australia) Pty Limited company
Bunurong/Boon Wurrung Country
28 Thistlethwaite Street, South Melbourne VIC 3205

Affirm Press is located on the unceded land of the Bunurong/Boon Wurrung peoples of
the Kulin Nation. Affirm Press pays respect to their Elders past and present.

New York Amsterdam/Antwerp London Toronto Sydney/Melbourne New Delhi
Visit our website at www.simonandschuster.com.au

AFFIRM PRESS and design are trademarks of Affirm Press Pty Ltd, Inc.,
used under licence by Simon & Schuster, LLC.

First published in the United States of America by Ecco,
an imprint of HarperCollins Publishers

10 9 8 7 6 5 4 3 2 1

A Cataloguing-in-Publication entry for this book is available
from the National Library of Australia

 A catalogue record for this
book is available from the
NATIONAL LIBRARY National Library of Australia
OF AUSTRALIA

9781923293267 (paperback)
9781923293922 (ebook)

Cover design by Allison Saltzman
Cover photograph © Christopher Testani/GalleryStock
Internal design by Renata De Oliveira
Proudly printed and bound in Australia by the Opus Group

MIX
Paper from
responsible sources
FSC® C001695

This book is for my parents, who gave me a wide-enough berth to take the leaps and make the mistakes; and for my son, who is the best reason to keep doing both.

Contents

Introduction

I graduated from college in 1996 and moved to New York with three things: a vague ambition to be a published writer, a yawning desire for validation, and a love of feeding others. My parents had taught me to keep my head down and do my work, accept what's offered, show up early, be polite, become indispensable. Beyond all that, I didn't have much of a plan for the rest of my life.

I learned to cook at a professional level, so that I'd have something to write about, and a practical skill with which to earn a living. I had the good fortune to stumble into the food world at a time when cooking and eating became an increasingly respectable and well-documented form of mainstream entertainment. Thanks to even more good luck and timing, I had the benefit of two superstar mentors.

The first was the chef, restaurateur, and TV host Mario Batali, for whom I worked as an assistant for nearly four years. He already had a high profile, but was still at the beginning of a wildly successful expansion of his business empire. Working with Mario was exhilarating and educational, and it opened up a world of opportunities for me.

The second was chef-turned-author-turned-TV-host Anthony Bourdain, who was nearing the apex of some high-altitude professional mountaintops when he hired me, a new mother burned out on corporate media, as his assistant. The job got bigger and more re-warding in the nine years I worked with Tony (the only name by which he ever referred to himself), until his death by suicide in 2018.

In different ways, my two mentors, Mario and Tony, built their careers and reputations on the glamorous appeal of wild excess, and for a long time, this gave me a plausible excuse to live the same way, in order to be successful, get attention, and fill myself up with everything that the world had to offer.

Under the cover of "creating experiences" and "having a good time," but really to blunt my big feelings of inadequacy, anxiety, and ennui, I became a self-destructive binge drinker and chronic pot smoker, dabbling in pills and cocaine. There were a few unambiguous alcoholics in my family, sure, but I didn't see myself that way; it took me a very long time to recognize the pathology in my own behavior. I almost always had a job, and when I occasionally fucked something up, I never considered my addictions to be a factor, and only rarely admitted to myself that they were addictions at all. I'd succeeded at becoming a published writer, and along the way I became a wife and mother. I was never arrested (because I was lucky), never crashed a car (because I stopped driving), or fell down a staircase (because I lived in a ground-floor apartment).

Every time I drank or got high, I was trying to re-create the ex-perience of chugging my first wine cooler and inhaling my first bong hit, during which my brain and body were flooded with a sense of relief and escape, weightlessness, a soft and sparkling departure from my overwhelming adolescent concerns: social and academic pres-sure, boredom, body shame. Everything was funny, and nothing much mattered. My life wasn't particularly bad—it was an ordinary teen life—but these readily available substances felt like a seductive shortcut to happiness. As is the case for many addicts, my emotional growth hit a wall at about age twenty-one; in sobriety, I am now catching up, and growing up.

In his review of a book about the life and death of Tony Bourdain, *New York Times* critic Dwight Garner wrote, "Most human beings have more desires than opportunities in life. Those whom the gods will de-stroy are provided with desire and opportunity in equal measure."

This is my story of being a (relatively) high-functioning addict in a world of irresistible temptation, led by a desire to emulate the char-ismatic men who guided my career. I kept it together until several successive implosions—careers, marriages, reputations, lives—showed me that I am in control of almost nothing beyond how I choose to care for (and feed) myself and others.

Care and Feeding

chapter 1

Hayseed

"You look like a complete fucking hayseed," said the man conducting the job interview. "What's your story?"

My story is fuck you, I thought, then forced a polite little laugh and said, "I guess my story is that I just graduated from college, and I want to be a writer."

It was 1996: the Unabomber was in custody, the US economy was unstoppable, and all the girls were dancing to the AOL dial-up modem sound, wearing WonderBras and clear acetate pumps. I didn't think I was a hayseed until this man said it, but then it felt painfully true.

Sitting in this man's office, I was unaware of the actual, visible seeds in my hair, picked up earlier that day on the sprawling campus of Brooklyn Botanic Garden (BBG), where I was an intern. I wore an ill-fitting navy-blue pantsuit, which constituted the entirety of my job interview wardrobe. Each morning, while I raked and mulched and mowed and weeded outdoors, the suit's synthetic fabric greedily absorbed all the complicated scents inside the BBG employee locker room.

In college, I had tried to obscure my small-town roots with various gestures of world-weariness (reading Anaïs Nin, smoking unfiltered cigarettes, getting diagnosed with mild clinical depression), but here in midtown Manhattan, the man across the desk saw me for who I was: a shy, soft-bodied twenty-two-year-old with a limited skill set. He may not have seen that I loved getting drunk and high and watching cable television, that I wanted a creatively fulfilling career and to be passionately loved (or at least lavishly validated), and had no idea what to do about it.

After multiple fruitless interviews like this one, during which there were typing tests to fail, and unanswerable questions about my strengths, weaknesses, and proficiency with Lotus 1-2-3 and Excel, I got offered a receptionist job at a financial recruiting firm, whatever that meant. They told me that the "opportunity" was contingent on my "joining a gym," which I realized was code for losing weight, so I passed. I didn't yet understand why I had to be thinner (which is to say, more attractive) to answer phones and open mail in an office full of men.

I then had two promising interviews for a household cook job, first with an agency rep and then with the employer, who then hired someone with more experience. It was all quietly excruciating, especially having to go back to BBG each morning and weed-whack along Flatbush Avenue, while people drove by, occasionally throwing full diapers or almost-empty drink cans out their car windows.

I was living in an illegal basement apartment in deep south Brooklyn, beneath my landlord's own sprawling Victorian house, which he shared with his wife, their two teenagers, and a golden retriever named Billy, who was friendly and sweet, but also a loud and unpredictable nighttime barker. The best thing about the apartment was the rent, which was $350 a month. The bathroom was spacious and well lit, with pleasing pink tiles, and a pink toilet and sink, which I liked very much. The worst thing about it was everything else, especially that it was presently my home, inhabited by me.

The apartment was only marginally apartment-like, with weak fluorescent lighting mounted into a drop ceiling, held up by unpainted cinder-block walls. The spiders were bold and numerous; the mice were timid but made their numbers known by their copious leavings. It was, as befits a basement, dark and damp, even during the hottest and driest summer afternoons. On move-in day, my older sister drove me and my stuff down from our parents' house upstate, and within ten minutes of our arrival, she had an allergy attack so intense that she could barely breathe. She left, wheezing heavily, while most of my stuff was still stacked in the driveway.

Shortly after I moved in, there was a heavy rainstorm that sent rivulets of dirty water under the bolt-locked back door and into the nearby closet where I'd stacked my winter clothes and shoes and some books. Eventually, the puddles subsided, but, never having experienced a flood, I didn't fully grasp that all of my shit had gotten wet and would soon be engulfed by mildew.

There was no separate means of egress to the basement; to get in or out, I had to pass through the family's living room and front door. I tried to be discreet and polite with my comings and goings, even the one Sunday morning following an after-hours party at an East Village club called Save the Robots, where I discovered how much more vodka I could drink while on cocaine. My new jeans were wet with my own fresh pee, and I crept inside clutching a handbag into which I'd quietly vomited bile and peach-flavored Snapple on the train from Manhattan.

The landlord himself was neither discreet nor polite. One weekday morning as I exited up the stairs and through the living room to the front door, on my way to work, he was right there, a few feet from the basement door, naked except for his flip-flops, fastening a collar and leash around Billy the dog's furry golden neck. I said nothing, didn't make eye contact, just kept going, down the steps and onto the sidewalk, muttering, "Oh my god, oh my god," over and over, until I got to the subway platform. Again, this was 1996; I didn't have a cell phone, so it was just me, talking to myself about having seen my landlord's flaccid dick bobbling weakly in the morning light.

I wondered if he'd had a robe close at hand as I waited for the train. I thought about his long balls and his droopy little boobs as I raked up cut grass. I thought, again, just briefly, about his wrinkly dick during my lunch break, when I took a stack of quarters to the employee payphone and called my answering machine, to see if my recent manic resume-faxing would yield any new interviews or offers.

There were no messages, which made me feel like a bit of a failure. I didn't yet understand that, while I was lonely and broke, insecure and underemployed and without a clear vision of what success might look like, I was actually doing OK. I was alive, and I had a bachelor's degree. I had seen an unwanted dick in an unexpected place, so now I had that story to tell. I had an apartment and a job, such as they were. I had my friend and classmate Alejandro, who lived in Manhattan and already knew, from his adventures in the after-hours scene, how to get and, crucially, share, cocaine. And I already knew that, when drug-sick and still drunk on the train, it was best to vomit into your handbag, if you had the option.

Objectively, I understood that twenty-two was the correct age to eat shit at a poverty-wage job that I hated, while living in a wet hole in the ground. Still, I resentfully compared myself to those friends whom I knew to not be eating shit. They were comfortably, even happily, living with their parents for the summer or longer, maybe traveling in Europe or spending a month at the Cape. Some worked meaningless jobs, if they absolutely had to, while studying for the MCAT, GRE, LSAT, or GMAT, with full use of their parents' spare Volvos and Subarus. Others were interning in labs or law firms or non-profits. They had vision, these friends; they had ambition, a path, and came from slightly higher socioeconomic backgrounds than mine. My family was solidly middle class: my dad a pharmaceutical chemist who roto-tilled our garden and snowplowed our driveway; my mom a registered nurse who clipped coupons and colored her own hair.

I didn't want to go to grad school, and I didn't want to live in a rural suburb of Syracuse with my parents. Anyway, they were selling the house, because the company was closing my dad's lab and transferring him to New Jersey.

I had moved to New York City, where I figured I had the best shot at an interesting life that would take an as-yet-undetermined shape.

In the meantime, BBG was paying me $7 an hour for the thirty-hour-a-week internship, which would run through the end of the year. I worked from 8 a.m. to 2 p.m., with a thirty-minute lunch break. That summer, New York's brutal heat felt incompatible with BBG's mandatory uniform: long pants and a heavy-duty cotton shirt. Some days, I worked closely with one of the master gardeners, performing delicate maintenance on the rose bushes, which could be tedious, but was largely solitary and quiet, which I liked. Other days, I ran a push mower up and down the steep hills of the Japanese garden, or pitched straw in an expanse of open field, or picked up broken glass and empty chip bags along the park's perimeter. I was invited to take as many courses as I liked, for no tuition. I took zero courses.

Working at a big botanic garden would have been a great opportunity for someone who planned to make a career in horticulture. For me, it was the thin thread of economic security that gave me the courage to move to New York, and one in a series of "cool" jobs that I'd hoped would make me attractive to dudes who drove Saabs and smoked weed, which is to say, the only kinds of dudes I thought I liked. I'd worked on farms, was a clerk at Collegetown Video, interned with a non-profit called Green Guerillas, and now, Brooklyn Botanic Garden. None of this work had had an appreciable impact on my anemic sex life. Rich hippie boys tended to like girls who didn't need to work at all, and now that I'd graduated, I lost contact with those boys, anyway. It was time to find an indoor job.

After several more sweaty late-afternoon interviews, I was hired as a receptionist for a public relations firm that promoted the interests and images of such clients as the Delaware Deli Meat Council and the Southeast Rutabaga Farmers Association. I quit the BBG internship and moved into a tiny, shabby two-bedroom apartment in Manhattan's East Village with the aforementioned Alejandro, who was working at a white-shoe insurance firm. We outfitted our living room with a cow-printed couch and a dressmaker's mannequin, both from a nearby thrift store. The day I vacated the Brooklyn apartment, I wrote a note to the landlord and placed it next to a neat collection of mouse turds by the kitchen sink. It said: "I saw you naked with your dog. This apartment floods and has rodents. Best regards."

In my new job, I sat at a desk facing the door, answering phones, receiving the occasional visitor, opening mail, and organizing and filing things. This was not difficult work, and I still managed to get plenty of it wrong. I couldn't master the intricacies of the interoffice phone transfer system, and had no gift for dressing myself in work-appropriate clothing.

A senior partner, Barbara, made this point quite plain one afternoon. She called me into her office, glanced in frank disgust at my chunky clogs, and said, "You need to dress neater."

I was wearing a loose, shapeless red sundress with big yellow flowers on it, and I suddenly, sickeningly realized that my ratty beige bra straps were wholly visible. "There's a Gap two blocks from here," she said. "Go get yourself some cute separates."

I did not want to buy or wear a tailored top in a fun print. I had no desire for a kicky shift or a slim pencil skirt. These clothes were uncomfortable and expensive and ugly and made me feel bad about my soft, undisciplined body. Feminine shoes hurt my feet. Barbara had made a reasonable, if blunt, request that I stop dressing like I was headed out on Phish tour, but standing in her office while she weighed and measured me with her eyes, I was mortified and angry. She was a monster, I thought, for daring to hold me to a standard, and the standard itself was monstrous, prioritizing aesthetic conformity over my personal comfort.

To solve the problem of being a shabbily dressed working woman in a hostile world, I started layering a sweater over my flimsy dresses, which hid my armpits and bra straps, and I put my interview suit into heavy rotation. I drank every day after work with Alejandro, who also hated his job, to which he wore a full-on suit and tie, shiny shoes, black socks. Alejandro didn't much enjoy weed, but he would occasionally smoke it with me, and we both smoked Gauloise cigarettes in bars, on the street, in the apartment, all the time. We went out almost every night of the week, often to parties thrown by Alejandro's friends at gay clubs. One night, we saw Celia Cruz perform at S.O.B.'s, and I danced salsa, clunkily, in my hiking boots.

I longed for an ally at the office, someone to shit-talk with, but my only age peer was a newly minted junior account executive who'd just been promoted out of my job. She politely held me at several arms' lengths, which in retrospect was probably professional and wise, but still I was lonely at work.

One morning, Laura the copywriter, a tall, slim woman in her thirties who dressed really well and seemed altogether way too fucking cool and smart for the job, and who was also marginally kinder to me than the others, stopped by my desk and asked me how it was going. I immediately got sweaty; the attention of anyone in any position of authority, which was everyone, made me nervous and inarticulate. Her casual kindness meant too much to me, after weeks of feeling like a wart on the bottom of a foot.

Laura asked me what my goals were, and I told her that I'd like to be a writer, maybe a food writer. I liked cooking, and I had started reading M.F.K. Fisher's *The Art of Eating*. She smiled warmly at me.

"Great," she said. "I actually need some headline ideas for this syndicated recipe feature." I had no idea what *syndicated* meant. "Would you like to give it a try?" I would!

She handed me the text, and I got to work. Just before I left to eat my homemade hummus sandwich on a bench in Madison Square Park, I printed out and handed Laura my list of draft headlines for the feature, which was written around a recipe for pork chops drizzled with blueberry sauce. I had made us of the phrases "jazzed-up" and "cheap meats" and "berry good" and "deep dark and delicious," and as she scanned them, she was like, "Hmmm," her perfect eyebrows forming a kind of frown, and then she kept her office door closed for the rest of the afternoon.

That evening, I returned home to a message on the answering machine, from a woman at the agency handling the private cook job that I'd really wanted. "It didn't work out with the candidate they hired, and the Smith family would like to offer you the job."

The next morning, I went to the PR office, typed up a brief letter of resignation ("Thanks for the opportunity, but I am not cut out for this environment. I quit, effective immediately."), made several copies, left one on everyone's desk, and was home drinking sensible, breakfast-sized Popov vodka shots and doing bong hits on the cow-printed couch by 10:30 a.m.

chapter 2

Fat-Free Reddi-wip

I was utterly awed the first few dozen times I entered the Smiths' home, where I would work as their private cook for the next two years. They lived in a massive penthouse apartment that topped a thirty-two-story building on Manhattan's Upper East Side, close to the park. The cathedral-ceilinged lobby was outfitted in dark wood and white marble and highly polished brass. A team of florists changed out the gigantic arrangements of orchids and lilies and roses every few days. A rotating cast of two guys, always two and always guys, stood in wait behind a high, wide reception desk, while a third guy opened the doors, hailed taxis, and/or simply stood outside the building, looking tough and immaculate, wearing a navy suit and *white motherfucking gloves.*

The apartment itself (4-bed, 3.5-bath!) was open and airy, with white walls and gray slate floors and mind-boggling views of the city from every room. There were two big caramel-colored leather couches, many large abstract paintings, and lots of little cacti grouped along the capacious windowsills. A giant television could be made to disappear into a custom cabinet, by remote control.

Mr. Smith was a finance guy with a large head and a mild god complex, and Mrs. Smith was a sweet, sheltered younger woman, an aspiring children's book author who was in thrall to her husband's fortune and intellect. She once asked me to verify that it was winter in California when it was summer in New York, which led to a tough conversation about the equator versus the Mississippi River.

Mr. and Mrs. Smith had a baby boy, Sam, with whom they maintained a distant but unfailingly cordial relationship. Sam had his own staff: a full-time nanny who worked banker's hours, plus two nighttime and weekend nannies, all three of whom lived rent-free in Smith-owned apartments on lower floors of the building. The full-time nanny's name, by coincidence, was also Sam, short for Samantha. To avoid confusing the baby, everyone called her Pepper.

I started the job with the cooking skills I'd picked up in the kitchen of Von Cramm Hall, a hippie-ish cooperative house located just off the Cornell campus. For a few hundred dollars a semester, I got seven vegetarian meals per week, and was part of a team that prepared dinner for the whole house membership, about forty students, each Tuesday night. My mother never had the patience or time to teach me to cook as a kid, beyond warming up canned soup or boiling water for boxed mac and cheese. It was in the Von Cramm kitchen, standing at the stainless steel prep table as the afternoon light filtered in through a grimy west-facing window, with someone's Pearl Jam / Bikini Kill / Paul Simon / Pixies mix tape playing in a portable cassette player, that a friendly, nerdy redheaded senior named Steve showed me how to line up four peeled carrots on my cutting board and rock the big chef's knife across them all at once, an efficiency that blew my mind. He taught me to tuck my left thumb across my palm, to keep from cutting myself as I held the vegetables steady, and demonstrated a technique for dunking sandy spinach leaves in a huge bowl full of cold water. This was the beginning of my kitchen education. Compost buckets, fruit flies, peanut butter as the base of a savory sauce: these were all things I saw for the first time at Von Cramm.

I supplemented these practical kitchen lessons with an intense personal study of my one cookbook, *Sundays at Moosewood Restaurant,* a collection of recipes and techniques collated from weekly "Ethnic Nights" (ahem) at the famous vegetarian Moosewood Restaurant, in Ithaca, which was about a mile from campus but an ocean away from my tight student budget. *Sundays* taught me how to press tofu, bake a decent focaccia, roast vegetables, and thicken sauces with a slurry of cornstarch and water, which still feels, to me, like a magic trick.

I stayed in Ithaca in the summers between school years, picking herbs and vegetables on a small organic farm on the weekdays, and on weekends, working with David, a restaurateur who vended falafel at music and community festivals. At first, I was a bad employee, just stuffing the salad and falafel balls and tahini sauce and pickles into a pita in any order, as fast as I could, especially if a line had formed in front of the tent. David noticed my carelessness and pulled me aside.

"People know my falafel from last year and the year before that," he said, "and they expect it to be the same every time. This is why it goes in an order: salad, falafel, salad, tahini, pickles, hot sauce." David was talking about consistency and nostalgia and pleasure, and at the time I resented the correction, but he'd planted a seed.

During the school year, I loved feeding homemade spinach lasagna and black bean soup and endless broccoli stir-fries to my hungry college friends. Cooking for others rescued me from the fear that I might not be much good at anything. At Cornell, I was a small fish in an exceptionally large and self-important pond, and I often felt unremarkable, even invisible. Every aspect of undergrad life felt like a competition: grueling exams graded on a curve; limited seats in coveted classes; and a scarcity of nice, good-looking boys among the pimply engineering wonks and aggressive future sex offenders of the Greek system.

I wasn't a standout student, not an athlete, wasn't especially popular or pretty, my family wasn't rich, and I didn't know what I wanted to do for a living, but I could cook well enough, and the validation was just enough to feed my hungry little ego.

The Smiths hired me without a cooking tryout; it was really my Cornell degree that qualified me for a place in their domestic retinue. Their half dozen executive assistants and household employees were all Ivy Leaguers. Pepper (née Sam, the nanny) had just completed a literary arts MFA at Brown. The household manager, Keith, was getting a PhD in philosophy at Columbia, and the overnight and weekend nannies were all Columbia nursing students.

The French cook whom I was hired to replace had been an outlier. She had no college degree, only a wealth of experience and an unwavering Gallic hauteur about butter that cost her the job, because, despite the Smiths' clear instructions, she was unwilling to serve food that tasted . . . *how do you say?* . . . like flavorless shit. Mr. and Mrs. Smith had caught her sneaking fat into the purportedly fat-free dishes that they believed would keep them from ever developing cancer, looking old, or dying. After two warnings, she was fired, giving me the chance to feed them the flavorless immortality they demanded.

I was thrilled to cater to their preferences, because I could do it while wearing a zip-front hoodie, loose jeans, and sneakers. Steaming vegetables and broiling chicken breasts didn't take up much space in my head, so, when not feeling skull-fractured by a gin hangover or the muddying effect of an occasional morning joint, I spent my mental energy ruminating on the short stories I'd started writing for my continuing-ed fiction course at NYU.

Because making dinner and the occasional lunch for two adults wasn't really a full-time job, I also did some light housekeeping and general-assistant stuff. Lina, an older woman from Guatemala, came three times a week to deep-clean, but every day I did Mr. and Mrs. Smith's laundry, changed their sheets, and emptied the trash in their bathrooms and bedroom. I kept the racks in their library stocked with the latest issues of business, finance, tech, and science magazines and several daily newspapers. I kept the supply closets stocked according to an extremely detailed eighty-five-page household manual that I was responsible for updating and distributing to the staff. I ensured that there were always twelve pairs of black Wolford stockings at the ready in Mrs. Smith's closet, and, in the pantry, eight bottles of organic fat-free tomato sauce, in two rows of four, labels facing front, just like the murderous husband demanded of Julia Roberts in the 1990 domestic violence/big hats thriller *Sleeping with the Enemy.*

One Saturday afternoon, when the Smiths were in California for a long weekend, I brought Alejandro up to see the place. I expected him to be impressed, but he wasn't. "They've got really boring taste for people with so much money," he said.

I felt personally diminished, slapped right across the face, by his low opinion of the apartment. This joint was far and away the nicest place that I had ever been allowed into. If something was clearly expensive, I thought that meant it was clearly good. Perhaps I was just a rube, like the excitable American man I'd once overheard on approach to the palace of Versailles, urging his kids to hunt for arrowheads. "A place this fancy, you know there's gonna be arrowheads!"

I'd been acquainted with a handful of rich kids at college, but save for the obvious tells (late-model BMWs, breaks spent in Gstaad, Clarins beauty products in the dorm shower), those kids were indistinguishable from the merely well-off. Cooking for Mr. and Mrs. Smith was my first hands-on experience with real wealth: the apartment, the gloriously clean and expensive food shops where I bought their food, the studio apartment they'd bought and converted into a home gym with all the right equipment. The Smiths paid me well, nearly twice what I'd made at the PR firm, with good health insurance right away, and three weeks' vacation. I was allowed to buy whatever groceries I liked to assemble my own lunch and given a lot of freedom to just do my job, without much management or supervision. I felt very lucky.

The Smiths and I had a pleasant-enough relationship, communicating mainly by email and engaging in small talk when we happened to encounter each other, but the more time I spent in their home, the more baffling and alien I found the whole enterprise of keeping them fed and cared for.

Mr. Smith was laser-focused on squeezing all chaos out of, and exerting complete control over, every aspect of daily living, from complex financial dealings, to the likelihood of terminal illness, to the correct height of a stack of towels in a linen closet (five). He tuned the machine of their domestic lives for maximum efficiency, like a hungry, dead-eyed mash-up of B. F. Skinner and Henry Ford, employing a large staff to enable his neurotic pursuit of frictionless perfection.

My job was about managing minutiae: things like assuring the optimal placement of their bedside garbage cans (so that they could successfully drop a tissue into one without visual confirmation that it was perpendicular to the pillow), and cutting their apples and raw broccoli florets into extremely specific bite-sized pieces, which I then put into open-top plastic bags (*not* Ziplocs, the opening and reclosing of which was deemed to be an egregious waste of time).

One evening, I arrived home after work to a series of increasingly frantic answering machine messages from Mrs. Smith, who'd wanted to make herself a (fat-free) yogurt smoothie, but, alas, she could not find the measuring cups, because they were not in the first drawer she opened. I spent the better part of the next day drawing a map of each of the cupboards, cabinets, and drawers, and indexing which items they contained.

Working for the Smiths became a powerful form of social currency. The stories about them were so grandiose and silly, and it was fun and easy to judge and feel superior to people with tons of money and maybe not enough humility and common sense for my tastes.

I spent many weekends on Long Island with my good friend Johanna, a college classmate, and her lefty-academic parents in their big, comfortable house full of dogs and books and food and visitors and art from their world travels. In Johanna's house, if you were smart and interesting, you were welcome to stay as long as you liked, smoke weed in the basement or on the back porch, join in and sing while someone played the old upright piano. Around the table or at the nearby beach with Johanna's family, I shared the weirdest stories of the Smiths' excesses, playing up the absurdity for laughs, and repeating on demand the greatest hits, which included the time they tried to sue the federal government over a can of whipped cream.

As you may well know, the 1990s were a simpler, arguably much stupider time in our ongoing American dietary nightmare. These were the days of the ThighMaster, of zero-fat blue cheese dressing, and SPAM Lite, days in which certain low-fat potato chip bags carried a mandatory FDA warning about "abdominal cramping and loose stools."

One afternoon, on my daily grocery run to Agata & Valentina, I added a can of fat-free Reddi-wip to my cart, thinking that the Smiths might enjoy a modest dab of it on their antioxidant-rich bowls of blueberries. The next morning, while stripping their bed of its Frette sheets and pillowcases, I saw the whipped cream can in the wastebasket, next to Mr. Smith's side of the bed. That day, I bought two cans, and the next morning, there was an empty can in each of the two bedside baskets. For several weeks, with zero discussion, this went on: two cans, every day, and six on Fridays, to get them through the weekends.

And then, an email from Mrs. Smith: "Have you changed the way you've been cooking for us? We have both gained some weight recently, and we can't figure out why, as we continue to eat fat-free and work out."

Uh-oh.

I replied: "No, I haven't changed the no-fat lunches and dinners. Has anything else at all changed, anywhere, in your day-to-day?"

Later that day, I got a rare email from *Mr.* Smith:

"Please discontinue stocking the fat-free whipped cream that we've recently enjoyed."

Seinfeld fans may recall an episode in which Jerry, Elaine, and George indulge in enormous quantities of fat-free frozen yogurt, believing that they can do so without consequence. When they do start to get fat (or, really, "fat,"), they have a sample analyzed by a food lab, and, guess what? There was fat in the frozen yogurt.

Like life imitating a TV show about neurotic weirdos, the Smiths had me find a lab that would test the fat-free Reddi-wip. The lab report showed that, because it contained trace amounts of milk and cream, fat-free Reddi-wip was only fat-free *per serving*, which was 2 tablespoons. When sucking down nearly five cups of the stuff, which is the entire 185-calorie can, the Smiths were consuming 35 grams of dietary fat, and 37 grams of sugar, not exactly gluttony, but enough to add a few pounds to a meticulously lean human frame, if applied consistently.

Eating too much fat-free whipped cream was an honest mistake, made by hungry people in the aforementioned very-stupid-about-food 1990s. The average man would've probably laughed it off. The well-above-average Mr. Smith briefly rallied a team of attorneys to begin the process of suing the FDA for "misleading labeling practices." When his anger eventually cooled and he calculated how much of his time this particular windmill tilt would consume, he backed off the lawsuit, and the Smiths resumed the practice of eating unadorned blueberries, like former heroin addicts making do with methadone.

As ridiculous and delusional as their money made them, the Smiths could also be kind and generous. A few days before my twenty-third birthday, Mrs. Smith wandered into the kitchen while I was whisking together a marinade (fat-free yogurt, vinegar, coriander, cumin, cardamom, cloves, ground chilis, turmeric, salt, and black pepper) for some planks of extra-firm tofu. She asked, politely but not without genuine interest, if I had any big plans for the weekend.

"Well, it's my birthday on Sunday," I began. "My parents just moved to New Jersey, and my mom might come spend the day with me in New York, but she's not sure she actually can do it."

Mrs. Smith looked at me quizzically. I was suddenly self-conscious but realized that I had no choice but to continue. "She, um, has multiple sclerosis? And it's hard for her to walk," I said. I then started to cry, mortifying the shit out of us both.

"I'm sorry," I said, laughing with embarrassment and dabbing at my eyes with a full-sized, heavy-duty Bounty paper towel, an extravagantly wasteful gesture that my mother would never have tolerated.

She had been diagnosed with MS in 1965, at age nineteen, and the disease lurked quietly within her for almost three decades before becoming ever more apparent and invasive, like a thicket of opportunistic knotweed slowly choking out a stream.

Mrs. Smith said something about how that must be so hard, and she was sorry to hear it, and I shouldn't apologize. She left the kitchen without whatever it was she'd come for. Later, as I was almost out the door, she found me again, and said that she and Mr. Smith would like to offer me use of their car service on my birthday, to pick my mom up at home, drive us around the city for whatever we had planned, and return her to their new home in the outskirts of Princeton.

To be ferried around in a sleek black town car by a near-silent man in a dark suit seemed almost too much for my mother, who had probably ridden in a taxi fewer than five times in her life. She was awestruck and grateful, to the point of discomfort. I found myself annoyed by the way she made herself small, adopting the posture and timidity of a country mouse in the city, which is what she was. In her own comfort zone, my mother could be quick, funny, observant, irreverent, especially after a few drinks. She loved pranks, gag gifts, puns; she had a favorite T-shirt, purchased for a dollar at a rummage sale, that said DON'T TOUCH MY TUTS," with ancient Egyptian iconography, strategically placed. Whenever I taught her some piece of filthy slang, she'd pretend to be shocked, asking, "Where do you *hear* this stuff?," but she'd also be laughing, and I could tell that she was proud of me.

Now, in the back of the car, cowed by wealth and hobbled by her illness, she was hesitant and fragile.

"You should never leave this job," she said, arranging her feet precisely on the clear plastic mat that protected the pristine gray carpeting. "They're so good to you."

She reminded me of me, walking into the Smiths' apartment

for the first time, thinking that it would never get any better for me. Did my mother really think that this was my mountaintop, making criminally simple food for rich neurotics, while occasionally catching some crumbs, intermittently flung, from the edge of their table? It was a comfortable existence, but I was already chafing at its limitations. I knew that I needed to engage in something more challenging than steamed cauliflower and Snackwells if I wanted to enjoy any success that was truly my own.

Shortly after that outing, while eating a goat cheese and arugula sandwich from Citarella (fourteen 1998 US dollars) on a lunch break, I paged through a copy of *New York* magazine that was bound for the Smiths' recycling bin. I'd been drawn to a story about what it was like to be a chef, a career in which a person could, according to this article, earn up to $85,000 annually. From all the details in the piece, I cherry-picked only that impressive number, pinned it in my mind to a vision of a professional kitchen where the work would be creative, fun, and easy, and decided to quit my job and go to cooking school.

chapter 3

Don't Freak Out

Three months later, in early June 1998, I started my training
at the French Culinary Institute. I was in a class of about twenty-five
students, led on that first day by a chef-instructor named Pascal.

"I'm gonna give you some advice," he said, "for the kitchen, and
for your life, which is gonna be the kitchen. OK? Here it is: It's hard
work. It's a hard life. Don't freak out. Freakin' out is not gonna help."

Too late, Pascal. I was kind of freaking out a little bit, in a running
sweat, my sockless feet cooked to sizzling in the kitchen clogs I'd worn
for the long walk from my apartment to the school.

We were a class of assorted ages, sizes and affects, all of us bound
up in the required uniform: chef coat, checked pants, an apron with
long strings, and a claustrophobic neckerchief, each item made from a
waxy blend of polyester and burlap. I had recently, impulsively, gone
off my antidepressant meds, just snipped away the pharmaceutical
safety net and let it drift to the ground, for no good reason that I can
now recall.

In the white noise of the kitchen exhaust fans, I could hear a roller-
coaster train ascending—that slow, sickening chain clatter, the turning
wheel, metal on metal: twenty-five thousand dollars in non-refundable,

bank-financed tuition for an education that I suddenly maybe didn't want. Cooking professionally was going to be a difficult and physically challenging job, and I was soft and weak and starting at the bottom, and it would be a long time before I'd be any good at it.

"Come get a toque," said Chef Pascal, pointing to a pile of paper rectangles on the steel table in front of him. "Wrap around your head, and fix with only two staples, no more, just two." He was a craggily handsome French man with a modest, dignified pot belly, and he wore the whole chef drag, too, only with a much taller toque.

Pascal next made us introduce ourselves, say where we were from, and why we had enrolled in culinary school. The first to speak was Liz, a flossy-looking Connecticut housewife, with shiny silver hair and big diamond stud earrings, who was thinking about opening a bakery, now that her kids were in college. (Liz dropped out before the end of the week, presumably forgoing her entire tuition.) Next was Manuel, a slight, soft-spoken man with wire-framed glasses who had just moved to New York from Mexico, leaving behind the Roman Catholic priest-hood to become a cook.

Mike, a shiny-faced white guy wearing a Rolex, who said he'd been a "highly successful criminal defense attorney for twenty years," was "ready to finally follow my passion for food and wine, wherever it leads me."

A handful young men had self-sorted into one corner, looking fresh out of high school or perhaps a year of college, their unruined bodies at beautiful, arrogant ease. Chip, from Macon, Georgia, said, "Ah intend to kick everyone's ass, and graduate at the top." Nervous laughter all around.

Next up: Dimitri, from Astoria, Queens: "*I'm* gonna graduate at the top of this class, after I kick everyone's ass." Jesus *fuck*. Chef Pascal frowned and held up his hands, palms out.

"Eyyy, guys, enough, guys. There is no 'top the class,'" he said. "We are not at 'arvard, OK? Don't freak out. Everybody's gonna do well, everybody's gonna get a job. There are sousands of restaurants in New York."

It was almost my turn. Why *had* I enrolled in culinary school? Because I had gotten bored of alphabetizing quinoa varieties for the mega-rich. *Don't freak out.* I closed my eyes, inhaled, didn't die, exhaled. God, I was being so stupid.

I said, "I'm Laurie, and I live here in Manhattan. I've been working as a private cook, but I don't have any training, and I want to learn how to actually cook."

Our formal culinary education started with a lesson on how to wash our hands, pull our hair back from our faces, remove and stash our earrings, rings, watches, and bracelets, and never again wear them into the kitchen. Pascal had us place wet paper towels under our cutting boards, so they wouldn't slip. We opened and examined the contents of our brand-new utility boxes, bright red and nubbly, which contained all the tools we'd need in the next six months of school. We learned how to hold, sharpen, and use our knives, how to properly peel and slice onions and garlic, saving the skins and trimmed bits for stock. We learned how to cut carrots into julienne, jardiniere, brunoise, macedoine, paysanne, and lozenge, using actual rulers to check the sizes. We learned the absurd and difficult art of tourné, shaping little seven-sided footballs from potatoes and turnips. We learned to crack eggs against the table, not the edge of the bowl, and to swipe out every bit of white inside the shell with two fingers.

Don't freak out. It didn't always work, but I did try not to freak out when I burned a roux or underseasoned my haricots verts, broke an emulsion, chopped an onion into pieces that were too large or too small or not uniform enough, cut off a sliver of fingertip and nail, or burned my forearm and the back of my hands in an angry cloud of steam. I was such a thin-skinned little baby, and I took correction and instruction as a personal referendum on what a complete idiot I was, how unsuited for this hard, hot kitchen life.

What was I so afraid of? It was just work, and I had already done plenty of work in my life, but much of it had been of the "sitting in a library or lecture hall" variety. Even my physical work experience—farming and gardening, hauling boxes for a moving company, chalking and postering on campus, trash-picking and weeding in Brooklyn, cooking for the Smiths—had been largely solitary and self-directed, no one yelling at me, no struggle for space, minimal physical danger.

Cooking professionally meant cooperating with and depending on others, and in culinary school, "others" included jacked-up eighteen-year-olds and arrogant middle-aged lawyers who liked to brag about their wine collections and their sports cars.

I had this fantasy of professional cooking, rooted in my time at the college co-op kitchen, as a nonstop party to which you were always invited, with music you chose, and plenty of time to stop for bong hits and to use the bathroom. In reality, I learned that you might cook for a decade before you were allowed to choose the music, if you were lucky enough to work in a kitchen that allowed music. There would be no instant feedback, no warm, validating stroke of the ego; you would never see most of the people who ate your food, and, anyway, most of those people were happy to believe that you didn't exist, unless you were Wolfgang Puck or Paul Prudhomme.

Cooking professionally required the unlearning of all my amateur kitchen habits, surrendering to authority, and following a fixed system of rules while wearing a uniform. Cooking professionally demanded deference, stamina, precision, and humility. The kitchen rewarded the athlete's team-player mindset; I had quit running track in seventh grade, after two practices made it obvious how much slower I was than the other girls.

I began to have intrusive thoughts about butchering a human body. We practiced for speed on stacks of cheap and versatile chickens, breaking them down into their parts: pop the legs out from their sockets, run your knife through the loose skin and wiggle it in next to the ball joint (and do not lose *ze fucking oyster*); carve out the wishbone with a paring knife, hack off the wing tips, crack the sternum with the heel of your hand, separate the muscle from the rib cage, hack up what remains for stock. Repeat, repeat, repeat, stacking the parts in separate hotel pans, using your knife to scrape up detached globules of yellow fat from the scratched surface of the white plastic cutting boards, which always smelled faintly of bleach.

What would it be like to detach my own femur from its hip socket, slice through the tendons, and flop the fatty thigh muscle onto a cutting board? I'd pinch and knead at the joints of my hand, feeling around for the place a knife would go in, to make neat separations. I could, in theory, gently bubble a stock from my own cartilaginous fingers and feet. Which would be a more tender roast: my chubby buttocks or my modest breasts? While I had no desire to injure myself or anyone else, at least not in such an overt way, and was repulsed by the idea of consuming human flesh, cannibalistic butchery fully occupied my mind, sometimes running in the background while I cooked or read or watched TV or drank on the couch while trying to fall asleep.

Was there another path for me after graduation, one that would sidestep the presumed misery of the restaurant kitchen? Shortly after completing Level I, the first of four units of study, I went to ask this question of the dean of students, a retired French chef named Marc.

"Maybe you want to be a private cook, or a caterer, or a writer for a food magazine," said Chef Marc, "but they will not take you seriously if you don't cook in a restaurant. When I began to work, I had a pain in my heart, much like you do now. But one day, you'll see, it's not there anymore." It wasn't what I wanted to hear, but it was an answer.

Despite all my self-doubt, school wasn't entirely without its rewards. I did well on the frequent written exams, thanks to my dusty book smarts, and though I never tired of shoving hot bread, profiteroles, spoonfuls of crème Chantilly, and fried potatoes into my maw, I actually lost weight, because I was on my feet all day, and too tired to eat much at night.

It was a revelation to learn how many delicious things a person could make from a handful of humble commodity ingredients, using only basic technique and proper seasoning. Onions, flour, potatoes,

leeks, eggs, milk, salt, pepper, a metric fuck-ton of butter, and sometimes stocks, or heavy cream, cheese, or sugar: these were the building blocks for such new (to me) wonders as pâte à choux, pommes
Anna, pommes boulangère, gratin dauphinois, crème anglaise, potage
parmentier, and soupe à l'oignon gratinée. Every day, we learned to
prepare something deceptively simple, and this, I recognized, was
powerful knowledge, whether or not I'd ever make these things as
a professional cook.

One morning, there was a new student in the classroom. He had
long brown hair, neatly pulled back into a ponytail, and big, dark eyes.
I chose the work station next to him and introduced myself. He was
Adam, a nighttime student, making up a class he had missed, which
was the highly anticipated lobster class. I could tell from our brief chat
that he was smart, and he spoke with an intoxicating outer-borough
accent.

"I'm interning at Mario Batali's new restaurant, Babbo," he said.
"He has another restaurant, called Pó. This guy's incredible; he's on
the Food Network, and he cooks with a map of Italy. You ask him a
simple question in the kitchen, and he can give you, like, an ency-
clopedic rundown about the history of tortellini, or, like, the entire
curing process for ten different kinds of salami."

I'd heard of Pó, but the chef's name, and the name of his new place,
didn't ring any bells for me. I didn't have cable TV service, and could
only afford to eat out at Meat Deli, an Avenue C bodega with a fantastic $2 burger. Adam was cute; it would have been nice to have him in
class for more than a day.

Adam told me about his direct supervisor at his internship, a
daytime sous-chef whom everyone called the Hammer. "First day, this
guy tried to run me off. He made me brunoise a case of portobello
stems, and after I did that, he threw them in the trash while making
direct eye contact with me," said Adam, laughing, and I laughed, too.
"Then he told me to get him a bucket of steam, so I held a hotel pan
under the milk foamer on the espresso machine and captured some

steam under plastic wrap. After that, he stopped fucking with me."
I kept laughing. I loved this story, and I hated it.

We were joined at the work table by Laura, who was born and
raised in Manhattan by parents with significant cultural and financial capital. Laura was sharp and talented, and she also had a kind
of blithe, rich-kid confidence that hurt my feelings by virtue of its
existence. It wasn't personal, and it wasn't her fault—I was automati-
cally resentful and jealous of anyone who presented as happy, well-
adjusted and/or financially solvent—but I was always so nervous
around her, talking too much, making dumb mistakes.

Chef Pascal walked around plopping down wet, blackish lob-
sters on the stainless steel tables, one between every two students.
When everyone had their beast, he demonstrated the humane dispatch technique, driving his knife down vertically into the animal's
head, tip-first.

Apprehensive about my first kill, and particularly hung over that
morning, I carelessly severed the lobster's head from its body with
a clean *horizontal* cut. To my shame and horror, the now-headless
lobster skittered around the station, primitive nerve impulses inter-
minably activated by my brutal fuck-up.

"You cut it the wrong way!" Laura yelled, laughing, then stepped
back to let others observe my mistake. No matter how many more
times I bisected the animal, each resultant part continued to spasm.
Chef Pascal came by and said, simply, "*C'est la catastrophe.*"

chapter 4

Inflammation and Swelling

I woke with my usual hangover and a straight line of hives, tender and pink, along the inside of my right forearm. It was 6:30 a.m. on a Monday, mid-September, the halfway point of my formal culinary education.

I walked to school along Houston Street, shored up with coffee and Advil to blunt the pain in my head. The hives became darker and maddeningly itchy as the school day wore on. I spent the morning whisking a huge batch of aioli, peeling and julienning a case of celery root, then dropping and retrieving green beans and spinach leaves out of heavily salted boiling water, shocking them in a big ice bath. I fantasized about running the large-holed cheese grater over my skin.

That evening, I sat at my little kitchen table, studying the recipes in the course book, any two of which we'd be required to prepare, from memory, on an upcoming practical exam—terrine d'aubergine et poivrons rouges "arc-en-ciel" (a "rainbow" terrine of nightshades and peppers); moules gratinées à aïoli (mussels broiled under a thick blanket of mayonnaise and fucking *whipped cream*); linzer torte, or the dreaded crêpes soufflé: one must prepare for any eventuality.

Later, I slouched on my little cow-printed couch, sipping Popov out of a coffee mug and reading a borrowed paperback copy of Jennifer Belle's *Going Down*, a novel in which a newly destitute college student turns to sex work and the unhelpful counsel of a near-deaf therapist. I envied Belle's skill, her sharp voice, and her success; I'd read some-where that Madonna was going to make a movie based on the book.

How did she, or anyone, find the time, the quiet, the space, the confidence, the knowledge, to really write anything that someone else might find worth publishing? Since starting culinary school, I'd stopped taking writing classes. I now spent my free time drinking at home while re-watching my VHS tapes of *Party Girl* and old *Ab Fab* episodes, or sometimes in the cheapest East Village bars, taking dirty little key bumps when they were offered.

By the time I went to bed that night, the hives had faded to a gentle blush. *Good*, I thought, *that's done*, but by the next morning, there was a new crop of them, behind my left knee, and the day after that, I found a straight line of them in the space between my right eyebrow and my ear.

I'd never had allergies, so I guessed that maybe the hives were a physical manifestation of my uncertainty about the future. I didn't want to spend the money or time to see a doctor, so I bought some generic Benadryl and a tube of hydrocortisone. The hives would go away, I hoped, when I got a job and stopped paying the rent with high-interest cash advances on my Visa card.

At school, we transitioned from the relative tranquility of the classrooms to the kitchen of the student-run Restaurant L'Ecole, where any member of the public could walk in and roll the dice on a modestly priced three-course meal. Your lunch might have begun with an expertly clarified and perfectly seasoned consommé, in which the exact right number of uniformly brunoised vegetables floated at tasteful intervals. On the other hand, you may have ended up with a wet pile of thickly julienned celeriac, drenched in broken mayonnaise, and coated with sandy, haphazardly chopped flat parsley leaves (and stems!). Your main course *could* have been a crisp golden skate wing grenobloise, punctuated with suprêmes of lemon and fried capers, or an unremarkable chicken breast with a tomato concassé, or a tragically overcooked omelet full of chewy, greasy nubs of half-rendered bacon. For dessert: perhaps a mini-croquembouche of flabby choux pastries, stuck together with gummy caramel, or a perhaps a flawless crisp strawberry napoleon! You can't win if you don't play.

We students rotated daily through the kitchen stations in fixed groups of three. I really lucked out with my partners: Chatty David, with whom I engaged in daily companionable shit-talk, and Quiet David, who was planning to take over his father-in-law's kosher pizzeria in Brooklyn. Quiet David never tasted anything in the entire six months of school, and he gave me and Chatty David all the pastries, quiches, soups, and bread he made in class.

There were seldom more than thirty guests at any given lunch, and yet the daily pressure of getting our mise en place ready by noon often put us deep in the weeds.

"Ziss is nothing," one of the chef-instructors would say, if he saw one of us looking stressed. "Wait til you get into the real world," at which point I would have to take a deep breath and remember Chef Pascal's entreaty not to freak out. We had left Pascal behind in the teaching kitchen and were now in the hands of a few different chefs.

There was one very old Swiss guy who oversaw the guest chef demos, receptions, and private parties hosted by the school. He would intuit which group of students was the most overwhelmed with the day's prep, then shuffle over to that station with half of a hacked-over cured salmon fillet and a loaf of rye bread or a baguette swiped from the bread program.

"We have event tonight, wiss bankers," he'd say. "Make pretty hors d'oeuvres."

You'd then have to scavenge aioli or crème fraîche, dill or chives, a lemon, maybe some capers, from your fellow students' stations, and do your best to fashion thin slices of fish into elegant rosettes on toast, with tasteful garnishes. He would come by again at some point to look at your work. There were two assessments: if he was pleased, he would silently nod and walk away with the tray. If he was displeased, he would jab a finger at individual hors d'oeuvres and hiss, "Zeez look like the *ass*hole of the *cat*," before popping one into his mouth. He'd still take the tray, and the hors d'oeuvres would be served, but you would go home in shame, knowing you'd wound the salmon a little too tightly.

Our daily supervising chef was Marvin, a rare American on a faculty full of Europeans. He looked like Barry Manilow's sinewy and extremely disappointed-by-life younger brother, down to the curly mullet, and he took every opportunity, through word and deed, to cheerfully convey how thoroughly his spirit had been broken by the business of cooking. I was afraid of him, but I found his grim realism refreshing.

While the ancient French deans and Swiss-German senior instructors were on super-high alert the day that Julia Child came for lunch at L'Ecole, Marvin was demonstrably nonchalant, and this I appreciated. We were urged to do our very best work in the hopes that Julia would order something off our station, but I couldn't get it up for her. I had never watched *The French Chef* on PBS and hadn't read her books.

I knew who Julia Child was, but only because of Dan Aykroyd's imitation on *Saturday Night Live*, which had (wrongly) cemented her in my mind as a signifier of the haughty country club élite that mustered my family's middle-class defenses. Our food was not Julia's food. My mother cooked ground-beef meatballs, surrounded by a jar of Ragú, in an electric frying pan, and Duncan Hines cakes covered in canned frosting. The only thing French that came out of her kitchen were hand-cut fries cooked in bubbling Crisco, in a countertop deep fryer. My mother loved chocolate-covered cherries and cheap white wine. I think she was lukewarm on the day-to-day grind of family dinner, but she enjoyed cooking for company. In the summer, she made pitchers of strawberry daiquiris, using berries from our garden, and something called frog eye salad, in which tiny balls of cooked acini de pepe pasta are suspended in a matrix of whipped cream, pineapple juice, mini marshmallows, and canned mandarin orange segments. In the fall, she baked Concord grape pies for the neighbors and fed codfish gravy with cornbread to my dad and his friends on opening day of deer hunting season. Every spring she made wild leek soup, long before I'd come to know them as "ramps."

Julia Child, for her lunch at L'Ecole, ordered canard rôti with sauce à l'orange off the meat station. My team, on fish, was responsible for saumon en croûte with pike mousseline, a real dinosaur of a dish that only two customers ordered. At the end of service, Julia very briefly lurched through the swinging door between the dining room and the kitchen, burbled, "Merci beaucoup!" with a stiff wave, and retreated before the collective applause had even begun.

That day, a line of hives wound down my neck, from jawline to collarbone. I had an appointment after service with the school's career counselor, Jennifer. She was just a few years older than me, and very kind. I told her the same thing that I'd told the dean of students, that I really didn't think I was cut out to be a restaurant cook, and I asked for her advice on skipping that part and going straight to another type of job. "I'm so stressed out that I have hives," I said with a dry little laugh. I wanted her to pull me onto her lap, spoon-feed me hot chocolate, and tell me that *Gourmet* had an opening that was perfect for a smart, sensitive young person like me, with a $95,000 starting salary, full benefits, no dress code, and a town car to and from the office every day.

Jennifer said, "No matter what you want to do, you've got to work as a restaurant cook first, for a minimum of six months, to establish credibility. No magazine or TV production or publishing house is going to hire you without any cooking experience, and anyway, it will be good for you to get over your fears."

A few days later, she sent me on an interview for a garde-manger job at a not-quite-yet-opened restaurant on Second Avenue, about a ten-minute walk from my apartment.

"Don't tell the chef that you want to be a writer," Jennifer warned me.

The chef, who was also the owner, met me at the door with a crushing handshake. She was a tall, masculine woman with a swoop of short, dyed blonde hair. Her name was Deana.

"Come on in," she said. The space was half-gutted and dusty, lit with a few dim hanging construction lamps in the corners, which illuminated the exposed electrical wiring. There were mismatched dining chairs stacked everywhere, big round oil stains on the ancient hardwood floors, evidence of the smoked fish retailer that had previously occupied the space. Deana's new restaurant concept, she said with pride, was "Very fun and cool, open twenty-four hours, but not a diner."

She told me that she had run a few restaurants in Provincetown; this was her first New York venture, and her first time as an owner, and she'd brought a handful of her most-trusted crew down from the Cape, including the sous chef, Nick, whom she pointed out to me as he carried a stack of sealed cardboard boxes through the dining room to the staircase.

It was hard to imagine this deconstructed space transformed into a functioning dining room, but the depth of disarray was comforting; if I got the job, I wouldn't have to start anytime soon.

Deana handed me a typed copy of her opening menu, which I scanned quickly. Coming off garde-manger, there would be a green salad, a citrus salad with mussels, a clam chowder, a seaweed salad, a deviled egg plate, and chicken wings. It seemed like a lot. She asked me where I was from and how school was going, then, to my surprise, offered me the job.

"By the time you start, Nick will have written the prep list, and all you'll have to do is follow his instructions."

"I can definitely follow instructions," I said. I was a pleaser, and I was almost completely out of money.

"It's eight dollars an hour, with a raise after three months, but you gotta fuckin' earn it."

We agreed that I would stand by for Deana's call and start work when the restaurant was three days out from opening, an unknown date that was entirely dependent on when ConEd turned on the gas. I could relax a little bit, knowing I had a job lined up. The hives didn't go away, but I thought maybe they would subside when I got my first paycheck.

Two weeks later, Deana left a brief message on my answering machine, while I was in school. I took a few long pulls on the one-hitter, ate a few bites of the apple brown butter tart I'd made that day, then called her back.

"Congratulations," she barked.

"Oh, um, thanks?" I was pretty stoned, and not sure what she meant. I scratched at the row of hives on my ankle and washed down a Benadryl with a glass of tap water.

"I caught Nick shooting up heroin in the basement this morning," she said, "so he's obviously fucking fired. Everyone is moving up a notch. You're gonna be my pastry chef. Don't do drugs at work."

Fuck. *Fuck.*

"This is a big opportunity for you. You're gonna be supervising two employees, making eight plated desserts, breads and muffins for brunch, and special event cakes. I'll give you nine dollars an hour."

If running garde-manger was like riding a bike, running pastry was like flying a small plane. Pastry work takes a level of skill that I lacked in spades. I could've maybe become a decent pastry *cook*, with months of practice and a patient boss, but I was in no way qualified to be a pastry chef. I gave it my best effort, for three days, during which I broke a huge batch of buttercream, made some apple pies that the chef called "too skimpy to serve," and baked several dozen hard and dry cinnamon rolls. I felt like I was drowning every second. On the fourth day, Deana wisely fired me with a phone call. "We need someone who can come in and turn it out," she said. "No one has time to train you." I never got paid. The place closed within five months.

The morning after I lost my first real cooking job, I took the French Culinary Institute final exam, a closed-book practical in which I was randomly assigned the sautéed mushroom cake and a half chicken with tomato concassé, some of the easiest dishes. There was an afternoon graduation ceremony, at which they gave us diplomas and the big tall toques. I didn't go out with my classmates afterward; I had $60 in my checking account, persistent hives, and no job.

That night, exhausted, baseline drunk, a little bit stoned, and desperate for clean laundry, I stripped my futon mattress of its fitted sheet. I decided to turn the mattress over, to redistribute the lumpy filling a bit. I pulled its indistinct edge toward me with both hands and lifted it up. On the underside of the mattress were several—dozen? Hundred?—slow-moving, black-ish brown bugs. An infestation. My soul evaporated; my brain reverted to its factory settings. I shouted all the curses I knew, but mostly *fuck*. I didn't have hives; I had fucking *bedbug* bites. And I'd been living with them for a while.

I slept on the couch every night for the next several weeks.

At that time, bedbugs were almost unheard of in New York City. I told the landlord, who sent an exterminator, who sprinkled boric acid powder around the perimeter of my bedroom, and urged me to throw away everything: the futon mattress and frame, all my bedding, the clothes stuffed under the bed, and the delicately striped throw rug I'd paid way too much for in a moment of stoned self-indulgence at an ABC Carpet sample sale.

"Gotta be honest, these are the first bedbugs I've ever seen," he said, pointing his flashlight at a crack in the baseboard of the wall that separated my bedroom from the adjacent apartment. "This is where they're coming in. Your neighbor's got a major infestation."

This information was not a surprise; my next-door neighbor was a rail-thin middle-aged alcoholic who often hosted shouty, weekend-long parties that spilled out into the hallway. The previous summer, he and a few of his friends, very visibly shitfaced, had decided to slide an old refrigerator down all five flights of stairs on a Saturday afternoon. It was a hilarious good time to them, until they cracked a hole in the second-story landing and one of the guys fell through, breaking an assortment of brittle bones. A bunch of cops and EMTs showed up, and the next day, there was an eviction notice taped to my neighbor's door, which hung there for several days, then disappeared. He was still living there, presumably with thousands of bloodthirsty bedbug roommates.

After the exterminator left, I called Jennifer the career counselor to tell her I'd been fired, and that I'd graduated, and to ask what I should do next.

"Well, I think you should look for another cooking job, but I do have someone looking to hire an assistant," she said, with a mild reluctance. "There might be a little cooking involved, but it's mostly administrative, and there's the potential for some writing. Have you heard of a chef named Mario Batali?"

"Oh, yeah," I said, recalling what that guy Adam had told me. "The chef with the TV show and the map and the new place called, like, Booboo? Sure. I'd love to meet him."

chapter 5

Coke Can Dick

I showed up at Babbo at 6 p.m. on a Thursday and approached
the podium, standing behind which was the maître d', a man with
precise facial hair, pointy incisors, and a red-and-blue paisley cravat.
He coolly assessed my fake-ermine-collared, fake-leather trench coat,
a thrift store special, under which I wore my least-pilled black sweater
and nicest jeans. I couldn't tell if he disapproved of my clothes, was
just doing his job, had a bad personality, or what.

"I'm here for a job interview with Mario," I said.

Behind him, the dining room was bathed in warm yellow light,
full of people with good hair, easy smiles, fine jewelry, white teeth.

"Have a seat at the bar, dear," said the maître d', then muttered
something to the young blonde standing next to him. She nodded,
turned, and walked through the dining room and past the swinging
kitchen door. I hopped up onto a wide barstool whose seat was covered
with a leather cushion the color of butterscotch sauce. A bartender
with sad basset hound eyes and a clean-shaven head said, "Welcome,"
and placed a dinner menu and a cocktail list in front of me. Both were
printed on yellow parchment paper, the same color as the light in the
room. I was down to $17 in my checking account.

"I'm sorry, I'm just here for a job interview," I said. "Sorry."

He nodded, took the menus away, filled a glass with water from a pitcher, and placed it on a paper coaster in front of me. I hadn't brought anything to read, so I just sipped my water and watched him move back and forth behind the bar, greeting other guests, filling wineglasses, punching the buttons on a little machine next to a cash register. I turned my gaze to the coat check girl, a tall brunette with a silver ring through her septum, deftly handling real fur and leather coats and big puffy down numbers, briefcases and hats and shopping bags. The blonde hostess returned to the podium, and the maître d' approached me.

"Sorry dear, but Mario's gone home for the night."

I laughed awkwardly, feeling that *I* had somehow fucked this up. Was it the right day? Was there even a job?

"I guess he really does need an assistant," I said, and dismounted the barstool. The maître d' didn't hear my little joke; he'd already turned his attention to the small knot of new guests wriggling out of their coats, peering past him into the dining room, looking at their watches.

The next morning, Mario called me. He was all brisk business and made no apology. "I decided to go home and see my kids last night. Let's try this again," he said. "Come to Babbo at two on Saturday."

On Saturday at 1:55 p.m., I pulled the restaurant door open and he was standing right there, wearing shorts, although it was like 20 degrees, with slush puddles in the street.

"Hi, I'm Laurie."

"Mario Batali." He shook my hand hard and fast, and motioned to a small table between the bar and the front window. He gave off a crackling energy, somewhere between eager and aggravated. He had my resume in his hand, and before I sat down, he said, "So: organic farm, Natural Resources degree, Green Guerillas, Brooklyn Botanic Garden—what are you, a hippie?"

I laughed from surprise. "I mean, maybe?"

"Why do you want this job?"

"I really like cooking, but I want to be a food writer, not a cook. Jennifer at French Culinary told me that you're working on a new cookbook."

"You want to be a food writer? I'll introduce you to every editor in town. They're all on my dick, trying to get a reservation. Access is power, baby," he said with a leer that made my face flush. "What have you been reading?"

"There's this great book called *Unmentionable Cuisine*, about eating all the parts of the animal, that I used as the basis of my final project for school. Oh, and I just read *Tender at the Bone* by Ruth Reichl." This answer seemed to please him; Reichl had written a surprising three-star review of Babbo for the *New York Times*.

"I wanted you to meet my business partner, Joe Bastianich, but he's got a new baby that he's barely met, so he's not coming in today. Come on back to the kitchen," he said, standing up from the table. I followed him.

The Babbo kitchen was a much more compact and infinitely busier version of the one at French Culinary, full of cooks and dishwashers and porters, steam and convection fans and Spanish and English conversation, walk-in and lowboy and oven doors opening and slamming. I spotted long-haired Adam from cooking school in one corner, pouring olive oil into a blender, his back to me. My head swiveled; I tried to make myself small, to stay out of the way. I was well aware of the imposition created by even one extra body in a kitchen.

"This is Roger, my chef de cuisine," said Mario, his meaty hand coming down hard on the shoulder of a tall, dark-haired chef in black and white striped pants who had his back to us, with a portable phone between his left shoulder and ear. Roger turned around and said, "Roger, hi," with a big friendly smile on his face, but in a tone that could just as easily have been "Fuck you," his laughing demeanor clearly a thin disguise for some volcanic impatience or anger or suspicion. He turned back around to examine the clipboard hanging on a nail next to the pass, to which was clipped a long prep list.

I followed Mario back to the dining room, and he called over James, the general manager, who was as languorous as Roger was manic. James moved and spoke with the pained care of a grievously hung-over iguana, a demeanor I instantly recognized.

"Pleasure to meet you," said James with a warm southern accent, at odds with his funereal expression and the yellowed whites of his bloodshot eyes. He smelled strongly of cigarette smoke, and cradled a can of Fresca in both hands.

And that was it: Mario offered me the job, for an annual salary of $26,500, with health insurance after six months, and it never occurred to me to negotiate for even a dollar more. I was so relieved, so thrilled. He would later tell me that I was the only person who'd applied for the job. I had been at the right place at the right time; I could now justify having gone into debt for culinary school. I'd get to work on a cookbook, and get right up next to the magnetic heat and excitement of the restaurant business, while avoiding the risk and damage inherent to the endeavor.

My first day on the job, Mario took me with him to meet a field producer (what did that mean?) and a cameraman at a grocery store on the Upper West Side, to shoot "Chef on a Shoestring," a CBS morning show segment about cooking on a budget. He hailed a westbound cab on Waverly Place, opened the door, got in first, then patted the middle of the bench seat and said, "Slide those thighs on over."

Those thighs. I laughed. Was he joking? I couldn't tell. He held my gaze. I froze for a few seconds, then put my shoulder bag on the seat between us.

"You ever been to Cirque du Soleil?" he asked, smoothing over the moment. I shook my head, and he described having gone recently. "It's extremely gay," he said. "It's a bunch of dudes in tights, like, balancing each other." I was three-quarters listening, moving my face in all the right ways while I metabolized his come-on, or his joke, or whatever had just happened.

Had he really expected me to fucking *cuddle* with him in the first five minutes of my first day on the job? I mean, I'll admit I was flattered that he found my plump thighs appealing, because to me, they had always been a lethal liability. It would take me many more years to understand that it had nothing to do with my sex appeal; it was a power flex. He was testing my boundaries. This was the real job interview, just like him standing me up that Thursday had been the real job interview.

The field producer, a slight, nervous-looking young woman about my age, was waiting on the street outside the grocery store as we pulled up. Mario paid the driver, handed me the receipt, and jumped out to grab the producer in a bear hug that nearly knocked her off her high-heeled boots. She laughed as he let her go. Mario took off his waxed canvas winter coat and cashmere scarf and handed them to me.

"This is Woolie, my new assistant," he said to the producer, and so within thirty minutes of starting the job, I had a nickname. She smiled briefly at me before turning her attention to Mario, who had already grabbed a red plastic shopping basket and charged into the produce aisle, with the cameraman trailing him.

I followed at a distance, watching as he pinched off and rubbed a sage leaf between his meaty thumb and forefinger, then grabbed and squeezed two lemons in one hand. In the next aisle he admired a big green bottle of olive oil and did a little "hey, buddy, how you doin'" with a butcher who handed over a paper-wrapped package of pounded veal cutlets. That was it; they would do the cooking part in the studio, live, on Sunday morning. He handed the shopping basket to the producer. We cabbed back downtown to Babbo.

"Let me take you to lunch. I know the best place in the neighborhood," Mario said, and when we got out of the car, I followed him a few blocks up Sixth Avenue to Gray's Papaya, a walk-up hot dog counter. He ordered four dogs with sauerkraut and mustard, two for each of us, then turned to me and said, sweeping a hand toward the wall-mounted menu, "Get any drink you like."

"I'll have a small papaya, please," I said to the counter man, and Mario said, "Good choice, Woolie. Classic."

We stood at the little counter along the window inside the shop,

facing out onto West Eighth Street and eating too quickly to neces-
sitate any more small talk.

Back at Babbo, Mario fished half a yellow legal pad and a pen out
from the maître d's podium and handed them to me. "You'll keep
track of my messages. People are gonna call for me on the kitchen
phone and on the main restaurant number. I need you to be crisp on
the details. Lotta important people calling for reservations. I have
five tables blocked out every night, and I am the only person who
can book them. No managers, no cooks or waiters or anyone else is
allowed to take those tables."

"Of course," I said.

"And a very important job, very exciting," he said, his tone now
telegraphing Wonka-esque menace and glee. "Go look inside that
big box, in the coat closet." He watched me as I went in. The file box
on the floor was stuffed with hundreds or maybe thousands of yellow parchment cards. I picked one up; it had a woman's name and a
Larchmont, New York, address written on it, along with a note that
said, "Best pasta ever!!!!!"

Mario's frame filled the doorway. "Comment cards," he said.
"You're gonna write each one of those people a personal postcard,
thanking them for dining with us, and then you're gonna use their information to build a customer database." Oof: *database* sounded like
the kind of challenging computer thing I hated. "There's a few more
boxes full of these in the basement," he said.

"And listen," said Mario, his eyes narrowing angrily, his voice
a rasp, "You're *my* assistant. You don't work for Joe, you don't work
for Roger, you don't work for James. They're all gonna try to get you
to do stuff, but you belong to me. They ask you to do stuff for them?
Tell me about it," he said.

"Got it."

His face softened a bit. "We're gonna get going on the cookbook
immediately. I need you to start talking to the cooks, catalog every
technique on every dish we've had on the menu since we opened.

Have dinner here every night, until you've tried everything, so you know what we're talking about."

"OK!"

"Have you ever been to Atlantic City?"

I *had* been to Atlantic City once, the previous summer, with Alejandro. We'd bought $15 bus tickets that came with a $10 refund, in quarters, meant to be wasted on slot machines; I had saved mine for laundry day. We spent five hours on the beach, eating homemade baloney sandwiches and drinking cans of beer, entering the closest casino only to use the restroom.

"I'm doing a cooking demo thing at a casino next month, basically stirring the sauce for a bunch of mooks from Jersey and Philly," Mario said. "You'll come along, see how it works, help me with whatever I need. I'll make them give you your own room. Go ahead and invite a girlfriend to keep you company. And call the casino and make them give you your own room."

This was exciting. Was anyone else from cooking school getting a free trip to Atlantic City, writing a cookbook, eating dinner for free at Babbo every night?

I called the casino, arranged my own room, and started to settle into the job.

From 10 a.m. to 2:30 p.m., my desk was any table in the Babbo dining room. At 2:30 p.m., when the opening staff came in to set up for dinner service, I tried to carve out a little space for myself in the cramped basement office, shared by all the managers, wine stewards, and Roger, the chef de cuisine. It was stacked with cases of wine, dish and glassware samples, street clothes, binders from the cleaning supply and produce companies, active ashtrays. The plumbing for the kitchen's slop sink was located directly above the corner that became "my desk." The morning I arrived to find a stack of mail, phone messages, and recipe notes saturated in disgusting greasy water, I learned never to leave anything on the desk.

I spent my days hand-writing those postcards, then typing each address into a Word document that I hoped someone else would turn into "data." I established a wholesale account with Mario's publisher, so that we could sell signed copies of his book, *Simple Italian Food*, to Babbo customers. I printed out every iteration of the menu since the opening six months prior, scrutinized them all, and cross-referenced them with the binder of kitchen recipes, which Roger would reluctantly allow me to borrow for an hour or so each day so that I could start to puzzle out recipes for the book.

On Wednesdays, I cut out the *New York Times* restaurant review and taped it up on the walk-in door. Mario made the cooks read the review each week, to see what the competition was up to. Fridays, I walked to a magazine shop on Bleecker Street to buy three copies each of *Gazetta dello Sport* and *La Repubblica*, imported Italian-language newspapers that we would stock in the Babbo bathrooms. It was a clever bit of set-dressing, implying that the restaurant was a stand-in for home, while making sure that most of the guests wouldn't linger on the shitter with a newspaper printed in a language they couldn't read.

All day long, I took calls from the editors and staff writers of all the major and minor New York newspapers. I took calls from the editors and writers at glossy food, travel, lifestyle, fashion, business, finance, and news magazines. I took calls from producers at the three big network stations and all the local TV stations, cable producers. I took calls from meat and fish purveyors, upstate farmers, the parents of Mario's kids' preschool classmates, chefs and wine reps, and people Mario once worked with or had just met at the greenmarket or the dentist, all asking for the same thing: a reservation at Babbo. They used flattery and name-dropping and intimidation and the occasional offer of an outright bribe. They sent books and CDs and tickets to games and shows, knives, peppermills, toys and DVDs for Mario's kids, chef coats, wine, chocolate, poetry, hand-made artworks. This was the central drama of each day, delivering all the reservation requests to Mario and watching him do the inscrutable power calculus to decide who would get the tables, and whether they'd be offered the prime 8:15 p.m. slot, the lesser 6:15 p.m., or the 5:30 p.m. or 10:45 p.m., which were only attractive if you wanted to eat before or after going to the theater. The restaurant had about seventy seats and routinely fed more than two hundred guests per night.

I was excited by the proximity to power, money, charismatic and attractive new friends, endless booze, and rich food. I felt very lucky to have the job, which could be a straight path to being a food writer, and much better and easier than being a restaurant cook. It was 1999, and I was twenty-five years old, deep in debt, and thirsty for attention and alcohol. I was ready to work hard and get fucked up.

About a month into the job, I joined Mario on an early morning trip to Martha Stewart's TV studio in Westport, Connecticut, so that he could film a cooking segment with her. They sent a black town car to pick us up; Mario napped for the first thirty minutes of the ride, and once we merged onto the Henry Hudson Parkway, he snapped his eyes open and said, "Emeril just did a book event in Atlanta that had traffic backed up for *miles*. It was like a state of emergency, there were so many people there. I'm not there yet, but that's what I want. I want to be bigger than Emeril Lagasse. I want to break a major city's traffic infrastructure."

"OK," I said, unsure whether this was a command or just a guy sharing his feelings, or what. He closed his eyes again and kept them closed until the car pulled into a circular driveway in front of the studio, an old-fashioned stone fortress that could have easily been the town library or a WASP-y Presbyterian preschool. Martha herself was waiting to receive us, flanked by a few serious-looking, smooth-haired young women in fashionable coats. Just before exiting the car, I spotted something moving down the arm of my own coat: it was a bedbug, a lone survivor on the march. I opened the door and flicked it onto the wet ground, just before shaking Martha's surprisingly warm hand.

The shoot went exactly as you might expect: Mario was ebullient but deferential to Martha, who was then on the cusp of taking her company public and becoming a billionaire. She was impatient and short with the set dressers and food stylists helping to produce the segment, and there was an unmistakable sense that everyone on site was somewhere between stressed out and scared shitless. I did not envy these people their jobs.

A few weeks after that, on a cold Saturday morning, Resorts Casino of Atlantic City sent a stretch limousine the color of vanilla ice cream to Babbo, to collect the four of us: Mario, me, a young sommelier named Paolo, and my close friend Jessica, whom I'd invited along at Mario's suggestion.

Paolo was quite knowledgeable about the hundreds of Italian wines that comprised the restaurant's list and was skilled at selling those on the high end, but his demeanor made him an odd fit for a brash and lively restaurant like Babbo. He was a classic Italian mama's boy, shy, skinny, socially awkward, and perpetually in a defensive crouch, especially around Mario. Climbing into the limo, he seemed cautiously excited about the trip, like he couldn't believe his luck at being invited to go but suspected that things might go sideways.

Mario put on his sunglasses and fell asleep as we exited the Holland Tunnel on the Jersey side. The rest of us focused on the TV and attached VCR, which was playing the movie *Devil's Advocate* (gee-shucks young lawyer Keanu Reeves works for big bad Al Pacino who, spoiler alert, is literal, actual Satan).

Two unctuous entertainment managers met our limo as it pulled up to the entrance of Resorts. Well, to be precise, two unctuous entertainment managers met our limo one minute after it pulled up to the entrance. As soon as the car stopped, I went to climb out, and Mario grabbed my arm to stop me.

"Woolie, we are not getting out of this fucking car until someone from the hotel fucking greets us," he said. "Your *job* is to call ahead or otherwise make sure that I don't ever stand around holding my *dick*. Look at that fucking mess at check-in," he said. I could see out the window a line of about two dozen people at an outdoor check-in desk. "We don't wait in lines." *Shit.* This, I had not anticipated. I didn't know what I didn't know, and I didn't know what to do about it.

"How about I get out and find someone to help us?" I said, just as the entertainment managers materialized on either side of the car and opened the doors. These guys could have been twenty-nine years old or seventy, all Vaselined teeth and sharp suits and gold jewelry. They handed me their business cards and all our room keys. They walked us smoothly past the gen pop check-in and assured us that we were at Atlantic City's best property.

"Resorts is a classy place, with all the ele-GAHNCE, the ambi-AHNCE," one of them said, making the two descriptors rhyme. Jessica giggled. While we all stood waiting for the elevator, a middle-aged woman in a purple velvet tracksuit approached Mario.

"Oh my god, Molto Mario, I'm a huge fan!" she said, and his face relaxed into a welcoming smile. "I'm gonna be at your cooking class later. I have so many questions!"

"Thank you," said Mario, who then put an arm around me and Jessica and said, "These are my prostitutes, Dottie and Matilda." The elevator door slid open and we entered, leaving her cackling with laughter. Jessica and I widened our eyes at each other and said nothing.

"Get settled in your room, then come down to my room in thirty minutes and I'll order us some lunch," said Mario to us, and to Paolo, he said, "Paolo, I'll see you downstairs at 4."

It turned out that it was my job, and Jessica's, too, to hand Mario two hundred copies of his book, *Simple Italian Food*, so that he could scrawl his signature on the title page of each one, while seated on a dark green leather armchair, next to which was arranged a bucket of iced bottled beers and six chicken club sandwiches. He put MTV Spring Break coverage on the enormous television.

"Look at those tits," he said maybe a half dozen times, and we did, we looked at those tits, and each other, no longer bothering to suppress our giggles.

Then it was showtime. Mario was contracted to do two forty-five-minute cooking demos, at 4 and 6 p.m. Audience members had paid $50 each to attend the demo, eat a hotel kitchen version of the food he cooked onstage, drink wines chosen and poured by Paolo, and then get ushered the fuck out with an already-signed book, ideally to spend more money on casino games and alcohol.

"Just stand where I can see you during the demos," said Mario, and that's what I did for three hours, just stood there close to the stage, watching as he mesmerized rows and rows of delighted fans with his brainy, fast-paced olive oil evangelism and the cooking of ziti al telefono, a very simple dish involving pasta, tomato sauce, and cubes of fresh mozzarella cheese that, he told the crowd, resembled coiled telephone cords when they melted in the sauce. It was the end of the twentieth century, the twilight of the telephone landline.

Mario made fun of the crowd to their faces, using a heavy Jersey Italian lady accent as he imitated uncultured restaurant guests asking for their pasta cooked "al Dante." They responded with semi-scandalized screams of laughter. "They fucking love me," Mario said, as we left the second show.

One of our suave, now-lightly-sweating entertainment managers led us from the hotel lobby, across the entire casino floor, which was at full-tilt smoky Saturday night jangle, and up a series of escalators to the elaborately carved white wooden door of Capriccio, the fanciest restaurant on the property. As soon as we were seated, Mario grabbed the wine list away from Paolo and ordered a bottle of Italian Chardonnay from the reserve list, which he then smilingly sent back after slurping up a tiny sip. He then ordered a second expensive white, along with a magnum of Barolo, and the only French wine on the list, a vintage Krug.

"What's everybody eating?" asked Mario.

I'd had a full chicken club in Mario's suite and wasn't terribly hungry. "I might just do the spinach salad," I said.

"Absolutely fucking not, Woolie, no fucking way are you getting 'just a spinach salad,'" he said. "When you're out with me, you will order a cocktail, an appetizer, a mid-course pasta, an entrée, a dessert, a cheese course, and an amaro or a grappa, and we will drink a shit-ton of expensive wine."

His demand was oppressive, but there was also a glimmer of

something appealing about his commanding me to overindulge. It wasn't my choice to overeat and get shitfaced; it was my *job*.

Between the lobster risotto and the veal chops, Mario made everyone at the table tell the story of losing their virginity. This was fun. It felt great to make them all laugh when I said, of my fumbling high school beau, "He was basically two pushes and a squirt."

When it was Paolo's turn, Mario said, "We know you're still a virgin, Paolo," and waggled his empty wineglass at the waiter in a bid for a refill.

Paolo's big wet eyes and thin, downturned mouth betrayed his humiliation. It was super-shitty, but I already knew better than to defend him. Mario crushed everything in his path, and if you were lucky enough to be spared, you didn't remind him that you were still standing.

Apropos of nothing, Mario leaned toward Jessica and said, "You know, I've got a Coke can dick. There's a jacuzzi in my suite. I'm gonna hold you by your ankles and dangle you over it." She and I locked eyes and roared with laughter, and she said, to Mario, "OK," her tone in those two syllables masterfully communicating flattery, amusement, rejection, and just enough respect. The conversation moved on.

I was thoroughly entertained, more than half in the bag, and only marginally ashamed of myself for finding it all so hilarious. Why would anyone go to grad school or work for some earnest non-profit when you could be doing *this* for a living?

When we finished dipping our spoons into a big spumoni sundae topped with rainbow cookies and biscotti, Mario waved over a waiter, handed him some $20 bills, and said, "Where's the best strippers?"

Ten minutes later, the four of us were in a filthy minivan taxi to Bare Exposure, on the city's seedier side. Mario paid $20 apiece to get us in the door, and we sat down on folding chairs arranged around a folding table. But for the blacklights and disco balls and AC/DC's "Highway to Hell" on the sound system, the whole place had the same sort of low-ceilinged, damp-carpeted vibe as every church basement and American Legion Hall of my youth. On stage, two completely nude women engaged in a tepid little makeout, followed by artless, bottomless full splits atop a pile of one- and five-dollar bills.

Mario shoved a $50 bill across the table at me, and cheerfully barked, "Go get us some shots, Woolie!" I took the money and looked around for the bar, but there wasn't one, so I approached the fully-clothed middle-aged woman who'd collected our cover charge—she could have been a catechism instructor—and asked where I might buy some drinks. (Wasn't it Mister Rogers who advised us to always look for the helpers?)

"It's BYOB, honey," she said. "There's a liquor store across the street."

It was very much my job to go and buy a bottle of Jack Daniel's and four plastic cups, so that my boss could ogle boobs and drink without interruption. When I got back into the club, Mario had a six-pack of Coors Light in front of him and was cracking open a can.

"Mario stole that beer off someone's table," said Jessica, laughing.

"It was just sitting there unattended!" he said. I set out the cups, opened the bottle, and poured us each a shot of the whiskey.

"Lap dance for Paolo!" Mario shouted, and I'd like to be able to tell you in great detail what happened next, but the truth is, the blackout curtain had begun to descend. I went to use the bathroom and caught a glimpse inside the dancers' grim changing room. There were more rounds of shots, only Paolo wasn't at the table anymore. Jessica was sitting on Mario's lap. Then two big dudes were rather theatrically frog-marching skinny little Paolo out of the club.

"He touched the girl!" Mario cackled, tickled. "I told him this was a full-touch place, and that fucking idiot believed me." This was why Paolo had been invited.

"We should bring him his coat," said Jessica.

"Nah," said Mario.

Somehow we were then back at the hotel, sitting at a bar just off the casino floor. I drank a vodka shot and sang "The Gambler" for an audience of Mario, Jessica, and a young blonde bartender who found us amusing enough. Mario gave me and Jessica each $100 to lose at the blackjack table. He once again invited Jessica to his jacuzzi, and she once again artfully declined. Jump cut: Jessica and I were back in our room, laying waste to an enormous snack basket that had been left for us by the hospitality managers. Our TV was on, but it was impossible to focus on anything. I had driven the truck of myself for eight hours, at top speed, into the wall. I was sick, many times.

I woke up a few hours later on the bathroom floor, my head on a folded towel, my mouth a bile dump.

By 9 a.m., we were in another limo, this one mint green, and headed back to New York. Paolo remained silent and avoided eye contact. How had he even gotten back to the hotel from the strip club? He still didn't have his coat.

Mario slipped on his sunglasses and appeared to fall asleep immediately. Big free dinner, all that booze, getting his little punching bag Paolo roughed up at a titty bar, two reasonably cute young women by his side for the evening, and a $50,000 fee for his two cooking demos: he was living a fully consequence-free life.

I tried to sit as still as possible in the hopes of not vomiting and, failing that, I asked the driver, very quietly, if he happened to have a plastic bag. Mario slid his sunglasses down and leaned forward toward the driver. "Pull over."

As I stood vomiting on the Garden State Parkway, Mario stood by, out of splatter range, laughing. "You did a good job, Woolie," he said.

chapter 6

Lamb's Tongue

Late one Sunday afternoon, about three months into the job,
I was sitting at my damp little makeshift basement desk, hand-writing
a message, over and over again, on a stack of Babbo postcards, one for
each person who had completed a comment card after their dinner.

> *Thank you for joining us at Babbo. We look forward to seeing
> you again soon!*
>
> —MARIO AND JOE

Given the restaurant's extraordinary popularity, the whole exercise of personal outreach to each customer felt, to me, deeply unnecessary. Every reservation was spoken for, every night, and the barstools and walk-in tables were always occupied, with an impatient scrum of other guests waiting for those seats to open up. The general vibe in the dining room was fun and loud and sexy, with an ineffable quality of cool that the first and all subsequent waves of positive press reinforced, in a breathless, glamorous loop, again and again. Babbo was an impossible-to-score reservation, and would remain so for many years. Still, I suppose a fickle public can never really want you enough.

Mario rarely came down to the basement office, especially on a Sunday, but suddenly there he was, right behind me, clamping his hands onto my shoulders and squeezing hard. "We got a no-call, no-show from the new guy Kevin. Put a chef coat and an apron on, Woolie; you're the garde-manger."

That the new guy Kevin was a no-show was not really a surprise to Mario or to me. Kevin had only worked at Babbo for one week, Sunday through Thursday. On Friday, which was payday, he came in wearing crisply ironed jeans and very white sneakers, to pick up his first check. I'd been sitting at the bar next to Mario, going over the day's phone messages. When he saw Kevin, Mario jumped up and said that he had to check on something urgent in the kitchen.

"Stay here, Woolie, I'll be right back to finish this up."

It was late afternoon; the waiters, runners, and bussers were upstairs in their daily service meeting, and the cooks were finishing prep before a busy Friday night. There were 175 guests on the books, and walk-ins would boost it to well over 200. A manager whom everyone called Crusher stood by the front door, ready to hand out paychecks and keep customers from entering the dining room before opening time, 5:30 p.m.

Kevin took his check from Crusher and headed toward the exit, tearing open the envelope as he walked. He pulled out the check, peered at the attached statement. His face registered shock and then rage.

"Sixty-five dollars? Nobody said anything about four unpaid training shifts? What the *fuck*?"

Kevin clearly needed and had expected all of the five hundred dollars or so that he'd earned that week; this training shift thing was a really shitty and deliberate power play. I was angry on Kevin's behalf. I knew what that urgent need for money felt like.

Joe Bastianich, who had been hovering in the back of the service meeting, strode through the dining room, past Kevin, and out the front door, driving away in his giant black SUV just as Kevin asked Crusher, "Who's gonna fuckin' fix this for me *today*?"

Crusher had the height and bulk and voluminous pinstriped suits of a nightclub bouncer. He never lost his temper and was always smiling, a disarming comportment that conveyed its own special menace. From my barstool, I watched him gracefully but forcefully escort Kevin out onto the sidewalk and away from the restaurant. He returned, chuckling softly, just as Mario returned from the kitchen.

"I told Kevin to go home and take it up with his manager at the beginning of his next shift," said Crusher to Mario.

"He was pretty pissed," I said. "He seemed like he needed that money."

"This is not an emotional issue, Woolie," said Mario. "It's a management issue, and he can take it up with his manager at the beginning of his next shift."

Now it was two days later, Sunday afternoon, and the beginning of Kevin's shift started, but there was no Kevin. Roger parceled Kevin's prep list to Adam and some of the other cooks, and then, an hour before service, Mario came down to the office and plucked me off the bench.

Was I a scab? Not technically, and anyway, there was no time to ponder labor politics; I'd been given an order. I jumped up from my desk and hustled over to the small mountain of clean linens, fishing a size medium chef coat and an apron out of a plastic-wrapped bundle. I ran up the stairs and through the still-empty dining room and into the kitchen, excited and terrified.

I knew that the staff would treat me with grudging respect to my face, because I was Mario's assistant, and quiet derision behind my back, because I didn't really know what I was doing, and so they'd have to absorb my inevitable fuck-ups.

I didn't want to be coddled, but I also didn't want the full fire hose of abuse that I suspected was waiting for an inexperienced new cook in such a high-pressure, high-volume kitchen. At least it was a Sunday, which would be quieter than Friday or Saturday, but really, there weren't any quiet nights at Babbo.

Mario walked into the kitchen. "Have a good service, everyone. Good luck, Woolie!" He was headed home to cook dinner for his family, his regular Sunday-night routine.

As I washed and dried my hands and tied a dining room napkin around my head like a bandana, I reminded myself that I'd already written drafts of some of the recipes, for the in-progress *Babbo Cookbook*. I knew what all the dishes looked like on the plate, and tasted like on the fork and spoon, having recently eaten my way through the menu, at Mario's insistence.

Garde-manger was considered an entry-level station, but busy enough to require two cooks for service. There were more than a dozen hot and cold dishes coming off the station, and so many details to get right or fuck up. A copy of the night's menu was taped up on the wall, and Adam talked me through the plating on all the items as quickly as possible, while he continued to strain bright green oil from a blender pitcher into a squeeze bottle, through a funnel.

As the number two on the station, I'd be responsible for the amuse-bouche, which was always the same: a slice of Sullivan Street Bakery's sourdough bread, toasted and topped with garbanzo beans that had been marinated in olive oil, balsamic vinegar, olive paste, garlic, rosemary, and red pepper flakes. Like most of the food on the menu, it was rich, savory, salty, and acidic, with contrasting textures that made it a messy pleasure to eat. It was also cheap and easy, both essential qualities of a thing you give away for free.

A well-prepared cook would've had a stack of freshly sliced bread at the ready and would be holding a container of garbanzos at room temperature, so that guests wouldn't get a mouthful of cold beans and coagulated oil. I was not a well-prepared cook.

"Pull out two quarts of beans and throw one in the microwave," said Adam, who was crouching down in front of another lowboy, grabbing up hunks of cheese wrapped in plastic. I didn't know where to find the bread, how thick to slice it, whether I should toast it in the oven or on the grill, or whether to use a solid or slotted spoon to transfer the beans to the toast. I turned to ask Adam these questions and saw him exiting the kitchen, presumably for a cigarette and a piss before service began.

I don't think I've ever tried harder to do everything right than I did that first night in the Babbo kitchen. Chef de cuisine Roger was the expeditor, responsible for calling out the orders when they came in and coordinating the timing of every table's food. His energy was like a menacing storm cloud in the room. Much like Crusher, he didn't lose his temper, just smiled harder and talked louder and made sharper-edged remarks, sometimes disguised as jokes, as the pressure intensified.

"This prosciutto is way too fucking thick," he said, when I put my first plate of San Daniele up on the pass. He grabbed all four slices and shoved them in his mouth. "Adam, re-plate the fucking ham for the new girl right now."

"Sorry about that," I said. I was living that nightmare of being in the play without knowing any of my lines.

"Nope, not interested in sorry. Just watch Adam, and do it exactly like that next time," said Roger, still maniacally chewing ham as the tickets poured in.

Thank god for Adam, who was fast and worked clean and kept a cool head. In the few seconds of relative quiet we had that night, it was easy to make him laugh with a subtly rolled eye or a whispered, cutting remark. He told me I was cute, and I could feel a palpable vibe between us.

Maybe this could be fun? After two years of fat-free cooking, six months in school, and a few months writing postcards in the basement, this was finally some real-life, big-time cooking, oxygen, and heat and sweat, some stakes.

At the end of the night, while I was wiping down the station, a few of the cooks told me, sounding sincere and surprised, that I'd done well for my first night on the station. Roger came over and handed me a quart container full of beer. "Thanks for stepping in tonight," he said. "Mario wants you to cover the station until we hire someone new, hopefully just a few weeks."

I drank the entire beer quickly while cleaning up, then walked home, stopping a few blocks from my apartment to squat down and pee between two parked cars, the dignified alternative to wetting my pants. When I got home, I wrote the following in my journal:

> *Tonight I cooked at Babbo. A real back-on-the-horse experience. That feeling of instinctive movement, fast and efficient, turning shit out. What a nice surprise. I'm really glad Mario pushed me to do it. Almost makes me wish I was cooking for real, except that I know my experience is different, because it's temporary, and I have nothing to lose. All of the positive feedback makes me feel great. Couldn't be simpler than that. I almost can't handle it, it feels too good, embarrassing, the way I am processing it as "everyone likes me." This euphoria will fade, no doubt, but tonight was phenomenal.*

For the next several weeks, I did both jobs, answering calls and writing out postcards and handling shit for Mario in the morning, then four hours of prep and about six hours of dinner service in the evening, five nights a week. The other two nights, the station was covered by Bill, a line cook who regularly ran the pasta and grill stations.

Every night in the kitchen, once the tickets started coming in, the pace was relentless. Each table ordered at least two dishes from the antipasti section. Both of the multicourse tasting menus, which required the participation of the entire table, featured two dishes from garde-manger. VIP guests—who could be business or media big shots, wealthy friends of Mario or Joe, esteemed family members, celebrities, neighborhood regulars, the Clintons, or Bono—would get the "AA AD SM" treatment: "augment appetizers, augment desserts, send Moscato," which made for some particularly high-stakes dishes coming off my station.

One of the most popular items was a lamb's tongue salad with arugula, black truffle vinaigrette, pecorino, and a three-minute egg— a delicious dish, intriguing because of the truffles and provocative because of the tongue. If you broke the yolk on the pre-poached egg while plating, the whole dish went into the trash: you lose, start again. I did it once, and then figured out how to gently but quickly get under the egg with a large spoon, and never broke another one. A small win! A waiter came into the kitchen one evening to gossip about the actors Liv Tyler and Joaquin Phoenix, who were making out in a corner banquette. Roger called out for a lamb's tongue on the fly, which the food runner presented to them as a gift from the kitchen. They politely sent it back, on vegetarian principle.

There were two sformatos, baked savory custards: one made from acorn squash, one made from peas. The challenge in prep was to mix the custards well without incorporating air bubbles, which would make the baked texture dry. The challenge in service was dislodging them quickly and prettily out of their foil cups. In my first week, I'd cover my banged-up custards with a few too many roasted shiitakes or chiffonaded mint leaves, but eventually I learned to tap the inverted cup against the warm plate, rather than slashing it all up with a paring knife. Another small win.

I had four years of high school Spanish, but one evening I called out to the dishwasher for "platos fritos" (fried plates) instead of "platos frios" (cold plates), which were what I needed, and for the rest of my time in the kitchen, the cooks and dishwashers called me Frito.

To plate the tripe dish, I had to sneak slices of toast onto and off the grill, without crowding everything being cooked there, and without getting in the grill cook's way, which I occasionally did anyway. To plate the testa (house-made head cheese) and prosciutto, it was essential to work cold, clean, thin, and fast on the slicer. Sometimes I'd get it just perfect, like Adam had shown me that first night, and other times the slices would still be too thick, or too thin, or I'd accidentally lay the first one onto a hot plate that would melt the delicate fat, and I'd have to start over.

I hated watching Roger tip my finished dishes into the trash because they weren't pretty enough, fast enough, clean enough—but there were also lots of plates that went out pretty, fast, and clean during those six weeks, until finally they hired a permanent cook.

Mario and Roger both thanked me for doing a good job. I saved the kitchen a couple thousand dollars on payroll. I didn't get kicked out of the kitchen. I got a nickname. My cuts and burns were minimal and healed quickly. I never cried where anyone could see me.

chapter 7

Whole Panties Hangin' Out

Resuming my place as a civilian outsider, no longer essential to the machinery of the kitchen, was a bit of a letdown.

Once I got over my fear, I'd found kitchen work addictively exciting, and was entertained by the wide spectrum of humanity I bumped up against every day: rough dudes carrying big boxes of fish or whole animals; Gina the pastry chef, who was warm and sharp and sardonic and sometimes hysterical in both senses of the word; the pretty, dramatically self-absorbed waitstaff, always performing; the other cooks, the porters and dishwasher, alternately kind and tough; and Joe and Mario, lords of it all, sitting and standing wherever they wanted, changing the traffic and weather in the room.

I loved the sense of purpose I felt among like-minded people as we grouped together, split off, regrouped. Standing at my station, breaking animals and vegetables down into edible parts and useful scraps, then combining those elements in appealing and lucrative ways, I felt focused, motivated, useful, and alive.

There was something almost spiritual about the whole enterprise. When I was *in it*, and everyone was else is *in it*, too, and I took a few seconds to look up and observe the functioning of this improbable human machine of a restaurant, pushing back against entropy, something larger than any one of us could execute alone—I felt I was seeing perfection, evidence of god, even, in this human cooperation toward a common goal. It moved me, the way I had once been moved by singing the easy-rock Catholic hymns and ancient Christmas songs of my small-town youth.

There was no time or space in the kitchen for politics, climate change, terminal diagnoses and chronic illnesses, black mildew in the shower, whether the bills are paid late. It didn't matter where I grew up or went to school, who my parents were or weren't, what I looked like. There was only the food, the plates, my knife, my station. Work fast, work clean, listen and respond to the chef; do not fuck up—make it flawless, *now.* Cooking this way was a form of controlled danger, risk, excitement, outsized rewards. For me, cooking was also very much about sex.

I found it an ego blast to work that way, animalistic and carnal. In the middle of a busy service, I had these brief flashes of private arrogance. I imagined myself an athlete, an artist, a fucking genius— even if later, after metabolizing the adrenaline and dopamine and vomiting up the beer and hot dogs, I would remember, with a thud, that I was not truly any of those things.

My first few years living in New York had been a mostly celibate wasteland, despite my desire to love and be loved. I had little confidence, no game, and nothing clever to say to strangers in bars or the occasional friend of a friend who might have been single.

Pinch hitting at Babbo gave me a bit of swagger. I now cooked more proficiently and drank more strenuously. My inhibitions melted away like chicken fat, and the things that I really wanted to do and say came crackling up to the surface. I became a louder, bolder, more confident version of myself, capable of slicing ham at the correct width, then crushing at karaoke and talking my way into some grubby cook's bed. Right or wrong, the casual sexual availability of restaurant people made me feel that I wouldn't die alone.

Tying on an apron and holding a knife, telling and laughing at all the meanest, grossest jokes while working at full speed made me feel part of something that I'd assumed was off-limits. I was no longer intimidated by the work or the other cooks, like I had been in cooking school.

And oh, these cooks! These adorably dopey boy-men with their laissez-faire hygiene, who were only rarely available to socialize! They had appallingly filthy apartments, always with greasy, dusty copies of *Larousse Gastronomique* and *Le Répertoire de la Cuisine* and *Art Culinaire* stacked atop their mostly empty fridges. In their gross homes, in the middle of the night, these guys would open a stolen bottle of '95 Barolo, poured into Riedel sample glasses stolen from the manager's office. They would cook a stolen rib eye, for example, showering it heavily with stolen Maldon and coarse black pepper, then searing and then lovingly spoon-basting the meat with French butter and Italian olive oil in a stolen carbon steel pan that cost more than they made in a week. These petit larceny meals would be consumed before or sometimes after an artlessly vigorous fuck that was occasionally stymied by whiskey dick. As weird and loveless as these nights could be, it was the best thing going, and I craved more and more of it with my whole deeply lonely and super-horny little heart.

Nothing ever advanced beyond a flirtation with my garde-manger comrade Adam, despite our chemistry. It wasn't in the cards: he didn't drink very much, often went home right after service, and spent his days off fishing or foraging in the wilder reaches of eastern Queens and Long Island.

There were other intrigues, though. Between the kitchen, the bar, and the waiters, I had a handful of crushes simmering at all times, and there was one guy who had a crush on me: Bob, the bald-headed bartender who'd given me a glass of water the evening Mario stood me up for my first job interview.

One afternoon before service began, another bartender, whom everyone called Mama Maria, walked into the kitchen to collect a quart container of sliced citrus fruits for cocktail garnishes. When she saw me working, she came over and said, "You know, Bob told me that he likes you. He is so great, like a guy you can introduce to your mom. He loves his sister! I work Sunday nights at Union Square Cafe. You two should come in for dinner at the bar, and I'll take good care of you."

Bob was an aspiring playwright, perfect on paper, and I knew that he would respect me or whatever, but I just didn't want to be gently courted by a sensitive, family-oriented cartoon giraffe, and in that moment I hated Mama Maria for suggesting it.

A few nights later, however, I was out in a shitty NYU bar with a group of cooks and waiters and found myself talking to Bob, who turned out to be surprisingly funny and sharp. Emboldened by vodka and reconsidering my aversion to him, I told Bob what Maria had said about his crush on me. He looked down and said, "Yeah, well, I don't want to get you fired, and I need to keep my job, too."

"What do you mean?" I said.

"Mario overheard me telling Maria that I liked you." Bob laughed a little as he said this, but he looked sad and embarrassed. "He told me, 'My assistant is fucking *off-limits.*'"

This was news to me, and the guys in the kitchen seemed to have missed the memo, too, because soon after that, a cook named Noah asked me to get dinner with him on his day off. Noah was from Vermont and didn't believe in deodorant, just let himself smell like an old sausage left in a hot car. It was an obnoxious, almost admirable flex, to just go around smelling like a raw fucking human. He wasn't particularly funny, good-looking, kind, or smart, but I got drunk at dinner and fucked him anyway, perhaps to spite Mario, though I didn't actually want Mario to know.

I fucked Noah because he was willing, and who was I to turn down the willing? Having this disgusting secret made me feel interesting to myself.

There was something weirdly sexy about how little Noah cared what the world thought of him. I didn't love the way he smelled, but I didn't hate it, either. Our thing was a secret; he was already dating a sweet young waitress. This was good, because I knew I'd never have to introduce him to my friends, who would've certainly objected to his spicy body odor and his bad personality.

I kept sleeping with Noah, even when some filthy part of his body gave some filthy part of mine a yeast infection; even when he told me that he would always choose the waitress over me, because she was "way hotter" and "more of a girl." This was my first hatefuck, a real milestone, and it was exhilarating and exhausting and degrading, a mixture of eroticism and fear and self-loathing that made me feel perversely alive. Afterward, washing the bedsheets and taking a scalding hot shower were variations on my hangover recovery ritual. Whether getting wrecked by and then recovering from booze or some gross guy, I was happy for an excuse to be gentle with myself for an hour or so.

Once things ran their course with Noah, there was the sometimes-terrifying chef de cuisine Roger, who actually *was* smart and handsome and funny. He was from Southern California, and believed in deodorant. He was fourteen years older than me, and I'd never even considered him, since he seemed so far out of my league. Roger had just ended a long-term relationship with a woman he'd hoped to marry and have kids with, only she didn't want that kind of life. The general consensus around the restaurant, where everyone's business was everyone's business, was that the newly single Roger was all fucked up and on the rebound, which I saw as my great good luck.

At Roger's invitation, I met him on his evening off at the Holiday Cocktail Lounge on St Marks Place, a scuzzy dive bar that even now continues to resist the evolution all around it. We drank several small, watery vodka tonics apiece while talking about Babbo and our co-workers and Mario and, very selectively, ourselves. We smoked Camel Lights and fed dollar bills into the jukebox to play songs by Bob Dylan and Neil Young and Radiohead. We kissed on our bar-stools, then got into a cab and went back to his tiny apartment on Park Avenue South.

There was a brand-new mattress with no sheet or blanket in the middle of the carpeted floor, the heavy plastic delivery wrapper sticking out underneath it. A few feet away lay a moldering tangle of dingy white athletic socks and undershirts, a pair of black denim jeans, and a pair of black chef pants with a thin white pinstripe. A dozen or so empty Beck's bottles were lined up on the windowsill, a few of them stuffed with beer-engorged cigarette butts submerged in blackish sludge.

I couldn't possibly presume to immediately sit on his bed, such as it was, so instead I sat down on the floor. Roger took off his shirt, stretched out on the mattress, and said, "Come here," which I did. We rolled around together for an exquisite hour or so, and then he fished a $20 out of his wallet, pressed it into my hand, and told me to take a taxi home. I put the cash in my wallet and decided to walk; it was summer, and my mind and heart were chaotic, explosive.

The late-night light was orange-gray, the summer air humid and dank. I knew that fooling around with Roger was like standing on the tracks while a speeding train came screaming at me. If he even wanted to see me again—and boy did I hope he wanted to see me again—he was definitely going to use and discard me; I knew there was no future here. It would probably feel really fucking good for a while, and then it would feel really fucking awful. Still, I believed I was ready for it. I had been listening to a lot of Lucinda Williams and Emmylou Harris, and I wanted to try living my life like a country song: drunk, immune to logic, impulsive, corny, lonely, and rooting around in bad places for something that could pass for love.

The fun part lasted a month, during which Roger and I would eat dinner out on his nights off, drinking heavily and smoking cigarettes between every course. We'd go back to his apartment, to the bare mattress, which I enjoyed very much. With each successive week, though, his fresh heartbreak and rage would bleed a little more through the table chatter and pillow talk.

Toward the end of that month, Mario had a cerebral aneurysm, a thing I had never heard of before, but learned was quite serious and often fatal, though he was one of the lucky ten percent who survived with no apparent damage to his cognition or physical abilities.

I went with Nancy, a manager at Pó, to visit Mario at St. Vincent's hospital a few days after he'd had emergency brain surgery. We didn't know if or what he could eat, but we swung by the Great N.Y. Noodletown to pick him up an order of sea bass with flowering chives and some pork dumplings, just in case he was hungry.

Sitting up in his hospital bed, with a patch of his long red hair shaved off on one side of his head, post-surgery Mario was a temporarily defanged version of his essential self: softer-spoken and tired-looking, but still quick to joke that the nurses were giving him hand jobs, and eager for gossip. Nancy had to leave before me, to open Pó. As soon as she left, I was seized by a fit of melodrama and felt compelled to disclose something important, as if I were visiting him on his deathbed.

"I think you should know that I've been seeing Roger," I said. He looked genuinely surprised and puzzled, then said, "Thanks for telling me."

What was I doing? How could my private life actually be his concern, in a company with the HR structure of a spiderweb?

I left St. Vincent's soon after, hoping that Mario was sufficiently addled by heavy painkillers to forget what I'd told him. Walking east across Tenth Street, I kept hearing a woman's voice, somewhere far behind me, yelling, "Hey, lady! Lady! Hey, lady!" She couldn't have been talking to me. Why would she be talking to me? I walked faster, the cross-body messenger bag I carried everywhere bouncing against my hip.

"Hey, lady!" I felt a warm breeze high up on the backs of my legs, though I was wearing a sundress with a hem that fell a few inches below my knees.

"Hey, lady!" she screamed. "Your whole panties is hangin' out!"

I turned around then, and realized that she had been talking to me, about me. The skirt of my dress had gotten caught up in the long double strap of my bag, and had been ticking up, little by little, with each preoccupied step I took. My light pink silky underpants were indeed now *hangin' out*. I furiously tugged the skirt down and held on to it with my right hand as I walked the rest of the way home.

On his next night off, Roger suggested we have dinner at a French bistro called Les Halles, a few blocks from his place. We shared a plate of boudin noir with thick wedges of caramelized apple, a frisée lardons salad topped with a wobbly poached egg, steak tartare, and fries.

"The chef of this place just published a really good, really funny essay about restaurant life, in the *New Yorker*," said Roger. "You should read it." I had a bunch of unread issues stacked up next to my bed; I'd have to look for it.

After dinner, I soaked in Roger's tub and told him about showing my whole ass to the East Village on my way home from the hospital.

He said, "That's hysterical," but didn't laugh; he seemed bored. He was eating a vanilla Häagen-Dazs bar covered with sweating chocolate. There was still a gob of foamy white ice cream clinging to the wooden stick when he dropped it into my bathwater, laughing meanly.

"Here, have some ice cream," he said.

I waited a few more minutes in the water, to see what he would do next. A small film of butterfat broke apart on the surface of the water. When he ashed his cigarette into the tub, I pulled the plug and got out.

The next week, Roger had to cover someone's shifts on his nights off and couldn't see me. The week after that, because he wasn't yet medically cleared to fly, Mario sent me on his behalf to accept a culinary award at a big Napa Valley winery. It was exciting to drink Wild Turkey in my reclining business class seat, and novel to drink whatever brown stuff was in the white limousine from SFO to the fancy Spanish colonial hotel, but I was mostly miserable and anxious about the devolving Roger situation. I drank glass after glass of red wine at the dinner, during which a woman sang strenuously literal songs about each of the six chefs receiving the award, and there was a big unveiling of the gigantic, Van Gogh–style portraits that a local artist had made of the chefs. This was my first boondoggle, though I didn't know it at the time.

The week after that, Roger called me at work on his day off. He said that Mario was making him go on a date with his wife's friend Sasha, who was rich and knew a lot about art.

"By the way," he said, "I don't know why you told Mario that you were seeing me, but he's fucking pissed at me."

That *motherfucker.*

I asked if I could come over to his place, right after I was done for the day, just to talk, to explain myself. He said no.

"Please," I said, trying to swallow the sob. "Give me ten minutes."

"OK," he said. "You can come talk to me in my hallway."

When I got out of the elevator at 6:15 p.m., I saw him down the hall, standing in the open doorway of his apartment.

"Hi," Roger said, which sounded exactly like *fuck off.* "Here's what's gonna happen: You're gonna go soak and steam and get a massage at the Russian and Turkish Baths."

We had been talking about going there together, sometime soon. I was being bought off. He held out a small sheaf of $20 bills, and I took them, trying to touch his fingers, which he snatched away. "Then, you're gonna go see *American Beauty* at Union Square. It's really good. I saw it this afternoon. I think you'll see a lot of yourself in the Kevin Spacey character." He shut the door.

I walked to the Russian and Turkish Baths, used Roger's cash to pay the entrance fee, watched the attendant lock my wallet into a tiny locker behind the desk, and took a key to the women's locker room. I took a terrible brown towel and a navy blue robe and a set of plastic slide shoes. I sat in the super-hot Russian room and the regular steam room. I looked at the cold pool, in which was floating an enormous water bug, on its back, spinning on an unseen current. I went upstairs for my scheduled massage, administered by a fit older man named Dag. At the end of the massage, while I was on my back, he placed a hand very deliberately but gently at the top of my thigh and asked if there was anything else he could do for me today. His hand felt good there, and I knew what he meant, but I didn't know how to say yes, so I said, "No, thank you." When he left the room, I quickly got myself off, for no extra charge.

I considered skipping *American Beauty*, but then thought maybe if I saw it, I would better understand what had happened between me and Roger.

American Beauty did not help me. If Roger thought that I was Kevin Spacey's character Lester Burnham, a middle-aged man in a mild existential crisis, what character was he supposed to be? None of it made sense to me. Lester Burnham was happy with his choice to smoke weed and lift weights and sell hamburgers. I wasn't happy with my choices.

How was a person supposed to make the right choices, or even know what they wanted? How would I ever care about anything more than getting wasted and pursuing love, however wrong-headedly? Roger had an important job and a vision for a certain type of happiness and success. My job was a space holder, and I was ready to scrap it if it meant I could feel the way I felt that first night with him on his new mattress: free and desirable and alive.

Roger and I didn't sleep together anymore after that. He would still occasionally invite me out for dinner or drinks or to see a movie, on rare nights when he wasn't taking out some more-accomplished, more-beautiful, more-age-appropriate single woman. I'd always say yes, then drink way too much and try and fail to get him to sleep with me, sometimes crying or starting a fight. Later I'd wonder, nauseated with confusion and shame, why hadn't this extremely brief rebound fling with a man fourteen years my senior, a fling of which our boss disapproved, become the great unlikely love story of all time? I had no answer. I was twenty-five, and I knew almost nothing.

My heart is an idiot, I wrote in my journal. *My heart is a garbage can, my heart is a Speak & Spell. My heart is an absolute cock slut.*

More than six months had passed since I'd started my job, and my health insurance finally kicked in, so I started seeing a therapist, hoping she could help me sort it out and tell me how to live, how to become a good writer and find real love and lose twenty pounds and manage my Discover card debt and frequent bouts of diarrhea and tell me why I was so tired all the time, and couldn't be the kind of daughter I knew my mother wanted me to be, and whether it might be a good idea to go back on a small dose of antidepressant medication.

My therapist's name was Joan, and her office was just a few blocks from Babbo. During our initial intake session, I talked mostly about my job. I told her about Atlantic City, that it was the most fun I'd maybe ever had, but also that Mario had humiliated Paolo and that I might have given myself alcohol poisoning. I told her about Roger and about my discomfort with the way I'd seen Mario treat people, like Kevin the cook, getting fucked on his first paycheck. I also told Joan that I knew how lucky I was to have this job, with its proximity to so much power. Mario had set me up with important editors who were giving me freelance assignments, and he'd even said I might get cover credit on the Babbo book.

Toward the end of the forty-five minute session, she said, "I think we can definitely work together, but I need to disclose the fact that I live in the same building as Mario and his family."

I started to laugh, and she laughed a little, too.

"Mario and I are not friends," she said. "I saw him on the street a few weeks ago, and there was zero recognition in his face. His wife might know me, because our kids are about the same age, but I don't think I'm on his radar. So, you tell me: Can you live with this coinci-dence?"

I wanted Joan to be my therapist. She was warm, and a good lis-tener, with a gentle demeanor. She took my insurance, was accepting new clients, and her office was so conveniently located. I told her that I could live with this coincidence.

chapter 8

Dogs

I'd been sleeping with Bill the line cook before he left Babbo to work for a year in Rome, and I hoped to be sleeping with him again, when he came back to New York. He was from rural Indiana, and I found him hot in a solid, corn-fed Irish Catholic way, which made a nice contrast with his nihilistic worldview and constant smirk. Every time I ended up in bed with him, I felt my life moving forward, away from Roger, away from vulnerability, and toward becoming bullet-proof.

On our only real date, Bill and I passed a polite, companionable hour at the Tasting Room, a twenty-five-seat French restaurant, sharing leeks vinaigrette and duck confit. When we'd finished the bottle of Viognier, he leaned across the table and said, "When do you think you and I might fuck?"

The answer was: about an hour later, at his place, with a brisk, soulless passion that bordered on violence. I woke the next morning with deep purple bruises on my upper arms and thighs, which pleased me very much. They made me feel like I had Really Done Something.

As I was leaving his apartment, Bill asked if I'd like to hold his roommate's new puppy, a tiny white French bulldog named Donkey who had been asleep in a nest of blankets, inside a crate, before he'd plucked her up and held her out toward me. Donkey fit easily into one of his giant hands. She yawned wide, and I could see all her little teeth, and the black freckles inside her pink mouth. I could feel myself about to make some embarrassingly tender noises toward the animal, so I said, "No, thanks," and left.

Back home in the shower, I pressed my fingers into the bruise marks, expecting to feel some soreness that wasn't there. I wanted people to see these bruises, and to draw conclusions about me. I wore a sleeveless shirt to work that day, but soon got chilled in the air-conditioned dining room and had to put on a gray cashmere cardigan that I found in the coat closet. Mario was out of town, so I used the morning to finish editing an article for *Time Out New York*, about tasting menus focused on a single luxury ingredient. I was annoyed that the editor had cut the line "truffles are to sex as truffle oil is to sniffing panties." It was no dirtier than the magazine's sex advice column. I put it back into the piece.

The next time I slept with Bill, it was spontaneous. I was in a westbound taxi on Twenty-Third Street, on my way to see a performance of Bob the bald bartender's off-off-Broadway play. I looked out the window when the car stopped at a red light, and Bill was in the one next to mine. He saw me, too, and stuck his big tongue against the inside of his taxi's window, like a friendly dog, for comedy. After the performance we shared tripe stew and a bottle of cheap Rhône red at L'Express, then went to my place for another thrillingly brutal night, during which I discovered my appetite for being slapped and slapping back. On the way out the door, he asked to borrow my copy of *Kitchen Confidential*, which had just been published, and which everyone was reading, and I said, "Sure." I'd blown through it in a day and a half, enchanted and deeply envious of Bourdain's compelling, assured, and hilarious writing.

After I had a few more encounters with Bill over a few more months, he left New York to work in Italy, and I looked elsewhere for fun, always with the aid of alcohol, and often using the power and novelty of my job, dropping Mario's name if I thought it would make me more interesting to someone.

I slept with a wine guy, a journalist, a bartender. I went out to dinner with Mario and a visiting chef from Australia after a charity event, and the Australian followed me to the bathroom between the steaks and the boozy milkshakes. He pushed me up against the wall in the restaurant's dark vestibule and stuck his tongue in my mouth. I wasn't particularly attracted to him, but I was drunk and flattered, and I stayed with him that night at the W Hotel, where we had mediocre sex in a beautiful bed.

Another night, I went to a bar on Leroy Street with a bunch of cooks. I drank multiple negronis at a table, sniffed a smidge of someone's coke in the bathroom, and smoked my own weed on the sidewalk. Mario liked to say, "Nothing good happens after 2 a.m.," so at 1:50 a.m., on the mottled edge of a complete blackout, I left the bar. A slim man materialized next to me as I tried to flag a cab on Seventh Avenue South. I didn't recall having seen him in the bar, though he may well have been there all night.

"I can go home with you?"

He had a heavy accent, French and something else. Although he was wearing stiff jeans and a beige windbreaker, the official uniform of the sex offender, I wasn't afraid of him. I only thought, *This is interesting.* I probably outweighed him by thirty pounds or more.

"OK, sure, yeah." I just wanted to see what would happen. I wasn't even sure that he was real, such was the state I found myself in, yet again.

We kissed in the back of the cab and got out together on the corner of First Avenue and East Ninth Street. I was staying alone in a friend's apartment that week, looking after her cats. No one would know that I'd been picked up by a literal stranger on the street. If I lived (spoiler: I did), I'd tell all my friends about this wild thing I'd done. What would be the point of doing it otherwise?

Our congress was fun, brief, ostensibly safe, and satisfactory to both parties. He left shortly after. I typed an email to my friend Johanna, who was now a married grad student, living in Boston. Her life was nothing like mine.

I just hd random encounter with literal stranger! He spoken broke English, went down on me and then I jerked him. Off. I am extreme very drunk. What is my life? Good night? Do you think I havE A problem.

My headache and nausea that morning were the same as all the other headaches and bouts of nausea on all the other days. At work, I bragged about the negronis and the weed and the coke and the stranger to Charlotte, who answered phones, and Gina, the pastry chef, who'd brought a plate of cookies out to the dining room for us. Charlotte laughed and asked for details; Gina frowned.

"You're becoming a bit of a boozehound," she said, which stung. What did she know about me, anyway? "I'm worried about you."

Before I could say, "I'm fine, don't worry about me," Mario blasted through the restaurant's front door.

"Woolie, we've got a big fucking problem," he said, looking furious, and I felt sicker than I already did. He was going to Tuscany in five days, and he'd left his passport in the pocket of a pair of shorts that his "fucking idiot housekeeper" had unwittingly run through both the washer and dryer.

"Now it's all fucked," he said, tossing the desiccated thing onto the table.

I was on the phone with an express passport service within five minutes, and had the ruined document sealed into a FedEx envelope within fifteen. I knew that none of this was my fault, but I spent a few minutes wondering if I could have somehow prevented it from happening.

A few weeks later, my cordless phone rang, and it was Bill, calling from Rome. I had been working on recipes in the dining room, which was slowly filling up with waiters and busboys. I got up from my make-shift desk on table 20, took the phone into one of the bathrooms, and locked the door.

"How are you?" I asked.

"I'm OK. Lonely, honestly. I work all the time. It's so expensive here. Today's my only day off and I'm just lying in bed, reading. I'm running out of money. I'll probably have to come back to New York a few months early." His voice, always a kind of petulant drawl, sounded especially beaten down.

"How's the work?" I said.

"It's fine. I killed a dog," he said. I sat down on the closed toilet lid. It was cold in the bathroom, though the light was warm.

"What? What do you mean, you killed a dog?"

"I poisoned it," he said. "I'm staying with this family that owns the restaurant, outside the city. The neighbors have a dog that barks all fucking night. I work like fourteen hours a day and then I can't sleep because of the barking, so I stole a steak, soaked it in rat poison, and tossed it over the fence. Now it's dead." There was a boyish pride in his voice.

"Wow." I felt sick.

"You're the only person I've told. I figured you'd get it."

"Sure, I mean, you did what you had to do. A person has to sleep." He didn't say anything, so I added, "I'm glad you told me."

I could hear the staff chattering to each other in Spanish and Bengali and English in the coffee station, just outside the bathroom. Wooden boxes full of silverware rattled as they ran with them up and down the carpeted stairs. It was 3:30 p.m. in New York, 9:30 p.m. in Rome.

"Got any gossip?" Bill asked. He loved gossip. Every cook loved gossip.

"Let's see," I said, trying to think of something. "Um, Mario's college buddies came in last week with nine people on a six-top reservation, and they had the tasting menu and drank a shit-ton of wine, and then Mario comped the check and they didn't tip," I said. "Gary the waiter got fired for smoking weed on the roof during service, and now he's a backwaiter at Union Pacific."

"Huh," he said, still sounding pleased.

"The cooks hired a stripper for JB on his birthday. She was dancing in the kitchen, right next to the pasta cooker, but JB got really mad and started crying, so they had to stop her after about thirty seconds," I said. This made him laugh.

"Anyway, what about you?" I said. "How's your social life?"

"I don't have one," he said. "The language barrier is really a problem. I just jerk off a lot. I'll probably jerk off as soon as we get off the phone." I could hear him smiling.

"Why don't you do it now?" I said. "I'll talk dirty." I had never talked dirty to anyone on the phone, and didn't actually want to.

Someone pulled hard on the locked bathroom door, then said, "Fuck."

"OK, do it," said Bill.

"Oh, shit, sorry, Mario just walked in. I gotta go," I lied, and hung up before he could say anything else. I went down to the basement and worked on editing the recipes for the cookbook and thought about the dead dog. Was he even telling the truth? On my way out the door for the day, I ran into a few of the cooks standing out on the sidewalk, having a smoke before the first orders came in.

"I talked to Bill today," I said to them, and there were a few eye rolls. Anyone who'd left Babbo was seen as a traitor, especially if they went to Italy, which was something that Mario strongly encouraged, but almost no one (including Bill, it would seem) could afford to do.

"What's he up to?" said Frank.

"Well, he claims to have killed a dog," I said.

"What?!" Frank laughed. They were all waiting for the story. I wished I'd kept walking. I wished I was capable of keeping one fucking thing to myself. I was such a gossip, a shit-talker. Sharing a little juicy info made me feel powerful, at least for as long as it took for the listener to react to me.

"Well, there was this dog next door to where he lives, and he said he fed it a poisoned steak because—"

Roger stuck his head out the front door and looked at the cooks. He had the angry clown smile on his face. "Time to cook some food now, OK?" His mouth was smiling but his voice was battery acid. I still felt a stab of something hopeful and shameful and bad when I saw him.

The cooks stamped out their cigarettes and muttered a few small remarks to each other about what I'd just told them: "Who fucking does that?" and "That's fucked up," and "I always knew that guy was a sick motherfucker."

I wanted to stop them and say that maybe he was just kidding, maybe he didn't really kill a dog, but instead I just said, "Good night," and walked over to the West Fourth Street station entrance, under the Duane Reade.

The next day, I had a therapy appointment with Joan. She was a vegetarian, and extremely tenderhearted toward animals, even the pigeons that stopped to shit on her office windowsill. When I told her about the phone call with Bill, and what he'd said about the dog, she twisted a segment of her long hair around her index finger and said, "I know you didn't ask for this advice, but I have to urge you to stay away from this person. I mean, *Jeffrey Dahmer* killed animals before moving on to people. It's not safe for you to be alone with him."

I told Joan that while I objectively understood her concern, I couldn't really agree. I wasn't sure he was telling the truth. I knew I'd see him again, if he wanted to, when he got back to town.

"It's kind of a bird in the hand thing," I said.

A few months later, Bill returned to New York and took an executive chef job with a high-volume catering company. Within a few weeks of his return, Mario had roped him in as a volunteer cook for a dinner at the Beard House, on a Monday night. I'd also been pressed into service, along with a few cooks who had the night off. In the comically cramped kitchen of James Beard's old townhouse, we cooked a five-course meal of those Babbo dishes that featured the fewest, cheapest, and most durable ingredients. We drank beer out of quart containers while we worked, and big glasses of wine while we cleaned up. Afterward, Mario took us out for seafood towers and steak frites and non-vintage Champagne and brandy at Balthazar. I sat next to Bill and kept my leg pressed against his under the table.

When dinner was over, I said to him, "Come home with me," quiet enough for only him to hear.

"No," he said. "I'm tired."

"Come on," I said, feeling slightly panicked. I hadn't expected "no."

"Why should I?" he said.

"Come on," I said again. I had no good argument at my disposal. I felt desperate, miserable. I was quite drunk, and I was willing to take my clothes off with this repellent dog killer. Didn't he like sex? Was there someone else? "Tired" made no sense to me. I couldn't accept "tired."

I walked to the corner of Crosby and Spring and waved at the driver of an idling a cab. When I turned around, Bill was there. He got into the car with me. It was a short ride to my place; I paid for it. He didn't talk. I keyed us into my building and he started to follow me up the stairs to my fifth-floor apartment. Two flights up, he stopped walking. "I'm only going into your place if you let me beat the shit out of you."

"What?"

"Beat the living *shit* out of you," he said, raising his voice. "Do you want it? That's what's going to happen, if you make me go up to your place."

I stood still. He didn't seem to be kidding. I felt very dumb. Why did everything have to be like this?

"Go home," I said. "Good night." I climbed the rest of the stairs to my fifth-floor apartment; he didn't follow me.

I wanted to go right to sleep for the next seven to ten years, but I felt sick when I closed my eyes. I made myself vomit into the toilet, then watched *Weird Al Yankovic: Behind the Music*, pausing every twenty to thirty minutes to be sick again. I woke up on the couch at 9 a.m., showered, and went to work. I didn't avoid Bill but I didn't talk to him much, either, and I didn't tell anyone anything.

The next Sunday, my friend and college classmate Jenny had a party to celebrate her graduation from Fordham law school. While she was in school, Jenny worked as a bartender, in a handful of cheap, busy downtown places: Cherry Tavern, Cocoa Bar, Sidewalk Cafe. Jenny lived with her boyfriend, Tim, also a bartender, in a run-down building in Williamsburg, located almost directly under the BQE. It had a green awning with "Paisano Estates" painted along the front. Was that offensive? No one could really say.

Jenny and Tim's inner social circle consisted mostly of bartenders and waiters, many of whom were also rowdy musicians or graffiti artists. Someone always had a little coke to share or sell at a discount. You know that slightly patronizing line from the top of the *New Yorker* live music listings, about how it's "advisable to check in advance to confirm engagements" because "musicians lead complicated lives"? Tim and his friends seemed to embody this. I always felt like a cop around them; it was hard to find conversational common ground. They didn't care about washed-rind cheeses or Lambrusco or finding out what the *Times* dining critic looked like.

I went to Jenny's party by myself at about 6 p.m., with a plan to meet Jessica and Alejandro there. The front door of Paisano Estates had been propped open with an upholstered ottoman, and the apartment door was open, too. There were a few dozen people clustered inside, talking, smoking, drinking. Tim was in the living room, seated on a bronze corduroy couch with two women and another man, watching a huge wooden console TV that stood in front of the fireplace. I paused in the doorway, watching, too. On the screen, a woman was on a mattress, on her hands and knees. One man stood in front of her face, his dick in her mouth. Another man kneeled behind her, his dick presumably lodged somewhere warm. The woman wore an orange trucker cap, backward; the men wore white tube socks with green stripes, pulled up to mid-calf. I found it interesting that the three performers were all in the frame, and that the camera seemed kind of far away, but soon the perspective changed, and there was a gruesome, sloshing close-up of her mouth and its turgid, veiny contents. Tim looked over at me.

"Hey! Welcome to our spit roast," he said, and everyone on the couch laughed. It was hot in the room, no air moving, no air conditioning, no fans. "You wanna do some X? Jenny's got tons, just ask her."

"I'm good, thanks," I said. I'd never done ecstasy, having been scared off by the myth of depleted spinal fluid.

I looked around and didn't see Jessica or Alejandro in the apartment, so I sat down on a chair in the corner to watch porn on the television while the sun was still in the sky, on a hot late-spring Sunday in New York, in the mixed company of relative strangers who'd taken ecstasy to celebrate Jenny's Juris Doctor degree. The girl on the screen, who was now being athletically face-fucked on one end and spanked on the other, looked sad and tired, but also only about twenty years old. Her hat came dislodged from her head and fell on the floor. One of the women on the couch giggled.

I got up to look at the bookshelf. Jenny had held on to the more interesting of her college texts—*The Marx-Engels Reader, The Lenses of Gender*, the complete poems of Elizabeth Bishop—adjacent to which were stacks of recent and less-recent issues of *Penthouse, Hustler, Leg Show, Oui, Beaver Hunt, Playboy, Screw, Swank,* and *Juggs*. I took an issue of *Leg Show* off the shelf. The cover photo showed a blonde woman in a red ice-skating dress. Her sheer stockings were held up with red satin garters, and she wore red leather stiletto heels that were also ice skates. She was lifting her leg high in the air to reveal a tiny slice of red panties. The big feature story was about Marilyn Chambers's love of being barefoot. There were also several photos of a very tall woman whose legs were described as "stunning skull-crushers." I put the magazine back on the shelf and went to find my friends.

The apartment opened out to a narrow backyard behind the building, where a few dozen more people were talking, smoking, and drinking. Jenny's sweet dog, Bear, roamed back and forth between indoors and out. I saw Jessica and Alejandro, sitting together in chairs by the fence. I went to sit with them, and Jenny came over to say hello.

"Congratulations!" I said, hugging her. I was not myself a big hugger, but that was how everyone greeted everyone. "I just spent some quality time looking at Tim's porn collection."

She laughed. "It's amazing, right? I kind of love it." Her pupils were huge. She looked really happy.

"Yeah, I love it, too," I said, surprising myself, and described the threesome video and *Leg Show* to Jenny and Jessica and Alejandro and a few random others. I was performing a monologue, desperate for laughs and to demonstrate how absolutely down with it all I was.

I stayed at the party for another hour or so, talking, listening, watching the dog and various humans come and go. I drank more tequila mixed with lemonade and smoked the weed I'd brought in my one-hitter. I tried to engage Bear every time he came by, but he was only interested in Jenny, his person.

It got dark, and I got hungry. There were a few bags of chips on a picnic table and an unopened plastic box of iced sugar cookies from Key Food. A whole watermelon lay on its side. A slice had been sheared off the top, and the seedy fruit inside the shell was chunked up and swimming in vodka. I scooped some into a plastic cup, but I wanted some real food. No one at this party was going to seduce me or offer me a new job or show up with barbecued ribs.

"OK, I'm going home," I said, and stood up. The volume on the music had been turned up, and a floodlamp now illuminated half the yard with shards of harsh, silvery light.

"Wait, did you try the watermelon?" asked Alejandro, and I could hear a teasing challenge in his voice.

"Yeah, I'm—"

He stuck his hand into the cavity, grabbed a handful of fruit, and smooshed it into my face. "It's delicious," he said, laughing, and I was fucking furious, humiliated, and inexplicably scared, though not of him. I started to cry and yell at him. I didn't want to play along; I didn't want to hit him back. I just wanted someone to be nice to me, for things to be quiet and calm, to be treated well and to treat myself well, which was something I couldn't even conceive of. I felt so fucking stupid and soft and self-indulgent. I couldn't even imagine saying how I felt without immediately making fun of myself.

Alejandro, of course, had no idea about what was in my head. He was drunk, and maybe on ecstasy, and playing around in a provocative way that had always been fine and funny to me before. I was already embarrassed by my reaction. I accepted Alejandro's apology and decided to stay for one more drink.

chapter 9

Chopper

On a chilly Monday morning in November, a day off from work, I walked to Cibao Deli, on the corner of Avenue B and East Fourth Street, for a self-serve coffee. The man behind the counter had his radio tuned to 1010 WINS, the AM news station.

As I passed my dollar across the counter, I heard the radio announcer say that an American Airlines plane bound for the Dominican Republic had crashed a short time ago in Queens, minutes after taking off from JFK, and that all 260 passengers and crew, plus a dog, were presumed dead. The bridges and tunnels were closed, all the New York City airports shut down.

"Stay tuned to 1010 WINS for more updates," he said, and then the radio played a cheerful ad for the new McDonald's Big N' Tasty. I took my cup and walked outside, where I could hear the various tones and volumes of fire sirens, ambulances, police cars: not close, but close.

It had been two months since 9/11, and parts of downtown still smelled like a tire fire. You'd occasionally see people wearing gas masks on the street or selling American flag–printed T-shirts with terrible slogans like I SURVIVE [*sic*] THE ATTACK or SEPTEMBER 11, 2001:

I CAN'T BELIEVE I GOT OUT. Most days, a wiry white man stood directly under the arch in Washington Square Park, yelling about how the hijacked planes had been chartered by Steven Spielberg, Mariah Carey, and the New York Mets.

Was this new plane crash more of the same, the next round of who knew how many rounds? Who had seen something, but didn't say something? Fear, and dread roiled my guts like wild animals fighting to the death inside me. I worried for a second that I might shit my pants but managed to make it home in time.

I turned on the TV to a local news channel. A reporter interviewed two eyewitnesses, a shocked young man and a sobbing middle-aged woman, who both described seeing the plane plunge from the sky and into their neighborhood. There was video of black smoke and fire rising up between bungalows, driveways, minivans, mailboxes. Firemen unraveled a hose in the street while houses burned. It was a sickening horror: both the immediate, visible reality, and the fact that it may have been a deliberate act.

I turned off the TV. We would learn within a few days that the crash had been a tragic accident, not a terror attack. The plane had wobbled after takeoff, the inexperienced co-pilot badly overcorrected, the vertical stabilizer came dislodged, and the plane fell out of the sky and into peoples' yards and houses, instantly exploding in a fireball. Later investigations would show a design flaw in the rudder.

It was the second-deadliest aviation disaster in US history, and yet because it was an accident, there was, in the atmosphere, a weird collective sense of relief about the whole thing, and a doubling down on the notion that "life is short" and "anything can happen," which caused people to act in unpredictable ways, running full-speed toward, or swiftly away from, danger and uncertainty. Among people I knew, there were sudden breakups and ill-advised marriages. If I hadn't already decided to quit my job, I would have done it then.

The day after the plane crash, I was back at work, editing recipes at the bar. Across the room, I could hear Durim, the new service manager, talking to a young phone girl.

"What did I tell you about blondes wearing pink?" he said, play-acting at scolding her. "I can hardly control myself around you!"

The girl, an NYU freshman, smiled up at Durim from the ban-quette where she was seated, taking call after call. Her face was sheepish, her laugh light. She was wearing a blush-colored oxford shirt that was buttoned to the top of her sternum.

Durim had been on the job for about six months. When he first started, I wondered if he was too polite and soft-spoken for the loose, fun, dirty-talking culture of the restaurant staff. The busboys made fun of his Albanian accent, a combination of Italian and Slavic with a bit of the Bronx, and the waiters pushed back against his stiff notions of fine dining service, which he'd honed in various four-star dining rooms. Durim must have spent some time quietly observing the pre-vailing horny ethos, because now here he was, pretending to be upset with a young employee because he found her fuckability a distraction.

It wasn't just Durim: Mario's vocal horniness had set a tone for everyone who worked at Babbo. His grabby hands and constant dirty jokes and innuendo signified that it was OK, even encouraged, to flirt with and grope each other. No one called it harassment, except per-haps when making jokes about it. I had a stack of publicity photos of Mario in a two-handed finger gun pose, a slight smile on his face. One morning before he came in, I took one from the stack and used a Sharpie to write the words "Free breast exams!" on it. I showed some female coworkers to get a laugh. Then I put the photo in my bag and took it home, to be safe.

It was an open secret that Mario pawed at the women on staff. One afternoon during set-up, I'd seen him reach for the cotton draw-string that dangled down the front of a pair of lavender sweatpants worn by a cute young backwaiter named Ariela. His knuckles grazed her crotch for a split second before he pulled her toward him, using the string. She jumped back and shrieked, in the showily playful way of an adolescent girl being teased by an adolescent boy. Was she acting, to keep the peace? I had no way of knowing.

Within my first few months of working for him, Mario, ostensibly sober, also groped me during the workday, while I was taking a call on the cordless phone, walking in a kind of aimless circle around the dining room.

There were a few people around—a porter hauling laundry bags down the staircase, a telephone girl, one or two waiters starting to take chairs down from atop tables. No one was paying any attention when Mario beelined toward me, from the front door of the restaurant to the middle of the dining room. While I had my back to him, he simply grabbed my ass with one hand, squeezed hard, let go, and moved on into the kitchen.

I was rattled and distracted, but ended the call, and found Mario in the kitchen, leafing through invoices on a clipboard. I went and stood at his elbow.

"Hey. Please don't do that again," I said, quietly. I could see that I had startled him, but he instantly regrouped to furrowed-brow, narrow-eyed, curled-lip contempt.

"What are you, a lesbian?"

I laughed, then left the kitchen and went down to the basement to cry. *It's not really a big deal*, I told myself then, and I think it now, as I write this. *It wasn't that big a deal.* I told Jessica and my sister that Mario had grabbed my ass but didn't discuss it with anyone at work. I didn't want it to get back to him as gossip, and I didn't want to burden anyone else with the knowledge.

Everyone had good reasons for wanting to be and stay at Babbo, which meant excusing the odd grope or weird innuendo. The front of house staff made great money, the cooks got the experience and the glory of working in a red-hot place with a red-hot chef, and even the phone girls and hostesses had access to the powers of saying yes and no to reservation requests.

Mario's generosity with connections and opportunities was what kept me on the hook. As promised, he'd introduced me to food and travel editors, for whom I was now writing my own freelance stories. Mario had shared bylines with me in *Paper* and the *Los Angeles Times* and *Wine Enthusiast*. He sent me to continuing-ed classes in recipe writing, Italian, and HTML, and trusted me with a lot of responsibility for his books and the recipes and guest bookings for his TV show.

And he threw me some substantial crumbs from his heaving table: tickets to a *Saturday Night Live* broadcast, a Willie Nelson concert, a Rangers game. A third-row seat at the celebrity-packed *GQ* Men of the Year Awards. Three more boozy, gluttonous working trips to Atlantic City, two to Aspen, and one each to Miami, Boston, Philadelphia. Endless free drinks and meals, and the occasional bottle of precious aceto balsamico. A Tiffany crystal football etched with the NFL logo. And his old laptop, in lieu of a cash Christmas bonus. (That one kind of sucked, actually.)

Mario could be tyrannical, irrational, and mean. I tried to move cautiously through each day to avoid triggering a flare-up of rage or the spark of a sudden vendetta. He put a lock on the restaurant's stereo cabinet, which prevented anyone from interfering with his carefully chosen music selections. When he discovered that I'd unlocked the cabinet so that a manager could remove a CD that had been skipping during service, he called me a "pathetic moron," told me I ought to remember whose team I was on, and hissed, "Have I not made it very clear that no one touches the music? It is *my restaurant* and *I control the music.*"

Later that day he tossed a bouquet of white roses and lilies onto my desk and said, "Sorry."

He was forever on the defensive, paranoid that anyone else might be getting something more or better, and apoplectic if it turned out to be true. After one of our Atlantic City casino events, featuring several chefs, he was super-pissed to discover that the hotel had provided round-trip helicopter service from New York for Daniel Boulud and his team, while we'd only been offered a limousine. "Next time, Woolie, you demand me a *fucking* chopper."

Deflecting his intrusions and absorbing his rage was the price of admission to a pool I nonetheless felt very fortunate to swim in. I had jumped into the water, and I knew it was wet. If I suddenly realized that

I couldn't swim, I thought, it was on me to find the ladder and climb out. I was one of dozens of women in his orbit who would laugh off his suffocating hugs and suggestive comments, the occasional tongue in the ear, the lacerating, humiliating verbal kicks in the back. We were too dependent on our jobs, too invested in maintaining a friendly atmosphere, to ever raise an objection, and anyway, wasn't it just the nature of the rough-and-tumble restaurant business we all loved? Would things really be any different anyplace else?

When I decided to give notice, I didn't consciously think, and never said, that it was because of Mario's behavior. I believed it was because, as a generalist assistant in a world of specific competencies, I had learned all I would probably learn. I had been treading water, neither front of house nor back, and inessential to Mario's burgeoning TV and writing careers. Six months out from publishing *The Babbo Cookbook*, he'd decided that my name would not go on the cover after all. It was close to the bottom of a long list of acknowledgments.

Also? I had drunkenly slept with too many coworkers, and now I wanted to meet someone nice, someone whose heart hadn't been corroded by restaurant life. I was always broke, and I was drinking a lot, all the time.

Did I drink so much because I was unfulfilled, or was I unfulfilled because I drank so much? I had no idea. Everyone I hung out with, my colleagues and my college friends, drank and drugged; to relax, for fun, for the management of moods. I never said no to a bump of coke, and never ran out of weed, which I now had delivered to me at the restaurant.

Given the paramountcy of loyalty in Mario's world, I was extremely nervous about leaving. Defectors were dead to him, for the sin of taking what they'd learned in his employ and applying it to someone else's success. It wasn't just Mario, of course; no one is happy when a valued, well-trained employee leaves, but Mario was ready to scorch earth over a hasty exit. I gave him twelve months' notice, which was absurd, but I hoped it would protect me from being blacklisted if I ended up working for another chef or restaurant.

It only occurred to me later that I'd also protected myself from a raise or bonus.

Close to the end of my lame-duck year as Mario's assistant, we went to Melbourne, Australia, for that city's Food & Wine Festival. Major sponsor Singapore Airlines gave us two business-class tickets, but Mario insisted on bringing two assistants, me and chef Mark Ladner, who at the time was running the Roman trattoria Lupa. I only managed to squeeze the airline for an extra coach-class ticket, so Mark and I would have to trade off sitting in business class with Mario, and alone in coach, over the course of our three flights to Melbourne.

We flew from Newark to Amsterdam on a Monday evening. I started in business class. I'd brought some Vicodin and Percocet that had been gifted to me by one of the phone girls with a side gig selling pills, and some Ativan that my primary care doctor, a huge Mario fan, had prescribed for my (fictional) anxiety about flying. I took the drugs interchangeably, one of something every few hours, washed down with white wine. Mario drank one beer and fell asleep shortly after takeoff. The pills made me feel dumb and dissociated but were no match for Mario's snoring. I did not sleep.

Despite a burgeoning head cold, I found the will to smoke three consecutive cigarettes in the smokers' lounge, which was a few folding chairs arranged inside a grim, glass-walled box. I took an Ativan, then boarded the flight to Singapore, and for the next twelve hours, I had a few infrequent and jagged ten-minute increments of sleep, dreaming I'd been left in charge of a wolf-like dog that I'd neglected to feed.

We had a five-hour layover in Singapore. Everyone was punchy. I'd lost track of the time of day, and the day itself. Mark and Mario and I drank big beers and ate bowls of steamy yellow noodles with pork and shrimp. I paid $20 to take a shower and $10 to sit in a recliner with a thin tube strapped to my face, inhaling purified oxygen. I took a Vicodin.

Back with Mario in business class for the final leg, I fell gratefully into my window seat, determined to sleep through the snoring this time. When the flight attendant offered him a drink, he said, "The lady and I will each have a Singapore sling."

The cool red cocktail went down like cherry Robitussin on ice, and then I had to pee. Mario set his empty glass down on his tray and depressed the seat-side buttons to elevate his legs and lower his head and shoulders.

"You know what, I actually need to get up and use the lav'," I said, just as he got fully reclined.

"I guess you're gonna have to straddle me," he said. I laughed. He didn't.

"Woolie, I have already made myself comfortable," he said. His voice had that high, tight tone of dangerous annoyance. "I *know* you're not asking me to adjust my seat because *you* forgot to pee. You want to get up? Climb on up and over, baby."

I was wearing a denim skirt that hit just above my knees, and I had to hike it up to scramble awkwardly across Mario's lap. I faced him, so as to not expose him to my actual ass, but I kept my eyes on the carpeted aisle. He reached up and put his hands on my hips as I moved across him, and again when I did the same crawl back into my seat. I wondered how I might have avoided this humiliation. I could have worn an adult diaper, I guess, or refused to go on the trip. I closed my eyes and did not get up again.

We landed in Melbourne and it was, incredibly, Wednesday evening. The festival director, Sandra, met us outside the customs hall with a driver in a slim suit, who loaded our bags into a Mercedes van. Sandra was a handsome silver-haired woman in a navy shift and pearls, a slash of coral lipstick, and a cheer in her voice that shredded my nerves.

We went straight to dinner at Flower Drum, a fancy Cantonese restaurant, where we joined a huge round table of a dozen or so other festival presenters. Sandra directed me to sit next to an elderly American man named Hank. His wife was a cookbook author who'd be speaking and doing cooking demos.

"Do y'all experience asparagus pee?" Hank asked the group as I pulled my chair closer to the table. He was a retired chemical engineer and had some unique insights on the topic.

I was wrecked with fatigue, my throat and head pounding, my nasal passages now a fountain of thin yellow mucous. I chugged two quick glasses of Champagne and took a sip of water before the waiters began delivering the food: glistening, translucent spring onion cakes, followed by scallops with lily buds and a whole roast sucking pig the size of a well-fed toddler, the meat tender, the skin like crunchy taffy. There was Murray cod fried in a rice flour batter and garnished with soy sauce, scallions, and cilantro, then thin slices of abalone that had been cooked for thirteen hours at low temperature, served with dainty baby bok choy. When the waiters retreated, Sandra told us that abalone retailed for $450 per kilo. Mario and Mark, seated across the table from me, both seemed somehow completely fucking functional, even chipper, whereas I was a mute shadow of a ghoul.

A waiter returned to let us know that there would soon be a duck course and a beef course, and that the chef and his cooks would then come out to introduce themselves before two dessert courses, which would be followed by coffee and brandy.

I did the math on how much longer we would have to sit at this table, then heard the sound of shattering glass from somewhere inside my mind. I started to cry, silently, feeling not so much sad as held hostage. I closed my eyes, started to nod off, and when I opened them again, I saw that Mario was staring across the table at me with narrow-eyed fury. Sandra was up from her seat, coming around toward me.

"Come on dear, let's leave the table," she said, grasping my elbow, leading me to a bench near the coat check. I sat down. Mario had followed us; he sat next to me. Sandra smiled tightly and retreated.

"Get a grip, Woolie," he hissed. "It's gonna be a long fucking week if you can't keep your shit together."

"I'm sorry," I mumbled, mashing my fingers across the tears on my cheeks. "I'm jet-lagged, I have a bad cold—"

"You've been taking some heavy fucking pharmaceuticals and

drinking for two days," he interrupted. "You can't handle that shit. What did you think was gonna happen? Go splash some water on your face and come back to the table." He got up and walked away.

I felt ashamed and furious, yet weirdly cared for, like Meadow Soprano being dressed down by her father, Tony. That the pills were a bad idea had never occurred to me. I took a few deep breaths, dug my nails into my palms, and went back to the table for the Peking duck, beef filet, milk-and-ginger pudding, and bird nest with almond soup. When the chef came from the kitchen to greet our table, he spoke only with Mario.

The next morning, soaking in a hot bath at the Park Hyatt, I coughed up green phlegm speckled with blood, like some clunky plot device foreshadowing my consumptive death, which I hoped would happen, so that Mario would feel suitably bad about scolding me.

Later, Sandra took us on a tour of the Queen Victoria Market, where for the first time I saw whole goats and lambs and kangaroos skinned and posed for display at a butcher's stall. The animals' intact eyes looked enormous in their bony faces. We ate sausage sandwiches and drank red wine for lunch, standing up in a corner, then went back to the hotel to prep for the first of Mario's three cooking seminars.

He talked to the capacity crowd in his usual intense and authoritative cadence about the "miraculous and celestial love story between this specific pasta and sauce," disparaged grocery store butchers, and hinted that whisking zabaglione was just like jerking off, while Mark and I worked furiously backstage, plating small portions of bucatini all'amatriciana in a hotel production kitchen down a long hall from the ballroom.

For the next four days, between seminars and panel discussions, we were obligated to a full schedule of boozy long lunches and dinners with sponsors, the other festival presenters, and their spouses. We ate and drank some extraordinary things: unfamiliar game birds and black truffles and huge prawns and tiny vegetables, Persian fairy floss and fair-trade chocolate, Australian Shiraz and vintage Champagne and well-aged Sauternes and some very rare and exclusive sake. I kept a close watch on the room, and after each dinner, once I gleaned that it was even slightly not rude to do so, I retreated to the hotel, while Mario and Mark continued on into the night, drinking and smoking and making new friends.

On the morning of our last seminar, Mark said, "You know, the big man is really pissed at you for not going out drinking with us. He said you're not being a team player, that you don't have his back."

I felt like throwing up. "Yeah, but I think I have, like, a sinus infection," I said.

"I don't know, maybe take some cold medicine and go out with us tonight," Mark said. "I'm just the messenger."

I'd failed to realize that being a drinking buddy wasn't a fun perk of the job; it *was* the job. On paper, I was there to help tong pasta onto plates and hold on to business cards, but really, I was there to be a punching bag, a co-conspirator, a wingman, a straight man, a convenient female body, whether or not I had a cold or jet lag or just simply wanted some time to myself.

What did I expect? For three years, I was a good-time assistant, taking the trips and drinking the booze and laughing at the awful jokes and sometimes making them, too. My mistake had been believing that it was always my privilege and my choice to hang out with Mario and keep him company while he drank.

I couldn't wait to be done with the job. I let Mark take the business class seats all the way back from Melbourne to New York.

A few days after we got back from Australia, Mario handed me a Babbo business card, on the back of which was written "TONY," above an Upper West Side street address.

"I met Anthony Bourdain at a dinner last night," he said. "Really cool guy. He's looking to hire someone to help him write a cookbook and I told him he should hire you. Write him a letter."

chapter 10

Meetings

I wrote a letter to Anthony Bourdain, selling myself as the right
person to help with his book, and I put the word out to the French
Culinary Institute that Mario needed a new assistant. We got dozens
of resumes, from students, recent grads, and people who were way
overqualified. Mario interviewed a few top prospects, then chose
Eileen, who was tall and thin and pretty, with sleek brown hair and
a wardrobe of Missoni knits, Marc Jacobs T-shirts, and Prada trousers. She was a few years younger than me and had also graduated
from Cornell, where she'd studied English literature and ridden for
the varsity equestrian team. She started the job two weeks before my
last day, so that I could train her.

At the end of her first day, Mario and Roger exchanged a look
behind Eileen's slender back as she exited out the front door. Mario
said to Roger, "Quite an upgrade, huh?" as if it didn't matter that I
had ears, and Roger answered with his maniacal clown laugh.

My last day working as Mario's assistant was a Saturday. Many of
my coworkers joined me that night for a boozy farewell gathering at a
bar called Jane, on West Houston Street. Mario brought along a B-list
film actor he'd recently befriended, had a few drinks, and picked up

the whole tab. I was alternately happy-drunk and performing sadness, the way you sometimes do when you're young and leaving a job and will miss the friends you made there.

The next morning, I flew to the Bahamas. Mario's friend Butch had arranged a generous discount for me at the Atlantis resort, which his family owned. I'd invited my sister to join me, but her new husband had said no, that he wouldn't allow her to travel without him. I filed that red flag away for another time and went on vacation alone.

Mario had pushed me to book at Atlantis, because Butch owed him a favor, and it never occurred to me to explore other options. Even with the discount, the cost of four nights in the hotel ate up most of my meager Visa credit limit. I scanned the prices on the menus posted outside the various dining rooms on the property, then I put on my backpack and walked two miles to the nearest grocery store, where I bought a loaf of sandwich bread, a jar of peanut butter, a half pound of sliced ham, and some guava paste. There was no air-conditioning in the store, and there were no other tourists there. The power went off twice in ten minutes. On the walk back, I stopped at a liquor store and bought a liter of vodka and a six-pack of beer. After drinking the first beer back in my room, I bent the empty can slightly in half and used a tweezer to puncture it with a few strategically placed holes. Now I had a janky pipe with which to smoke the weed I'd smuggled to the Bahamas in my underpants.

I spent the next few days swimming in the ocean, getting stoned on my tiny balcony, and lying in the big bed drinking and watching old game shows, Food Network, and *E! True Hollywood Story: The Barbi Twins*. I saw myself on a rerun episode of *Molto Mario*. I took slow, aimless walks through and around all the public parts of the resort. I saw a young mother seated on the floor of the casino, bottle-feeding an infant wearing a hot pink onesie that said "I'm a tease." I saw groups of athletic teens and their sunburnt parents leaving greasy paper napkins and huge plastic cups still half-full with soda on the beach. I was deeply lonely, but amid the messy humanity careless snuffling up resources and spitting out trash and wet towels, I told myself that I should be glad to be alone, if this was what togetherness looked like.

On my last afternoon at the resort, I rode a waterslide that corkscrewed though the interior of an archeologically suspect Mayan temple replica with a built-in shark tank. When I splashed down into the pool at the end of the slide, I felt self-consciously dumb.

I'd loved waterslides as a kid, but now I was a stoned, unemployed twenty-eight-year-old, staying in an overpriced, intensively family-friendly resort designed for people who lacked the courage and imagination to go to, like, actual Mexico (a group that would seem to include me).

When I got home to New York the next night, I had a voicemail from Anthony Bourdain, who identified himself as "Tony."

"Mario gave you the seal of approval, and that's good enough for me," said his recorded voice. He wanted me to edit and test the recipes for his new cookbook, if I was still interested. He said we should meet to discuss details at the end of the summer, and then start work in the fall. I called him back. His answering machine picked up, and the voice of Elvis Costello chided: "Sometimes I wish that I could stop you from talking when I hear the silly things you say." I accepted the position, with extreme brevity.

I needed a little immediate income, too, so I started cooking dinner twice a week for Olek, a wealthy landlord, and his young family. Olek spent a lot of time driving between his properties in Manhattan, Yonkers, and the Bronx. He loved a bargain and would frequently insist that I cook with something he'd picked up on clearance, like a box of split and weeping tomatoes or a bag of mixed mussels and squid bodies that had logged many warm miles in the passenger seat of his SUV.

I always got good and stoned just before walking over to Olek's place. I told myself that this made me more creative, focused, and spontaneous, that it got me into a flow, and made the work more fun. In reality, being so high led to lots of dumb little mistakes: I'd carelessly dice the potatoes before peeling them, add too much water to the rice, forget to season the meat before I put it on the grill. A few hours in, as the euphoria fizzled out, I'd be irritable and distracted and frustrated with my own torpor and stupidity and slowness. When I got home, I'd remedy that by having a few stiff drinks and smoking more weed.

Late that summer, I attended my ten-year high school reunion, in my little hometown of Chittenango, New York. I stayed with my parents, who had fled New Jersey and moved back upstate the second my dad retired. The reunion was held at the Rusty Rail. Tickets cost $30, and were good for unlimited well drinks and a buffet supper: dinner rolls, some unlovely carrot and celery sticks, and a few chafing dishes of baked ziti that was somehow both wet and burnt.

Being a high-achieving high school student had socially alienated me from my most popular classmates, which is to say the athletes, the pretty girls, the burnouts, and the kids with criminally permissive and/or absent parents. Back then, at the occasional weekend party, I tried to win the cool kids' validating approval, performatively smoking their ditch weed and drinking Coors Light. Now, ten years after graduation, I found myself still doing a pantomime of deviance for their acceptance, this time with brown liquor and joints rolled from the fragrant weed I'd had delivered to my home (I bragged), in darkest New York City. Many of my classmates had stayed local, gotten married young, and had kids right away; a few were already divorced.

When anyone asked about my work, I only said that I was a freelance writer and an assistant to a chef. I figured that if they'd heard of Mario, they'd be too impressed, and if they hadn't heard of Mario, they wouldn't be impressed at all.

The next morning, I sat at my parents' kitchen island, fixing my misery with a plate of cheesy scrambled eggs and a thin ham steak. My mother sat next to me, drinking coffee, her brand-new walker parked next to her chair. She stared at my hands for a few seconds. "Why are you eating like that?"

"Like what?" I asked.

"With your fork in your left hand and your knife in the right," she said. It was accusation.

"It's the European style," I said. "I took a table manners course last year, for an article. It's more efficient; you don't have to change hands when you're cutting your food."

"Oh, so the way that I do it isn't good enough anymore?" There was an unconvincing tease in her voice.

For fuck's sake, lady, I thought. "No, mom, I just like it better this way." She continued to watch me as I finished my breakfast. That I could hurt her with a fork and knife made me feel guilty, which in turn made me furious. Later, while she showered and my dad mowed the lawn, I filled a travel mug with vodka and ice cubes and sipped it steadily on the long train ride back to New York.

That night, feeling like shit, with nothing to look forward to but another drink, I called a young woman named Anne, who answered phones and hostessed at Babbo, and whom I knew had recently started attending 12-step meetings.

"I'm not sure, but I think I might be drinking too much," I said. She invited me to join her at a nearby Tuesday-morning AA meeting, just to listen. I said I'd see her there.

Monday night, Alejandro and I went to the soft opening of a new midtown restaurant, operated by a fellow French Culinary Institute graduate who'd reached out after seeing my bylines in *Time Out New York*. I was punchy and sad and scared, worried that this might be my last-ever night of drinking, and I'd better make it a good one. After a quick dinner, we moved to the bar. I didn't know what to do next with my life, and there was no one to ask. I drank too many vodka tonics, too fast. I was retelling old stories, detailing ancient grudges. I was jealous of everyone who seemed to have their shit together, which I assumed was everyone in the world but me.

I was speaking too loud. I spit on the floor. I was, yet again, teetering on the edge of blackout wasted, an absolute embarrassing disaster.

"Fuck this place," I yelled, for no reason.

"You need to stop," said Alejandro, quietly. As drinking buddies, we had been evenly matched for the first few years together in New York, but now it seemed my internal combustion engine, which ran on booze, had gotten stuck in the highest gear. He led me out onto the street and put me in a cab, then continued his night.

I woke up sick and sweaty, hating myself. I called Anne at home and told her that I was too sick to join her AA meeting. I called Alejandro at his office and said, "I'm gonna take a break from drinking," and I did, for six weeks, during which I still smoked weed at least once a day and poured myself endless glasses of iced seltzer with lime and bitters, to mimic the soothing sound and feel of a cocktail. Once I saw that I could make myself stop, I started drinking again, slowly at first, and then gradually faster. I never made it to a meeting with Anne. I didn't really want to get caught up in all that, and obviously didn't really need it.

There were other useful meetings, though. In a white warren of cubicles in the Condé Nast building, I met with a marketing manager at *Bon Appetit*, and got some lucrative copywriting work. I met Kathleen McElroy, then the editor of the *New York Times* Dining section, who wanted to hear my ideas, and gave me the chance to pitch and land my very first *Times* food story, about the homemade corned beef hash at a Brooklyn diner called Dizzy's. Mario called to congratulate me the morning the piece appeared in the paper, pretending to be a lumberjack looking for a hearty breakfast. I published another piece in the *Times*, about sake, and then another one, about unusual risottos. These short items didn't pay much—about $250 each—but there was my name, in print, in the *New York* Motherfucking *Times*.

And I met with Tony Bourdain for the first time, to talk about how we would approach the *Les Halles Cookbook* project. I expected him to be a French-inflected version of Mario: a man playacting as a pirate, swaggering, maybe a little handsy, probably quite mean. I steeled myself, but: in the warmth of his welcome and his overt gratitude for my taking the job, in his theatrical self-effacement and his slight, endearing awkwardness, Tony thwarted every one of my expectations.

We established and agreed upon a plan of action: using the recipes in the Les Halles kitchen bible, I would scale down the quantities and expand upon the methods to make them legible to the home cook.

I would then test and adjust the recipes and pass them on to Tony, who would write headnotes and sidebars laced with the hyperbolic, faux-threatening, "listen up, dipshits"-style writing that had made him a star.

Now that I was strictly a freelancer, I needed tax advice, so I met with an old, gravel-voiced accountant with wild white eyebrows, like filaments of mold on the abandoned spaghetti of his deeply lined face. After a brief review of my credit card and student loan debt, my projected income, my expenses, and my whole human person, he growled, "The best thing I can tell you is to spend some time and money, fix yourself up a bit, and find a good man with a good job." For that wisdom, I wrote him a check for $75. I then went to Kinko's, paid $6 for 30 minutes of internet time, and invested $39.95 in an online dating profile.

In the early 2000s, online dating was so novel a phenomenon that the *New York Times Magazine* commissioned an eight-thousand-word feature on the subject from future Pulitzer-winner Jennifer Egan. She framed web-shopping for love and/or sex as an enlightened, future-forward pursuit, eloquently sweeping away the loser stigma of personal ads:

> *Serendipitous love as a romantic ideal is a paean to cities*
> *and their dislocations, the unlikely collisions that result from*
> *thousands of strangers with discrete histories overlapping*
> *briefly in time and space. And online dating is not the opposite*
> *of this approach to love, but its radical extension; if cities erase*
> *people's histories and cram them together in space, online*
> *dating sites erase both cities and space, gathering people*
> *instead under the virtual rubric of a brand.*

I wholeheartedly embraced her generous perspective, and decided that my brand would be "smart / irreverent / blonde," while the brand I sought was "kind / gentle / gainfully employed (but not in restaurants)." To extend (and maybe torture) Egan's metaphor, if looking for serendipitous love in the three-dimensional world was like hunting an animal, or being hunted, then online dating was like choosing a cut of butchered meat at the grocery store, aware that the extra skin and fatty, gristly bits—mine and the other person's— would likely stay hidden until after purchase.

Anyway, that's how I met Alex, on a dating site. He was a welcome palate cleanser after all the dysfunctional restaurant randos I'd gulped down the previous few years. Alex spoke softly, was funny and mildly self-deprecating, loved cats, lived alone, and had a job working behind the scenes in live television news.

We were both lonely and in our late twenties. We both came from the same coupon-clipping stratum of the middle class, both grew up in the kind of small town that you were desperate to leave if you were an ambitious and disaffected weirdo, as it seemed we both were.

We liked some of the same music, and both liked to drink, smoke weed, and eat a lot.

On our first date, a late lunch at an unremarkable café not far from my place, we realized that we'd worked at the same event six months prior. It was a NASCAR awards banquet at the grand old Waldorf Astoria hotel. I was inside, helping Mario make and plate Istrian ravioli with poppyseeds and butter, while Alex was in a television van right outside, helping to produce the broadcast of the event. I had no faith system and didn't believe astrology, but I wanted this coincidence to mean something good.

I saw too much promise in our fledgling relationship to sleep with Alex right away, and he was cautious, too, even offering handshakes in lieu of kissing me after our first, second and third dates. For the fourth date, we met at his tiny place in Brooklyn, where he cooked us penne with broccoli, bacon, pine nuts, raisins, and black olives, while simultaneously talking one of his company's clients through a tech crisis over the phone. I was impressed by the multitasking, especially since we'd just gotten high before the phone rang.

We ate the pasta out of big white bowls, sitting side by side at his desk, which held two computer monitors and two keyboards, stacks of

CDs and papers, cords and connectors, and technical manuals. When we were done eating, Alex said, "Do you want to see a crazy picture of someone I went to high school with?"

I did.

He handed me a 4 x 6 glossy black and white print of a teenage girl on her hands and knees, wearing a one-piece sleeveless bodysuit, stretchy white lace, cut very high on the legs and very low on the bust. She had the gigantically crunchy blasted-out heavy metal hairdo endemic to certain public school girls of the late 80s and early 90s. Her eyes were heavily lined, which made them seem smaller than they were; her face was smooth and pale, but the skin on her shoulders was densely freckled. She looked up at the camera with open-faced desire, her small smile sly and inviting. Who had taken this picture of her, and for what purpose? On the back of the photo was written "Terra," a seven-digit phone number, and the invitation to "call me."

He hadn't called her, Alex said, because he didn't think they would have much to talk about, and this made me laugh.

"I don't know that she wanted to talk," I said. There was something about his abstract introduction of sex that made me feel ready to take my clothes off with this nice guy who reminded me more of me than anyone I'd met in New York.

Later that night, Alex told me about a former girlfriend who'd moved from New Jersey to Florida with him, while he attended a tech school in Orlando. She soon started fooling around with his roommate, and when he found out, he heaved the roommate through the screen on the first-floor window of their apartment. I found it weirdly hot that this gentle person could be pushed to the point of physical violence.

"I'm a conventional guy," he said. "I believe in old-fashioned love."

It was early days, but I brought Alex to my parents' house that Christmas. Soon after, we shared a disgusting bout of norovirus. He spent three weeks in Saudi Arabia, for work, and when he returned, at 10:30 on a Monday morning, I was waiting for him, in his bed. In the spring, his mother bought me a flight to Las Vegas, so I could join him there for his thirtieth birthday, which he spent working at a tech trade show.

When, after six months together, I invited Alex to move in with me, motivated by a sense of safety and intimacy and joy, I felt sure that my mature adult life was now on a singular straight track.

chapter 11

Parting Gift

From inside a hotel bathtub in Charleston, South Carolina, I said, to no one, "I might not be able to pull this off."

"This" was creating an irresistible cookbook proposal, and then writing that cookbook, with Celeste, who had hired me for that very purpose. I was alone, and in theory, writing, but I'd just used an empty Diet Coke can to smoke weed, and had no plans to leave the scalding water.

Celeste was a caterer with a small chain of shops that sold crowd-pleasing prepared foods: buttery grilled cheese sandwiches with pepper jelly, whole roasted chickens with herbs and lemons under the skin, fluffy scones, big chewy peanut butter cookies, pints of pimiento cheese. The literary agent who'd connected us had described Celeste's brand as "middle-class Alice Waters."

She had just published her first cookbook, and because it sold well, the agent insisted she write another one, quickly, but Celeste was stretched thin running her business, and not naturally a writer; she needed help from someone with a finger on the pulse of her demographic, whom I understood to be female real estate agents with smooth-haired children enrolled at good schools. These women vacationed with their families in the Virgin Islands and Maine, lavishly fundraised for breast cancer charities, made jam as a hobby, and thought about Sting or Bill or Hillary Clinton when and if they masturbated.

Celeste needed someone who could confidently craft an original and marketable concept for her second book, after she'd put all her best ideas into the first one. What she got instead was me, a stoner of limited means and experience, albeit one with Mario's powerful brand name on my resumé, and no agent of my own to stop me from accepting her first offer of $25,000 for proposal and manuscript, which seemed like a life-changing sum, but was in fact far below what Celeste's first coauthor had been willing to accept.

Celeste flew me to South Carolina and put me up in a hotel for a few days, so that we could work together in person on the proposal, really hammer it out. We both expected a lot more of me than I found myself able to deliver.

She'd hired me in New York, over a chatty lunch at Les Halles, where I had felt confident and competent. Outside the Charleston airport, the second I settled into the leather passenger seat of Celeste's Volvo SUV, with my empty notebook and reliable hangover, I sensed the yawning knowledge and culture gaps between us. I trailed her around her busy stores and her capacious home kitchen for two days, scribbling a few notes of dubious utility. We shared several polite meals, during which I drank too much white wine and stumbled my way through increasingly obtuse discussions about big salads and easy marinades and the many charms of roasted garlic. I kept turning the conversation to her omnipresent dachshund, Wendell, who was all too happy to burrow into my lap and fart at irregular intervals.

Immobilized in the hotel tub, aware that I was flailing, I thought about the books of Mario's that I'd worked on. I'd had nothing to do with selling *Holiday Food* and *The Babbo Cookbook* to the publisher; those titles were greenlit because Mario's voice and point of view were rock-solid and distinctive. He knew exactly what he wanted to do, and

he had lots of great ideas, backed up with deep knowledge, a charismatic TV presence, and a growing empire of hot restaurants. I had
simply followed his direction, manifesting his vision with my labor.
Celeste didn't have a vision for her second book, and the more I tried
to help her figure it out, the more elusive the answer became.

I have made a tactical error, I thought, while alternating bites
of a Twix and a Slim Jim from the minibar. Why couldn't I just get
someone to give me money to write an organ meat cookbook, or a
novel about drinking and the messy sex lives of young people in the
restaurant business? (I had not yet tried to do those things, which
both seemed very difficult and uncertain.)

The bath water had become cool. I pulled the plug, got out,
wrapped myself in the heavy hotel robe, sat on the bed, and tried
to soften my angst with an episode of *Pet Star*, a delightfully stupid
animal pageant show judged by Mario Lopez. I then smoked some
more weed, opened my laptop, and did the best I could to synthesize
my notes into a useful proposal. I emailed it to Celeste's agent, drank
a mini-vodka and a min-rum, and fell asleep, teeth unbrushed.

The next morning, the agent emailed me back, cc'ing Celeste.
"There are no IDEAS here," she wrote. "It's NOT in good shape.
This is not a sellable document. It needs a CONCEPT. Why does this
book need to exist? You've GOT to justify its existence." *Shit.*

When Celeste picked me up an hour later, her smile was small,
her voice slightly hard-edged. "Let's see if we can't fix this thing up
today before I take you to the airport," she said, and I nodded.

We settled at a picnic table in the back of her largest store, sipping
weak coffees out of paper cups. James Taylor sang about the copper-
line on the store's PA system. I opened my laptop and my notebook.
We were going to drill down on a CONCEPT. I couldn't wait to be
alone again.

"So, why *does* this book need to exist?" I began. Celeste chuckled
mirthlessly. We hadn't yet talked big picture.

"I suppose there's a demand for it," she said.

"So maybe we approach it from a fast-and-easy perspective," I said.

"How do you feel about frozen vegetables as a weeknight shortcut?" I asked.

"Hmm . . . they're . . . not *ideal*," she said.

"What are your best-sellers here at the store?" I asked.

"Honestly? Pretty much everything that was in the first book," she said.

I was so confused about what I was supposed to do, embarrassed by myself, and ever more shy in the face of Celeste's reticence. On the flight home, I squeezed and poked, shaved and padded the proposal, trying to force it into the shape of a "sellable document."

That night, I shared the new version with Celeste and her agent, who called me the next morning.

"Celeste is cutting her losses. You're not up to the task. Sorry it didn't work out."

As with the doomed pastry chef job, I was both miserable about my failure and relieved to be released from a bad fit. My ego was injured, but I didn't bottom out, perhaps because Joan, whose therapy office I still visited every other Tuesday, had recently convinced me to increase my antidepressant dosage.

When I told her that I'd been fired, Joan asked, "How do you feel about it?"

"I don't know. I guess kind of embarrassed?" I said. I was stoned. "And, not every job is for me. I need to focus on the things that I actually want to do."

"And what do you actually want to do?"

"I . . . think I want to work at a magazine," I said, "but I don't think I can get hired at a magazine." I found it impossible to say out loud what I wanted without immediately acknowledging the unlikelihood of my ever getting it. It was self-protection, cloaked in self-sabotage.

With magazines (as with any competitive field), there was a complex equation of education, skill and experience, inside connections, generational wealth, the right BMI, facility with a blow-dryer, good clothes without rips and oil stains, and an aptitude for knowing which asses to kiss and how much shit to eat, and when.

Fortunately, things were going swimmingly on the *Les Halles Cookbook*. Tony told me, via brief but hyperbolic emails, that he was happy with my work, and he paid me in full, on time, every month.

The recipe editing was easy enough, and when it came to the testing, I hosted frequent, boozy little dinner parties, at which I served the fruits of my labors: oeufs périgourdins (fancy deviled eggs stuffed with truffles and ham, then rolled in whipped egg whites and deep-fried in duck fat), tartiflette (a casserole of fried potatoes, bacon, and creamy Reblochon cheese), rabbit pâté, and French fries.

I was still cooking for Olek and his family, and had picked up work for another family with school-aged kids. I was working freelance for a few different catering companies and writing articles for *Time Out New York*, the *New York Times*, *GQ*, *Playboy,* and *Food & Wine*. I was always busy, keeping my name in print, paying most of my bills mostly on time, living with a Maine Coon cat named Squid, and Alex, my gainfully employed and non-threatening boyfriend.

Now, did it create an omnipresent ache of anxiety in my gut that our sex life had lately come to a near-standstill? Yes, but I blamed myself, both for having drunkenly asked Alex an unfair question ("Do you think I'm overweight?") and for then taking deep offense at his answer ("Yes, but I love you anyway."). I had set a sweet, guileless man up for failure.

I knew that I was, objectively, overweight. I never exercised and always ate as much of anything I wanted. I drank many thousands of empty booze calories per week and binge-ate when stoned, stressed, hungover, drunk, or bored, which accounted for most of my waking hours.

My sense of myself was impossible to extricate from how it was refracted back at me, existing only in relation to others—whether they found me attractive, could tolerate or ignore my flaws, whether or not they wanted to employ me or spend time with me. In the early months of our relationship, I believed that Alex found me and my body to be perfect and would never see, let alone name, any of my many flaws. To be disabused of this delusion made me feel intolerably vulnerable, and so I shut down.

One sweltering mid-August morning, I got a call from Eileen, the young woman who had replaced me as Mario's assistant.

"Mario's friend Rebecca needs a last-minute caterer for her boyfriend's birthday party," said Eileen. "Can I give her assistant your number?"

"Absolutely yes," I said. Rebecca was a Babbo regular, and the star of an extremely popular TV show. Once again, Mario had opened a door of opportunity.

I met Rebecca in her immaculate downtown loft apartment that afternoon. We sat opposite each other in the living room, on pink silk-upholstered couches piled with white velvet pillows, while Lisa, her assistant, fluttered in and out. The walls were painted a cool, pale gray and hung with two jarringly earnest paintings: an angel with the face and body of a teen beauty pageant winner, and a weirdly muscular dolphin, arcing out from the placid surface of a turquoise ocean.

Rebecca chatted amiably about the menu for her boyfriend's birthday dinner. She wanted whole grilled striped bass, corn on the cob, gazpacho, and "a gorgeous birthday cake," which I said I could definitely do, while wondering if I could actually do it.

"Fantastic!" she said with a wide smile. "Now, let's talk price. I don't like when people overcharge me because I'm famous and make a lot of money."

"Of course," I said, and accepted her first offer: $300, plus expenses.

This was one of the many ways that the well-connected rich stay rich, which is by underpaying young, ambitious skilled workers, trading on the promise of access to more rich and/or famous potential clients. Any rich person could pay top dollar for a catered dinner from Glorious Foods, but the real game was to find a hungry, unincorporated lone wolf like me, with a persistent doubt about her own worth, too polite and concerned about seeming greedy or losing the gig to negotiate for anything, for fear of losing out.

I took the subway home from Rebecca's, ruminating about shopping lists, timing, transportation. At $300, I couldn't afford to hire a helper. I'd be up most of the night, baking and decorating the cake. Was there enough room in my fridge for all the groceries I'd need to prep? Would Rebecca reimburse me for a car service? Did her fridge have an ice maker? Would her TV castmates be there, too? Would she tip me if things went well?

I was back home, looking through my purse for the Post-it with Lisa's phone number, when my window air conditioner groaned abruptly to a stop. The desk lamp went dark, the music on the stereo suddenly silent. I looked out the window and up at the sunny sky, not sure what I was expecting to see, then slipped on my sandals and went down to the street. All the stoplights on Avenue C were out; a few intrepid neighborhood guys had already taken up the task of directing traffic.

Outside Cibao Deli, about a dozen people were gathered around a battery-operated radio. I stood nearby, listening and bracing once again for something terrifying, shocking. After an Arby's ad, and one for an injury and accident law firm, the steadfast 1010 WINS announcer reported that there was a massive power blackout in New York that was spreading across the northeast.

To my relief, Lisa called to cancel Rebecca's dinner party. A few weeks later, she hired me to stock Rebecca's fridge, twice a week, with her favorite dishes from *The Babbo Cookbook*. When Rebecca's boyfriend proposed, we downshifted to zero-carb meals from the *South Beach Diet Cookbook*, so that she'd be acceptably skeletal for the wedding pictures that she'd pre-sold to a major fashion magazine. All those broiled tomatoes and extra-lean beef patties paid off: in the published photos, she had a praying mantis jawline and her shoulder blades and clavicles looked like gorgeous flesh-wrapped razor blades.

Near the end of my first day back at Rebecca's after her two-week honeymoon in Bali, she walked into the kitchen, opened the fridge, surveying the stacks of Pyrex boxes full of barley salad and roasted broccoli and lamb chops and Dijon vinaigrette. She closed the fridge and said, "Everything looks amazing, as usual. Thank you so much, you're a superhero, but we have to have a difficult talk."

My stomach lurched. She continued: "Now that I'm an old married lady and ready to start a family, I've hired this incredibly sweet Thai housekeeper who will cook *and* clean *and* take care of my babies, when I have them. But! I wanted to give you a parting gift."

I wiped down my knives and wrapped them up for the last time, slightly crushed, but ready to graciously receive an envelope of severance cash and referrals to her rich friends.

"I think you need to lose some weight," said Rebecca.

That day, I was wearing an XXL black T-shirt that said BUSH IS A WAR CRIMINAL, over brand-new black cargo pants in a size higher than I'd ever worn before. I was aware of how I looked, but what the actual fuck did it matter to Rebecca? *You're fired and you're fat* was a real tough-love combo platter. I swallowed hard.

"I'm gonna give you a month's worth of Herbalife, to get you started on your journey. Talk to Lisa to get the details sorted out," Rebecca said. I grabbed my bag and stepped my fat ass into the elevator, mumbling polite non-words until the door slid closed. I did not want anything to do with shakes and pills, which I politely conveyed to Lisa, when she called me later that day.

"God, I'm so sorry about that," Lisa said. "Rebecca is the worst. She put me on some insane pharmaceutical diet last year, and she told me that if she caught me cheating, I'd have to pay her back, and it was, like eight hundred dollars a month." Lisa laughed merrily. I wondered how much she got paid, and whether and how often she cried on the job.

"Anyway, if you need work, I can recommend you to my old friend Lilah. She just had a baby and wants someone to make good, healthy food for her a few times a week."

Lilah was another famous actress on another popular TV series. I'd enjoyed watching her play complicated, often-brilliant women on screen for years. Lilah's apartment was very close to Babbo, and she'd come in just once for dinner, reserved under a fake name. The next day, Mario told me that when he'd introduced himself at her table, she'd been a "weird, cold bitch," apparently immune to his charisma.

I personally found Lilah warm and friendly, though our interactions were infrequent and brief. She was utterly immersed in caring for her squalling newborn and was often surrounded by a benevolent scrum of postpartum employees and friends.

Lilah had me prepare enormous quantities of steamed spinach (stems removed, because she said they interfered with her milk production), curried chicken salad with tofu mayonnaise, grain-free granola with roasted walnuts and dried cherries, and big batches of brown rice, cooked in vegetable stock and seasoned with nutritional yeast. As her needs were so predictable, there seemed no reason not to get very stoned before shopping and cooking for her.

Lilah asked me to bake her a carrot cake for Mother's Day. I used the recipe from *Joy of Cooking*, set a timer, and pulled the layers out of the oven when the recipe said they should be done. I let the cake cool while I made the rest of the food and gave it a thick layer of cream cheese icing just before I left for the day. Late the next morning, I got a call from Lilah's assistant.

"The cake you baked for Lilah has, like, raw batter in the center," she said with cold disgust. "It's inedible. She's very disappointed."

"I'm so sorry," I said, and I was. It was such an embarrassing rookie move, and a stoner mistake, not to ensure the thing was fully baked. "I can go out and buy a cake right now and—"

"No, that's OK, thanks. But she won't be needing your services anymore."

Oof. I stopped getting stoned before going to work at Olek's, and this self-imposed penance felt good, at first. Clear-headed, I worked faster and cleaner, and sometimes I'd get home and actually sit down to write. There was this insistently juvenile voice in my head, though, that said every time I didn't get stoned before work was a missed opportunity. It gave me a thrill, bringing my dark little secret into some ostensibly wholesome environment where I had been given the trust and respect I probably didn't deserve.

After two weeks, having proved to myself that I could do it straight, I went back to working under the influence. And a few weeks after that, Lilah's assistant reached out to say that all was forgiven with the cake, and would I please come back and do a few months' worth of egg white quiche cups and sugar-free Jello and steamed spinach, to get her skinny enough for the Emmy Awards red carpet?

chapter 12

Executive Editor

More than a year into freelance feast and famine, my financial picture started to tilt in a bad direction, as I accrued a ballooning load of credit card debt. I had a patchwork of modest income from writing and cooking. I had expensive-but-shitty health insurance through Freelancers Union, and abysmal financial discipline. I had zero dollars saved; ordered takeout several times a week; took too many taxis; and indulged in restaurant meals and drinks (and drinks and drinks and drinks) far more than was reasonable for a freelance writer and cook for hire paying Manhattan rent.

I worked odd hours—weddings that wrapped at 1 a.m., all-day deadline sprints, 3 a.m. pitch emails about things like "what do celebrities eat in their panic rooms?" and "chefs with weird beards." I would sometimes cook for two or three private clients in a day, followed by several idle days in a row. I had several types of liquor, an ice bucket and a cocktail shaker, a deep stock of weed, and a two-foot glass bong, but often ran out of coffee, or salt, or milk.

I fantasized about predictable paychecks, benefits, clear expectations, fixed working hours. Bouncing around between catering kitchens, rich peoples' empty apartments, and my own dusty hovel had become lonely. I missed the misery-loving company of regular co-workers; I missed being consistently connected to something out in the world.

Could I go back to being an assistant? Yes, maybe, for the right person, at the right price. I signed up for job alert emails from New York Celebrity Assistants, a professional association I'd joined while working for Mario. At the few meetings I'd attended, I was struck by how many members, mostly women, seemed stuck in a mild fugue state, trauma in the eyes, but smiling.

The first job alert email came in:

"I'm hiring my replacement, assisting a celebrity cosmetic dentist. He's very nice, funny, demanding, and tough. He's all over the place, and this is an unstructured environment, working out of his office and his home, with no definite hours. Must have impeccable personal style, very thick skin, and be willing to constantly change gears with no notice. Travel to the Hamptons required. You'll deal with his TV appearances, pay his bills, and handle all of his personal affairs including medical appointments, haircuts, and socializing. You'll choose, buy, and send gifts, walk his dogs and take them to vet and grooming appointments, send out Christmas cards, make him dinner reservations at the best places, get him tickets to the hottest shows, often at the last minute. You will deal *with* his wife and teen daughter, but not work *for* them. Starting salary $40,000. Health insurance after one year."

Fuck that, I thought. Fuck *that*.

I unsubscribed from the job alert emails, but kept an eye on the *Times* and the culinary school job listings, and put the word out to friends and associates that I was looking for a full-time position. Within a few weeks, the *Times* ran an ad from the glossy hardcover food magazine *Art Culinaire*, which was hiring an executive editor, at a starting salary of $48,000, plus health insurance right away.

I thought about the commute from Manhattan to the Morristown, New Jersey, office. This wasn't one of those "just across the Hudson

River" deals; getting to and from work would take two hours each way, via subway, New Jersey Transit train, and almost two miles of walking. For the chance to skip all the in-between steps and become the top editor of a magazine, though, I would gladly schlep.

I sent my resumé, playing up what I assumed were the two most important terms: "Batali" and "Bourdain." I took the train to New Jersey for an interview with Hector, the magazine's publisher. He was a former high-end hotel chef who looked remarkably like cruel billionaire boss Mr. Burns from *The Simpsons*.

Though Hector was kind and curious when he asked me about my skills and experience, I found his softness disquieting. He was a European chef of late middle age, trained in and molded by a system that rather proudly ran on cruelty, violence, and humiliation. Had he also led kitchens this way, and was this how he ran his magazine? I hoped not. I wanted to work for a man who didn't scare me.

Hector called and offered me the job a few days later. I happily accepted, and took two weeks to wind down my private cooking gigs and finish outstanding writing assignments. Toward the end of that liminal period, Mario called me, looking for a favor: "I need blurbs."

He had a new cookbook coming out, this one squarely aimed at the middle American demographic that had been intimidated by the semi-obscure ingredients and fine dining pretensions of *The Babbo Cookbook*. To add to the new book's shelf appeal, he'd been advised to collect relatable endorsements from salt of the earth women, "real *nonna*-matriarch types," he said.

Would I please write three short blurbs in praise of Mario and this book, attributed to imaginary women with Italian-American surnames, from inland California, Pittsburgh, and the Southeast? He didn't mentioned compensation, and I didn't ask. I felt that I owed him, for all the professional doors that his name had thrown open. I had no ethical beef with the assignment, and kind of liked being in on a harmless little scam. Within an hour, I wrote:

Blurb 1:

"I've been a huge fan of Mario's since the first episodes of Molto Mario hit the airwaves, and can't wait to cook my way through his latest book. Thank you, Mario, for sharing your extensive knowledge and passion for Italian cooking."

—TERESA BIANCO, FRESNO, CA

Blurb 2:

"Another delicious treasure from my favorite Italian chef. His recipes are always surprising, but stay true to the soul of Italy. Mario is the undisputed king of cucina Italiana."

—MARY PALADINO, PITTSBURGH, PA

Blurb 3:

"More tempting recipes! More great stories! More good times ahead for my whole family. I love Mario."

—ANGELA VITALE, KNOXVILLE, TN

About six months later, when the new book came out, I stopped into the Union Square Barnes & Noble, picked up and turned over a copy, excited to see my fake blurbs out in the world. The back cover of the book said:

"Mario Batali is a madman and a hero. Is there nothing he's not good at? Great chef, successful restaurateur, an author, an intellectual, host of a ridiculously informative and much-too-good-for-television TV show, aficionado of fine rock and roll—and a man of Falstaffian appetites."

—ANTHONY BOURDAIN

I was disappointed but unsurprised. Tony was much cooler and more compelling than Teresa, Mary, and Angela. He had a travel show on TV and had recently published a book of essays and a new crime novel; his name was all over the food press, men's magazines, and Page Six. If my imaginary friends had to get bumped from the back of Mario's book, at least it was Tony doing the bumping.

For the many months that we worked in tandem on the *Les Halles Cookbook*, Tony and I had communicated only by email. He was now out of the restaurant kitchen entirely, traveling all the time for his TV show and the ongoing endeavor of book promotion, and responding to my recipe queries at odd hours. Shortly before the final manuscript was due, he asked me to meet him at his home, to do a last round of recipe edits in person.

When I arrived at his place, midmorning on a Tuesday, he answered the door in bare feet, wearing jeans and a long-sleeved gray thermal shirt, holding a lit cigarette. He seemed more relaxed than he'd been at our last meeting some eighteen months ago.

He said, "Welcome, welcome," in a tone laced with self-deprecating irony, warmth, and a slight impatience to get started, though I'd been careful to arrive five minutes early. He gestured toward the woman sitting cross-legged on the living room rug and said, "This is my wife, Nancy, and that's Molly."

Nancy was slim and elegant-looking in well-worn blue jeans, a black sweater, and elbow-length yellow leather work gloves, into which Molly, an energetic gray cat, was sinking her claws. Nancy encouraged this, making little teasing swats and jabs toward her.

She looked up, said, "Nice to meet you," and continued sparring with the cat. I followed Tony down a hallway to an office with a wall of windows facing west, over the glittering Hudson, and about a dozen potted philodendron and pothos plants crowding the windowsill, their shiny heart-shaped leaves greenly filtering the daylight.

Tony sat at his desk, and I sat on a cushioned folding chair across from him, and for about an hour, we worked through a checklist of outstanding changes, edits, and queries in the recipes. When we finished, he handed me a personal check for $3,000, an amount unrelated to any money I had invoiced him for.

"You've done outstanding work," he said, and it took me a moment to understand that he was giving me a bonus. A surprise couple thousand dollars was a big fucking deal, the difference between comfortably paying bills or getting the dreaded and lately all-too-frequent voicemail from my landlord, Mr. Batmaz: "Your rent is in arrears."

On my first morning as the executive editor of *Art Culinaire*, I woke with cautious optimism. It was the day before the incumbent George W. Bush would be re-elected president, a conclusion that I believed wasn't entirely foregone. I took the subway to Penn Station, the commuter train to the suburbs, and walked from the station to the magazine headquarters, on the first floor of a converted 1920 red brick schoolhouse. It was handsome, capacious, and flooded with natural light. Opening the office door, I felt like a thirty-year-old kindergartener.

Hector introduced me to my new coworkers. Tracy was the art director, and I liked her immediately: she had a friendly smile and a charming Texas accent. Amy, the administrative assistant, was guardedly polite. And then there was Becky, a recent graduate of the Culinary Institute of America, whom Hector had just hired as a three-month intern. There was no one else working on the editorial side. My name was at the top of the masthead, but the top was also the bottom. It hadn't always been like this; just a few years prior, when they'd done a feature on Mario, the magazine had an editorial and art staff of six full-timers.

Art Culinaire was known for its oversized, full-color, highly detailed photos of beautifully composed plates of food. For the first several years of its existence, it was one of the only ways for chefs to peacock their work for their peers and to keep up with what everyone else was doing. Now, in the first few years of the twenty-first century, the magazine was being nudged into obsolescence by the advent of the digital camera and the voracious creep of online media. That the internet gave everyone a platform was a thrillingly democratizing thing, but corrosive, too, to the existing systems of publishing. I knew that I was getting in just as the ship was taking on water, but I *was* in: I was the new executive editor of a still-respected publication, and I intended to squeeze every drop of juice from this soft, bruised old lemon.

Hector had a separate office, with a solid wood door, directly across from the employee bathroom. He went in there for a few minutes, then came out carrying a stack of envelopes and said, "I'm going to the post office."

From the huge window next to my desk, I saw his car pull out of the small parking lot and onto the street. Tracy clocked it, too. She jumped up and came over to my desk.

"OK, so I'm gonna fill you in real quick," she said, and then told me, in awful detail, about Hector's pattern of hiring, idolizing, growing disillusioned with, and firing or pushing out writers, editors, photographers, and art directors over the nearly two decades that he'd been publishing the magazine. One editor had enjoyed several months of golden child status, and was then abruptly fired for writing "stalk of celery" in a recipe, when Hector preferred "rib." Another editor had been fired for accidentally scraping the door of a rental car while driving to a shoot. A talented art director had won an award for photos she'd taken for the magazine, and within a few weeks of that victory, Hector decided she was no longer qualified to shoot anything, and he began to abusively micro-manage her until she quit.

This was a lot to take in. I appreciated the warning, but felt like a popped balloon. I would have liked a honeymoon hour or so before learning that my new boss was a sadistic, mercurial nightmare.

While Tracy talked, Amy answered a phone call that went on for several minutes, the intensity and volume of her voice steadily rising. I managed to mostly ignore Amy, focusing on what Tracy was telling me, until she yelled, "There's *three hundred dollars'* worth of pay-per-view porn on this bill, and you're telling me that Mister *Monster* wanted to watch it?!" She slammed down the receiver and glared over at us.

"My husband thinks I'm a fucking idiot," she said. "I mean, parrots *are* very smart. *Very* smart," she said, challengingly, threateningly, defensively, "but do *you* think a parrot knows the difference between cartoons and porn?"

I had no answer.

"There's Hector 's car," said Tracy, and she went back to her desk. Becky the intern, who had been standing by, listening to Tracy, pulled up a chair next to mine, and we started to look over the half-finished recipes and feature story outlines that the previous editor had left behind. Becky picked up a recipe printout and squinted at it.

"'Pickled sardines with ginger sherbet and mustard oil foam,'" she read, then pretended to stick her index finger down her throat, like a sitcom tween. "That sounds fucking *gross*."

There was something about Becky's close-set, feral black eyes and gravelly voice that reminded me of the rough, aggressive kids with whom I'd shared a mutual antipathy in elementary and middle school. By the end of the first day, she'd made it clear that she didn't give a fuck about *Art Culinaire*; she had just gotten engaged, she told me, and she didn't intend to ever get a job. Later in the week, she gloated about how low her taxes would continue to be, thanks to Bush's presidential re-election. I decided to put her on recipe testing, which meant that she'd spend each day in the basement kitchen, supervised by Hector.

Despite all I knew about Hector as a slow-tick time bomb, most days at *Art Culinaire*, I was happy. I was getting paid well enough to read and write and talk to people about things like artichokes, tempura, and meringue. I did a deep dive into Japanese savory ice cream, flavored with the likes of octopus, cactus, ox tongue, wasabi, chicken wing, and crab. I interviewed restaurant florists and hospitality professors, winemakers, farmers, publicists, fishermen, apron designers, and the great science and food writer Harold McGee, whose *On Food and Cooking* was (and remains) the standard reference on food science for cooks. I talked to chefs about their inspirations, their paths to success, their challenges, their plans for the future. I had health insurance. And, best of all, I got to travel to out-of-town photo shoots, on the company dime.

My first such shoot was in Chicago, with a grumpy but friendly-enough photographer named Dean, who complained bitterly about the magazine's stingy day rate and per diem, but he was professional when it mattered, and skilled at quickly getting the sexy close-up food shots we needed.

For the issue I'd been tasked with closing, Hector had asked Charlie Trotter—at the time, the absolute gold standard of American chefs—to name a mentor and a protégé, *and Art Culinaire* featured recipes and photos from all three chefs. Trotter's mentor was Florida-based fusion pioneer Norman Van Aken. His protégé was Homaro Cantu, a young Chicago chef who made use of lasers, a centrifuge, custom-engineered tools, and food-grade nitrogen at his restaurant, Moto.

American cooking was nearing peak "molecular gastronomy," which at its core is about using sound scientific principles to make better-tasting and more consistent food, but also gave rise to new techniques. Fine-dining plates in the molecular gastronomy era featured sauces transformed into foamy quenelles, gellified spheres, or little piles of powders. Chefs contorted brawny hunks of pork shoulder or veal breast into unnerving cylindrical shapes, using "meat glue," or cooked them at perilously low temperatures, in sous vide machines.

Some of what came out of this era was delicious and thought-provoking, and some of it was silly, unnecessary, and/or revolting. Reactionary critics and chefs who felt threatened by this weird new thing predictably clutched their pearls, while credulous younger food writers, myself included, offered maybe too much broad encouragement. On my watch, *Art Culinaire* published recipes for carbonated raw oysters, celery pudding with peanut soup, and blue cheese and egg yolk soda.

Chef Cantu's first name by birth was Omar, but as a young adult, he'd legally changed it to Homaro, a half-joking homage to the lobster (*Homarus americanus*), which, for flaunting one's devotion to the craft, was funnier, cheaper, and less painful than a knife tattoo. He was a smart guy, and a nice guy, to the best of my recollection. During our interview, he made many reverential references to Trotter, his mentor, and he expressed the sincere belief that he could change the world with his ideas about food.

After the interview and photo shoot, Cantu invited us to dinner at Moto, where we ate a poached scallop and "pearls" of squid ink sealed inside a polymerized shell made from a buttery saffron and seafood broth; beet-flavored cotton candy, sweet and earthy and fantastic; a menu printed on fully edible paper, with ink that tasted like a tangy aged Manchego cheese; and freeze-dried ice cream pellets with twenty-five-year-old balsamic vinegar, with the richness and complexity of a Sauternes.

Under Cantu's leadership, Moto went on to earn a Michelin star. He opened a second new restaurant, wrote two books, and established a foundation in Charlie Trotter's name when he died. Homaro Cantu was by all accounts a driven, cheerful, optimistic, happy person, but who knows, really? In 2015, he was found dead by his own hand, in the building he'd been using as a lab for new ideas.

chapter 13

Dinner Party

A few months into the job at *Art Culinaire*, when late winter began tipping into early spring, I got a call from a big-time novelist, Patrick, who needed a cook to help pull off a boondoggle, in the form of a dinner party.

He explained the set-up: his girlfriend Jill did publicity for a California winery, and she was trying to get them a foothold in the competitive sparkling wine market. Jill had Patrick pitch a story to a men's magazine about "how to throw a dinner party like me," the "me" being "a louche Manhattan party boy." In his piece, Patrick would name-check his girlfriend's client's brut rosé. The magazine bought it, and now Patrick needed someone to do the cooking. "Our mutual friend Mario Batali told me to call you," he said, and I could hear the smile in his voice.

I accepted because I was still pretty broke, despite having a full-time job, but also because I was desperately curious about Patrick's apartment, his life, his well-connected friends. Sitting in the quiet *Art Culinaire* office all day, I sometimes missed the high-pressure hustle of catering, using my wits to snatch victory from chaos.

The winery gave Patrick several cases of product, and hired a photographer to document the whole party, from set-up to clean-up, making sure there was a glass or bottle of pink wine in every shot. They also paid for rented chairs, linens, glasses, plates and flatware, and a team to set it all up; a maid service to deep-clean Patrick's apartment before and after the party; all of the food; and my labor. I charged them $1,000, and no one blinked. I should have charged more.

The dinner was on a Saturday night. At the end of most *Art Culinaire* work days, I would down a shot or two from one of the surplus liquor bottles in the office, then walk to the station, where I'd take some brackish bat hits at the end of the platform before boarding the train. By the time we got to Penn Station, I'd be coming down, my muscles lazy and my head dull and scratchy, and ready for a refill once or twice or more before bed. On the Friday before Patrick's party, I stayed sober, white-knuckling the boredom of the train ride, then shopping for everything I needed at Citarella and Jefferson Market.

Back home, deep into the night, and again early the next morning, I prepped for dinner. I crushed three dozen garlic cloves with the broad side of my chef's knife, then covered their shreddy surfaces with kosher salt and anchovy fillets and capers and a bunch of parsley, all of which I chopped and crushed together into a messy paste. I freed the two boneless lamb shoulders from their feathery red netting, rubbed them all over with the paste, then rolled them back up and secured them with twine.

I mixed up a mustardy vinaigrette with brunoised shallots and fished limp or ugly leaves out from bags of bitter salad greens. I toasted walnuts in the toaster oven and segmented grapefruits for the salad. I brushed sandy soil from the earthy surfaces of $149 worth of morels, chanterelles, and oyster mushrooms, then sautéed each type separately before making the pâte brisée crust that would form the base of a custardy torte. I wiped clean the lavender-pink bottoms of pearly baby radishes with a wet paper towel, trimmed their feathery roots with a scissor, and plunged them into quart containers full of ice water. I hard-boiled, shocked, and peeled a few dozen quail eggs, then mixed the crushed yolks with mayonnaise, mustard, and smoky pimentón, and packed this mixture into a Ziploc bag from which I would later snip a corner, for piping.

In discussing the menu, Patrick had insisted that no one would want dessert, only to keep drinking, but I thought there should still be something sweet on offer, so I made a quick rhubarb jelly, to be served with sliced baguettes alongside hunks of Stilton and Manchego and a few bars of great-quality dark chocolate that I'd break into pieces.

My plan was to arrive at Patrick's place at 3 p.m., though I hadn't given any thought to the logistics of getting there until late Saturday morning, when I got nervous. It was almost impossible to get a cab on Avenue C, where they rarely cruised.

I called Carmel, my go-to car service, to schedule a 2:30 p.m. pickup.

"Sorry, hon, we're very busy today," said the dispatcher. "I can do a stretch limo at 3:15 for a hundred and fifty bucks, plus tax and gratuity. You want it?"

Ah, fuck. Seventy-five dollars a mile! "Yes, please," I said. I called Patrick to tell him I'd be late; his machine picked up.

I was sweating heavily into my old French Culinary Institute chef coat as I hefted my tote bags of prepped food and equipment down five flights of stairs to the street. It had been more than twenty-four hours since I'd had a drink. It would have been good to have a partner, someone who could help me think of all these little details and help carry shit down the stairs, but Alex was away again, installing his company's software in a Dubai television station.

The limousine was pink, like a raspberry, or a rash. We hit a stretch of green lights going west on Houston Street, a nice bit of good luck. A uniformed doorman stepped to the curb as the car glided to a stop. When he opened the door and we made eye contact, I reflexively said, "Sorry, it's just me," because the car seemed to suggest the likes of someone exciting, like Charo, or Barbie's sister Skipper.

Patrick's apartment was on the top floor of a luxury building in the West Village. I'd met him once or twice before, with Mario, but when he opened his door, holding a glass of red wine, I introduced myself anyway, assuming that he wouldn't remember my face. His own face was round and impishly handsome: his mottled cheeks the same color as my limousine, his blue eyes red-rimmed, and his dark brown hair, curly and threaded with silver, immaculate.

I lugged the bags through his living room, on one wall of which hung a massive framed mirror, opposite a huge framed painting that contained a few seemingly unrelated images, rendered in different styles and tones: bright red salmon steaks, a gray and black assemblage of well-dressed adults in conversation, a big blue star covered with raindrops.

He noticed me noticing it, and said, "Just got that one. David Salle."

I smiled and nodded and said, "Ah," which was what I always did when pretending that I knew.

The kitchen was bright with the afternoon sunshine. The gray stone countertop had six gas burners set into it with a stainless steel oven beneath. The two-compartment sink was impressively deep; the fridge nearly empty, thank god, save for a few bottles of Fiji water, a package of salted Plugrà, and a large bottle of fish oil capsules. I unpacked everything perishable—the salad greens, the eggs, lamb, butter, cheese, mushrooms, radishes, the rhubarb jelly—while Patrick hovered around and briefed me on the guest list: a gossip columnist turned screenwriter, another novelist, a women's clothing designer, a famous painter's son, a music producer, a wine importer, Mario, and the famously vegan Moby, who, Patrick assured me, understood and accepted that there would be many animal parts and products on the table.

Jill, girlfriend and publicist, opened the apartment door with her own key. She was about six inches taller than Patrick, blonde and pretty. She spoke to me in a warm, conspiratorial way, acknowledging the boondoggle but ready to have fun with it. She and Patrick both said to me, a few times, that they were grateful that I was willing to do this weird job at the last minute.

Jill poured me a tumbler of cold white wine, my first since Thursday night, and after a few big gulps, I felt warm and energized. I quartered the tiny little new potatoes and tossed them, with olive oil and Maldon salt and several bushy rosemary sprigs, in one of Patrick's porcelain bowls that was glazed a brilliant turquoise and weighed a metric fuckton.

I divided and calmly rolled out the torte dough, catching a slight whiff of butter as I flopped the first circle over the heavy wooden rolling pin that my dad had made for me. I laid it gently into a fluted tart pan, pricked the bottom with a fork, scattered the precious mushrooms across the surface, and began to mix the savory custard, using outrageously expensive eggs with yolks the color of a late-summer sunset.

Jill came into the kitchen and introduced me to Greg, the hired photographer. He had a full-lipped mouth and big, elegant hands, with a silver wedding band on his left ring finger. He shook my own right hand, which was slick with butter, and asked what I was doing. He started taking photos of the food. Every time I looked up, he made direct eye contact with me, which made me feel shy and conspicuous.

Greg had a new DSLR camera, he told me, and kept coming over to the counter, leaning in to show me the test images on the little digital screen: a pile of radishes, the corner of a sofa, an empty wine glass on the table, his own plastic-lidded cup with irregular splashes of dark coffee on top. Was this flirting? What was his angle? I went to the fridge and refilled my wine glass.

The guests started showing up around 7 p.m., and Patrick brought each new arrival back to the kitchen, so that Greg could shoot him pouring and handing out flutes of sparkling rosé, the bottle label clearly visible, and me very much out of frame.

When Mario arrived, he beelined to the kitchen without waiting for Patrick. "Hey, Woolie!" he said, grabbing me in a lingering full-body hug. He was cheerful, clearly in his element, and trailed by a pretty young woman with a sleek dark bob, wearing a black blazer over jeans and a sheer white tank top, no bra, whom he introduced as "a superstar television producer."

From the kitchen, I could hear Jill making a brief speech before dinner, first talking up the wine, then thanking everyone for being in on the grift, which got a big laugh. Patrick and Mario came into the kitchen to let me know that it was time to plate the first course.

"Come on out and do a little show-and-tell on the food," said Patrick, and I stopped dead. I didn't want to talk to these people; I didn't want to be seen by them.

"Uhhh . . ." I said, trying to refocus on distributing the walnuts among the radicchio. "I'm not sure—"

"You want me to do it?" said Mario.

"Oh, my god, yes, *please*," I said, and he did, spinning out his usual flowery bullshit about the food, throwing in effortless references to Renaissance art and Tom Waits and the dewdrops on the nipples of a thousand angels. In that moment, he felt like a true ally.

Between the mushroom tortes and the lamb, the gossip columnist came into the kitchen and asked me to whip a half dozen egg whites, so that Patrick could make a round of pisco sours. I pulled the lamb from the oven, set it on the stovetop, pulled a carton of eggs from the fridge, and started cracking and separating them into two bowls while she stood there watching me with narrowed eyes.

"All the food has been so good. I'm constantly entertaining. I would love to hire you to do this at my place," she said. My wrist and forearm were on fire from the whipping.

"Thank you, I'd love to do that," I lied. She continued to stand there, not saying whatever the next thing might be, so I added, "I love money," and laughed weakly, and hated myself.

Patrick came in and kissed her on the cheek. "Ready for some?" he asked. He removed a framed black and white photo of a French bulldog that was hanging on the wall near the stove. He laid it face-up on the counter, pulled a little black bottle from his pants pocket, and deftly tipped out a pile of powder atop the image of the dog's velvety snout, which he fashioned into a thin line, using a paring knife from the countertop block. He then stepped back and the gossip columnist leaned in, daintily snuffling it up. She thanked him quietly and returned to the dining room. Patrick watched her leave, then turned to me.

"I love her to death, and I know she's a knockout, but I could never quite get it up for her," he said. "Chronic eating disorder. No meat on those bones." He arranged a second line and gestured toward it with an open palm and a raised eyebrow. Of course I accepted it. It was the most and presumably best coke I'd ever been offered. He then arranged a line for himself, consumed it neatly, and returned the dog photo to its place on the wall.

"The food has been fantastic, by the way," he said. "Everyone who actually eats food is very happy. Thanks again for doing this." He reached into the inside pocket of his navy blazer. "A gratuity," he said, and handed me a personal check for $1200. Later, the fact that he'd misspelled my first and last name would give me a bit of trouble over at Citibank, but it did eventually clear.

And at the end of the dinner, Greg the photographer helped me pack up my containers and bowls and knives and a few bottles of rosé that Jill had pressed on me. He asked if I wanted to come see his studio, on Delancey Street, really not all that far from my place. We got into an eastbound cab and talked a little shit about the guests all the way to Avenue C. He helped me carry my bags upstairs and waited by the front door while I changed into a clean sweater and jeans. On the way out, I grabbed a copy of the latest *Art Culinaire* and handed it to him, shyly. Might be good to get him on a shoot, I thought, although I'd be embarrassed to tell him the pathetic day rate that Hector offered.

We stopped at Cibao Deli for a six-pack of PBR cans, then walked and talked for several blocks through the damp downtown dark to his studio, which was a tiny apartment on the fourth floor of a tenement building. The room was full of books and lights and stands and big rolls of white paper, boxes of film, lenses, and, along one wall, a black leather sofa.

He played some jangly rock music I'd never heard, via an iPod connected to one large speaker, and we sat on the couch, our open beers on the floor in front of our feet, while he showed me images from a Gary Winogrand book.

He had a sexy voice and seemed hyper-alert to the world around him, to the potential of something beautiful in everything ordinary. He laughed a lot, he talked a lot, and he had opinions, stories, some of which were interesting (he'd just shot the inaugural Puppy Bowl) and some less so (he had a lot to say about the imagery in *Crouching Tiger, Hidden Dragon*, a few scenes from which he played on a DVD in a laptop).

While Greg talked, I thought about Alex, who so often shut down in social situations, and who was increasingly suspicious of the government. When we were together at home, we watched documentaries about 9/11 conspiracies and the Freemasons and Peak Oil and the Warren Commission.

We weren't even engaged yet, and I was already pulling away from him and into myself, building terminal little resentments about all the usual unsexy shit of adult life: snoring, dishes, laundry, garbage, money. Between his work travel and mine, his occasional late-night shifts, my late-night drinking and early-morning commute, we spent less and less time together in or out of bed. When we were together, I was either too fucked up, too tired, or just not into it, still humiliated by his honest acknowledgment of my body's actual size, and unable to talk about it with him.

I was worried about this sad state of affairs. It was a kind of happiness vacuum, especially in contrast to the dreamy relief and unselfconscious physical desire I'd felt when we first met, not all that long ago. And breaking up, and the specter of going back on the market or being alone forever, seemed worse than staying unhappily together.

If I walked away from Alex, who would change my adult diapers? Who would take me to chemo? This was how I saw the future: several decades of work and then the disgusting and expensive and boring and awful breakdown of the human body, made only marginally more bearable by having someone to witness your suffering.

Concerned about our vanishing intimacy, I made us an appointment for a couples therapist, to which Alex agreed. We really couldn't afford it and struggled to make time for our first and only session, at 8 a.m. on a Monday morning, on the far Upper West Side. For $300, the therapist listened to me describe our lack of connection, then suggested that Alex and I "do something fun together."

We went bowling at Port Authority. The music was too loud to have any kind of conversation, Alex couldn't find a ball that suited him, and we got into an argument that was and was not about how hard he'd pounded his fist on the electronic scoring machine when it malfunctioned. I was worried that we'd get into trouble with bowling alley management, but mostly I was upset about the way he was acting—sullen, petulant, depressed—and that I had no power to change his mood, or mine.

Now, sitting next to Greg the photographer in his studio, drinking beer with our legs touching while Alex was far away in Dubai, I wanted to prolong the whole Schrödinger's cat of it for as long as possible. I could feel Greg trying, performing, maneuvering, as if I weren't already completely in the tank for what was about to happen. I fucking loved that feeling, those moments, unsure but reasonably sure that all that accidental touching was on purpose.

And then there was a break in the conversation, and he did kiss me. We kept setting limits—just kissing. But let me touch your tits? Maybe you should take off your shirt. OK, but then you take off yours, too. OK well, should we just take off our pants, get comfortable, see how that feels? I was reminded of my teenage fumblings, when it felt so novel and so good to touch and be touched, electric and inevitable and laced with shame. We set rules for good and correct behavior, and then played right up against the line, eventually giving in once we'd sufficiently pretended that we wouldn't. It was the same way I'd start many evenings vowing to have just one drink, one hit off the joint, only a baby bump of coke.

I could not fathom saying no to what was happening, because it was exactly what I wanted.

And as soon as it was over, that little matchlight in my chest was extinguished, replaced by an acrid smoky wisp of longing and sorrow that persisted for days before finally dissipating into a dull sadness. That intoxicating desire and power that I'd felt with Greg was not part of my actual life. It hurt to know that there was another way to feel, a way I wanted very much to feel, only to get back to it, I'd have to continue behaving like the selfish, dishonest asshole I'd just proven myself to be.

For a while after that first night, I subsisted on longing and fantasy, delicious and painful in their own ways. This was a pre-smartphone era, still prohibitively expensive to send too many text messages, so Greg and I exchanged emails, which I only wrote and read at work. Six weeks passed before he asked me to meet him at his studio on a Friday evening. Like Alex, he traveled a lot for work, plus he was married and had a kid. I wondered if I was the only woman who met him there.

"I'm not in love with him," I told Joan, "but I love the way I feel when I'm with him."

In October, six months into the thing with Greg, I flew to Los Angeles for an *Art Culinaire* shoot, and by coincidence, he was there for work, too. The balance had shifted; I was suffering more than seemed right for such an ephemeral affair. I felt guilty for lying to Alex, and angry with Greg for not being more available to me, which I knew was unfair, and misplaced, but anyway, I started looking for things to hate about him.

We met for dinner at Spago on my first night in LA; I'd supervise a shoot there the next day. I was annoyed by Greg's shiny dress shoes, which he'd paired with jeans.

"Those shoes make you look so *Jersey*," I said, and he winced but laughed it off.

I rolled my eyes when he told me about the exquisite tits and angelic faces he'd seen at Jumbo's Clown Room the previous night. He flirted with the pretty waitress, asking her questions about herself and cracking jokes, which made me crabby and jealous. When she walked away from the table, I snapped, "You're so desperate for everyone to like you. Why can't you just leave her alone, let her do her job?" When his eyes filled with tears, I felt a tiny twinge of regret, but mostly I felt powerful.

Greg came back with me to my hotel, a scruffy little low-rise joint in Koreatown that catered to German tourists. We swam naked in the pool, and then he made me come with his hand, under a towel, on a chaise longue. A few minutes later, I started to cry. I felt trashy and sad.

"I don't want you to stay over. I don't want to do this anymore," I said, which was and wasn't true.

chapter 14

Techno-Emotional

On a damp spring Friday after work, I took two shots of vodka, left the *Art Culinaire* office, and walked to the bar across from the New York–bound train platform, where I had three vodka tonics. I read the *New York Times* and talked to no one before boarding the 7:36 p.m. Once seated in the half-full train car, I fell asleep. When I woke up, the car was quiet and completely empty, with none of the ambient low rumble and whooshing air of a live train. I pulled out my cheap cell phone, which was big and white, like a sanitary napkin that you couldn't fold. The display said "9:22 p.m." Assuming no delays, I'd been asleep at Penn Station for a half-hour.

I was drunk and ravenous and very much needed to pee, so I gathered my stuff and got up to leave, but the train doors were closed, and I couldn't pry them open when I tried. I was locked inside a New Jersey transit train. *Shit.* I laughed at myself and looked again at my phone, which had zero bars, because I was deep underground in 2006, when we (or really, *I*) hadn't yet heard of Wi-Fi, and our phones were still very dumb. Who would I call, anyway, 911? Seemed embarrassing.

I set my bag down at my feet and squinted out the cloudy plexiglass window and as far down the empty platform as I could see.

I hoped someone would rescue me before I was forced to use the grim stainless steel toilet at the other end of the train. I kept watch at the window. After about ten minutes, a uniformed conductor came down the steps and started walking toward my car. I banged on the window with the side of my fist well before I knew he could hear me, and yelled, "Hey! I'm in here!" When I heard my own voice, I felt a flash of panic, followed by a wave of humiliation. He stopped, opened the door with one of many keys hanging from a ring, and gave me a brief lecture about the danger of sleeping on the train.

I told my sister about it the next day on the phone, as a slightly ridiculous story, with me as the clown, but she didn't find it funny.

"Are you OK? You need to be more careful," she said, and only then did I hear it from her perspective: I'd gotten too drunk and passed out so hard that even the bump of the train stopping in the station, and the noise of the brakes and my fellow passengers departing, had failed to rouse me.

"God, whatever, I'm fine," I said.

In therapy, Joan never let on whether it was a good or bad idea that I'd stopped sleeping with Greg, and she offered no judgment on my having slept with him in the first place. She only asked, "How do you feel?" *(Sad, confused, like shit; guilty over resenting Alex for simply being the safe and stable person I had committed to a few years prior.)* And "What do you want now?"

I wanted unlimited access to that crackling, full-bore pleasure I had felt with Greg, without all the side effects. But also: I wanted a guarantee that I wouldn't waste my time chasing that pleasure, only to wind up regretful and alone.

I wanted to be smart and enlightened, impervious to the old patriarchal bullshit, but I didn't want to age out of the old patriarchal bullshit club. I saw unmarried women over thirty-five as terrifying cautionary tales of terminal loneliness. This fear was based on a handful of conversations I'd had with women five or ten years older than me, who were frustrated with dating and regretted having given up on the chance to have babies with imperfect ex-boyfriends.

I wasn't personally dying to be a mother, an endeavor that seemed like a huge fucking drag, a voluntary prison term of selflessness, with bodily autonomy, sleep, and solitude swept off the table, maybe forever. Here, too, my conclusions were based on anecdotal evidence. During the few times I took care of the Smiths' baby Sam, when Pepper the nanny had gone on vacation, I hoped to be hit by a bus, as relief from the grinding monotony of responsibility for such a tiny, helpless person. More recently, I'd spent a night with my sister and her infant twins, whose rude needs to scream and eat during the overnight hours had only reinforced my distaste for the sacrifices of motherhood.

Still, conditioned from birth to seek out a place within the rational order of marriage and family, it was nearly impossible not to surrender to sunk cost fallacy. I was thirty-one, ostensibly fertile, a decent commodity, and Alex was a willing buyer offering a fair price. Why would I contemplate a risky return to the open market? I was too scared and selfish to give up the security of this relationship. Who else would want me? I was overweight, deep in debt, lacking in both self-control and self-respect. What was I gonna do, get a roommate again? Disappoint my parents, who were huge Alex fans? No. The goal was to understand and root out my desire for extracurricular adventure, with the help of therapy, then ideally settle into this good thing that I had.

Once in a while, Alex would say to me, lovingly, "You're my soulmate," just trying to be offhandedly sweet and romantic, and it made me want to claw off my own skin. The concept of *soulmates* seemed like some weak New Age *bullshit*, not to mention completely antithetical to his strident atheism. I personally didn't believe in soulmates, and anyway, if I was his soulmate, what would that say about the state of his soul, or mine, which I had subjected to rot with my shitty behavior? Nothing good.

A soulmate was a teenager's fantasy, and marriage was a mature adult arrangement. I tried leaning hard into the idea that "no one person can or should be everything to you," a piece of wisdom plucked from somewhere in the ether, maybe a women's magazine advice column?

For Christmas, I bought Alex a gift certificate for a spa in midtown where the massages with hand jobs were an open secret. I put the envelope in a shoebox and wrapped it in a week-old copy of the *New York Observer*, which was printed on salmon-pink paper. I handed it to him on the morning of Christmas Eve, a few minutes before we left for his parents' place in New Jersey. He opened the package, read the name of the business out loud, then looked at me, eyebrows raised in bemusement. He'd never shown any interest in massage.

"It's a place where you can get a happy ending. I thought it would be a fun little dirty thing," I said, half smiling. It occurred to me with a mild dread that this was actually a gift for *me*. Buying my boyfriend a potential hand job for Christmas was a covert gesture toward balancing the scales against my bad behavior, without any real risk of having that behavior exposed.

(Years later, I would find the gift certificate in a drawer, never used and long since expired.)

I took on the project of feeling more relaxed and less self-conscious in bed with Alex, experimenting with various calibrations of booze, weed, timing, and the furtive browsing of a copy of *Playboy* with Denise Richards on the cover, decked out like a Christmas tree, which I'd bought because I had a short piece about napping in it. One evening after we'd managed to have a nice time together, Alex suggested I pick out an engagement ring, ideally something priced in the very low four figures. A few days later, at a vintage jeweler on the Lower East Side, I put a deposit on a $990 rhinestone cocktail

ring from the 1930s, then went back home and let him know where
he could find it. About a week later, when I got home from the long
slog to and from the office, Alex got on one knee in our grubby little
kitchen and held out a little blue velvet box. This pantomime of proposal made us laugh at ourselves, and each other. It was a lovely
moment, silly and sweet, and I felt a little lift of hope, tinged with
relief, undergirded with anxiety. In the subsequent days and weeks,
when I became overwhelmed by the truth of my own cowardice and
selfishness, the contrast between the very good thing I had and the
bad things I still wanted, I self-soothed with binge drinking, bong
hits, and Burger King fries.

Still: I was engaged. I told my friend Alexandra, who was an editor at the *New York Observer*, and she asked me to write regular posts
for the paper's fledgling Bridal Blog. It paid nothing, literally zero dollars, but that was fine with me, because I had the freedom to write
and publish a short weekly essay about anything I wanted to say about
wedding planning, a stage of life that touches on family, food, money,
fashion, religion, capitalism, media, tradition, culture, sex, happiness, and death. I wrote about refusing to rope my friends into being
bridesmaids; about getting stoned before wedding dress shopping (a
terrible idea, one of the very worst); and resisting the pressure to lose
weight.

That spring, I went to Barcelona for *Art Culinaire* with grumpy-
but-friendly-and-professional photographer Dean. We interviewed
and shot with five chefs in the city over the course of five days, during
which I wrote a Bridal Blog post in the form of an email:

Dear Alex,

*I have been in Barcelona for about eight hours. It's really warm
here. Those fleece-lined Adidas track pants felt so right in the Sam
Adams bar at EWR, and so wrong at the BCN taxi stand.*

I was sick on the flight. Which part of whiskey, Ambien, gin,

*and red wine do you think was the problem? When we changed
planes in Frankfurt, I saw (or maybe hallucinated) an extremely
tall and thin man in a pristine white jumpsuit pedaling a bicycle
through the terminal.*

*It's 8:30 p.m. and the sun is still fairly high in the sky.
My room overlooks a paved and red-painted play yard. Right
now there are several teenage girls on old-school roller skates,
practicing their moves and wearing identical blue skating skirts.*

*Young men and women in Barcelona have made a real
commitment to the mullet. It's hard to say whether they're being
ironic or earnest. I would love to get my hands on some Moroccan
hash.*

*I guess I'll go out and get some dinner soon. I have already
had one great meal, at a nondescript tapas bar: potato tortilla,
sausages, whole roasted red peppers, croquetas with ham and
bechamel, patatas bravas with aioli, and lots of cava. At the
grocery store, I paid 12 euros for contact lens solution, and less
than 2 euros for a really good bottle of rosé.*

*We should serve patatas bravas and cava at our wedding
reception. We should go to Barcelona for our honeymoon.*

*I know I am supposed to be excited about being in Spain, but
I am very tired and just wish I were sitting on the couch with you,
watching Aqua Teen Hunger Force and eating falafel.*

Love,

Laurie

At the end of the week, Dean and I picked up a rental car and a
translator named Jordi at the train station and drove two hours out of
town, to the Costa Brava, for an interview and shoot at El Bulli.

At the time, El Bulli was arguably the most exciting and well-
documented restaurant in the world, and the executive chef, Ferran

Adrià, a signifier for an explosion of Spanish culinary innovation. The fifty-two-seat restaurant was open for six months every year, serving eight thousand guests, though they claimed to field over three hundred thousand reservation requests annually, all well before the era of social media sport-dining.

Food writers and chefs had been aware of El Bulli for years, and the rest of the English-speaking world caught up in 2003, thanks to a fourteen-page feature in the *New York Times Magazine*. Soon after that, *Time* magazine included Adrià in a list of the 100 most influential people in the world. While shooting a documentary, *Decoding Ferran Adrià*, Tony Bourdain himself saw his own deep skepticism about "the foam dude" dissipate like an aerosolized shrimp bisque in a rich jerk's mouth.

It was a beautiful late spring day in northern Spain as we hurtled toward Cala Montjoi. Ferran's assistant Aintzane had warned us, politely but firmly, not to be late; his time was heavily scheduled, and I'd have exactly twenty minutes for the interview, before his brother Albert would start presenting the dishes for us to shoot.

We got a late start, losing several minutes helplessly idling behind a tour bus that was perpendicular parked in the middle of a busy Barcelona street, disgorging a full load of elderly passengers into the Maritime Museum.

The last few miles of road between us and El Bulli were strung together on a gorgeous, one-lane ribbon of terror, with numerous hairpin turns and highly distracting flashes of mountainside and the Mediterranean Sea. We arrived ten minutes before the interview was to begin. Aintzane met us in the parking lot and escorted us up a set of shallow slate steps and into the kitchen, where a few dozen men and two women moved silently around three rectangular work stations, overseen by an enormous wooden bull's head situated in the center of the room. No one looked up as we passed through to a cool, white-walled salon outside the dining room, in which two overstuffed chintz couches faced each other over a low glass table. While Dean quickly unpacked and assembled his stand lights, I reread the advance documents that Aintzane had sent me, which were required reading for anyone interviewing Ferran.

The first document was brief and more or less forbade the use of the term "molecular gastronomy" in Ferran's presence. (He preferred the terms "deconstructivist" or "techno-emotional.")

The second document was a twenty-three-point list called "Philosophical synthesis of El Bulli restaurant," which had recently been presented at a culinary symposium in Madrid, and which can still be found on the restaurant's website. Here's an example:

> *Point 21: Decontextualization, irony, spectacle, performance are completely legitimate, provided they are not superficial but are closely bound up with a process of gastronomic reflection.*

During the interview, all of which was passed through Jordi's translations, I read Point 21 out loud, and asked for an example of an "illegitimate" or "superficial" act of cooking.

Ferran had the distracted, put-upon air of a guy who was three pegs down the org chart from the Dalai Lama. He paused for an uncomfortably long few moments, then said, "Probably you've gone too far when what you do can be executed by someone who is not a cook. If you came here to eat and we covered your eyes, it's fine, but it can be done by anyone . . . it's one thing to do art with food, and a different one when food becomes art."

I nodded and fought back the urge to make the international gesture for jerking off a dick.

Now, listen: I respect the vast intellectual and financial resources required of Ferran and his team to execute the mission of El Bulli. I know how important and influential the restaurant was (and still is, despite having ceased operations in 2012). I know that the emperor had clothes, because people with more money and better access than me had seen them and reported back: the clothes were *exquisite*. And I knew that this was all just a little too fucking self-serious, and for what purpose, really?

If I were to ask, "Why is this brand of Spanish avant-garde cuisine so important?" then I would have to ask, "Why is anything important?"

I was lucky to be there, and when I got home and wrote about my experience at El Bulli, I wouldn't dare be remotely critical, because I was not a critic, and because my job was to describe for our cook and chef readership what it was like inside El Bulli. It was an impressive place, with impressive people making impressive food. I would never admit that I didn't fully understand it, or that it made me feel inadequate as a former cook.

At minute twenty, Aintzane pointed to her wristwatch, indicating that the interview was done, and a young male cook came and whispered to Ferran that the first plate was ready to be shot.

As soon as Dean finished shooting a dish, the two of us swooped in with our spoons and our fingers. We slurped cool briny oysters wrapped in a gossamer sheet of warm pancetta fat and topped with a sweet green pistachio emulsion. We frantically scooped up disappearing clouds of Parmesan "air" with muesli. We popped bubbles of melon caviar between our tongues and the roofs of our mouths. We crunched down on delicate coils of sweet and salty olive oil spring candy. It *was* delicious, surprising, strange, and fun to eat this food.

We finished shortly before staff meal, and with the help of three interns, we quickly packed up Dean's equipment and bundled ourselves back into the tiny rental car. Driving away from El Bulli, we narrowly missed the business end of a fifteen-ton Volvo truck that appeared at the crest of a blind curve.

We were still hungry, and decided to stop at a nondescript seaside restaurant, where we ate grilled sardines and planks of meaty, snow-white monkfish drizzled in olive oil and salt, with a few boiled potatoes and a carafe of rosé. The fish had been out of the sea for less than two hours, the waiter told us, and why would he lie? The sea was right there next to us. I'm not going to say that the fish and the potatoes and the wine were so much better than what we'd eaten at El Bulli, but it was all quite good, and a relief to sit in a chair, use a fork, see the charred skin, and pick out the bones.

chapter 15

Stewpot

When I returned from Spain and got back to the *Art Culinaire* office, Hector told me that he'd laid off Tracy, who had been the magazine's art director for nearly a decade. Subscription sales were cratering, he explained, bookstores were cutting back on their orders, and the few liquor giants who reliably bought ads had started to demand that their rates be slashed. He could no longer afford to pay Tracy's full-time salary, he said. He would take over art direction, and hire a freelancer when necessary. The ship was fast taking on water.

One afternoon a few weeks later, while I sat transcribing my tape-recorded interview with Ferran Adrià, Hector came out of his office and picked up a page from the tray beneath the big color printer. He then came over to my desk and slapped the paper down on my desk, next to the keyboard.

It was a photo of some dainty round dumplings, dressed with what looked like yogurt dotted with brown butter, onto which pine nuts, mint leaves, and chili flakes were strewn. Hector pointed at a few drops of white sauce on the edge of the yellow serving bowl. His face looked pinched and quivery, like Templeton the Rat from *Charlotte's Web*.

"We have a big problem," he said, smiling, jabbing his finger at the photo. "There is sauce out of place. This looks so sloppy. Why didn't you clean up the plate before Dean started shooting?"

I looked hard at the photo, which I didn't recognize as anything we'd shot in Spain.

"I'm sorry," I said, "whose dish is this?"

"Alison Barshak," said Hector. She had made her name as a chef in Philadelphia and was now cooking in a moneyed suburb.

"I wasn't on that shoot," I said. "I think maybe you supervised that one, while I was in Barcelona?" This was Hector's (extremely minor and totally fixable) fuckup, not mine, but I knew not to directly confront a man with evidence of his error.

"Oh," he said, after a long pause. "Well, remember for your next shoot. Don't let me catch you getting careless."

Go fuck yourself, I thought. "OK," I said.

I'd planned to stay in the job two years—it had only been eighteen months—but it seemed that Hector had already loosed the butter knife of Damocles. His business was failing, his personality was hot garbage, and I was getting sick of the commute: it was time to find a new job, before I got bullied or nitpicked or downsized out of this one.

One of the big national food magazines had an opening for a midlevel editor, and I got an interview, to which I wore clean pants and new-ish black kitchen clogs, my nicest shoes. I knew the editor doing the initial interviews; she was a friend of a friend, a kind and welcoming person who asked sincere questions at cocktail parties, and listened to your answers without looking over your shoulder for the more important people in the room.

"OK, so I'm going to be really honest with you," she said, after inviting me into her office and closing the door. "Once upon a time, this magazine was about great cooking, but we don't really do straight-up food stories anymore. Have you seen the most recent issue? It's got a whole package about white food, because there was a lot of white clothing on the fashion runways in Paris and Milan." She barked out a defeated little laugh.

"I know you want to write about food, but what our editor-in-chief wants is someone with connections to good-looking rich people who'll let us do photo shoots in their homes," she said. "We literally have a 'no photos of ugly people' policy. You know what I mean?" She laughed again. This was more intervention than interview.

"No one's copy ever makes it to print without being mangled to shit, by people who are not editors," she said. "The people who work here, who've been here for years, they're no longer happy people. I can pass your resumé up to the next level, if you really want me to, but I don't think you really want me to. I think this job would crush your soul."

I took myself out of the running, and kept quietly looking for a new job and chipping away at wedding planning. My mother mailed me a sample menu from our wedding venue, where she had put down a deposit for the last Saturday in June. It was printed on paper with a washed-out illustration of a beachy sunset scene, all sand dunes and palm trees and birds. There were words like "tropical marshmallow delite" and "wax bean salad," rendered in a stupid curlicue font that made me want to die in a house fire.

In the near-decade since cooking school, I'd developed a vicious snobbery about food, its presentation, and the language used to describe it. I planned to invite a number of friends from the food world to my wedding, and was worried about being exposed as a closet rube, because the people who ran our chosen venue thought we might want to serve "chicken franchise" (*sic*) to guests, whom I imagined whispering the kinds of cunty, judgmental things that I was thinking.

I turned this myopic panic about class, money, and food into fodder for the Bridal Blog, as a means of defense against future criticism, and because I couldn't express or even really acknowledge my more global concerns about getting and being and staying married.

Every time the *Observer* put up one of my pieces on the Bridal

Blog, I sent a link to a handful of people, trolling for praise in that fast-ending internet era before social media would give us a much darker definition of the word *trolling*. I was proud to be associated with the *Observer*, whose distinctive wit and style had yet to be destroyed by the dimwitted real estate scion and future First Son-in-Law who bought and wrecked it.

I shared my post about wedding food anxiety with Mario Batali, along with a note about how much I had enjoyed reading *Heat*, the book that made a case for Mario's genius, which had just been published.

This was a lie; I hadn't enjoyed reading the book. While gulping it down in great chunks, I was consumed by professional jealousy of Bill Buford, the book's author. In the opening chapters, Buford deftly described the world that I'd inhabited for nearly four formative years, though he'd spent much more time than me in the kitchen, and he'd gotten burned, bullied, cut, intimidated, and stuck with it anyway. He researched the book for years, and he had the luxury to do so, with the backing of the *New Yorker*, where it had started as a profile before he sold his publisher on a fuller story. He had a wife, his maleness, his age, his money, his status among the literati, and the blistering candor of his storytelling made it clear that he wasn't afraid of Mario.

Reading *Heat*, I was astonished at how Mario had behaved in the author's presence: drinking to incredible excess, digging through the trash for useable food scraps at Babbo, shoving scalding hot food in Buford's mouth with real menace, and saying dehumanizing, humiliating things to and about women and their bodies. In my experience, Mario had always been on his best behavior in front of the press, but it seemed that over his time with Bill Buford, he'd relaxed into his most unguarded self.

Heat was widely, positively reviewed, including by my *Observer* editor Alexandra, who wrote that "ninety percent of *Heat* is wonderful," while noting:

Though he's portrayed here as a genius, and certainly generous after a fashion, Mr. Batali also comes across as a thoroughly debauched creature, almost medieval—coarse, gluttonous, lewd, lecherous, mercenary, possibly homophobic, celebrity-toadying, drug-using, dictatorial to the point of sadistic, swaggering, with an ego the size of his massive belly. "You fucking moron! You fucking motherfucking moron!" he screams at Babbo's maître d' after the latter fails to recognize a record producer at the bar. His terms of endearment are equally profane.

I received an email from Mario the day after I'd sent him my note. "Tell your friend Alex I said thanks for the hate letter, and that she's a nasty asshole cunt," he wrote, "and tell her good luck ever trying to get access to any chef in New York or anywhere else, ever again."

I found his bedrock sense of entitlement to loyalty and discretion and freedom from consequences almost impressive, but the crass force of his words made me feel queasy and frightened. Would Mario punish me, too, for working with Alexandra, who had merely dared to say what was plainly obvious to any reader? I did not pass his message along to her, out of a desire to protect her feelings, and to protect him from himself.

Soon after that, I had a job interview at *Wine Spectator* magazine. When I sat down across from the editor-in-chief, his first question was, "Do you know which grapes comprise a Bordeaux blend?" (Apart from Cabernet Sauvignon, I did not!) The second question was, "Are you still on good terms with Mario Batali?"

"Yes," I said, and hoped I was right. Mario was among a clutch of very famous chefs who always appeared at the magazine's marquee wine tasting events. If I was on his shit list, it was over for me, anywhere in food media.

After two more interviews, an edit test and about ten excruciating days during which the publisher considered coming in from East Hampton to interview me (he ultimately didn't bother), I got an offer: associate web editor, $50,000 salary, plus benefits. There was a strict "no freelancing" policy, so I'd have to give up the Bridal Blog, but: I could walk to and from work.

On my last day at *Art Culinaire*, I uploaded to the home screen of my desktop computer an image of the German battleship *Bismarck*, engulfed in black smoke and sinking into the sea. It was petty and mean-spirited and the closest I'd ever get to telling Hector to go fuck himself.

Art Culinaire had been a nice training ground for me, a stab at legitimacy, with low stakes. I did a lot of writing for each issue, but suspected that not too many subscribers, of which there were ever-fewer, were actually reading it. They wanted to see which chefs were in the issue, what their dishes looked like, what their recipes were.

When I reread my text now, several years out, I see some decent writing, and some bombastic nonsense bullshit. I see that I was struggling to land on a confident point of view, a voice, a clear sense of my audience. Was I talking to chefs as a peer? Was I talking to food enthusiasts, trend chasers, culinary students? Was I meant to be credulous, or probing? I had no one telling me what the magazine's vision was, because the vision was the visual. I don't think Hector gave a shit about the writing, the voice, and probably most of the chefs who subscribed didn't give a shit, either. It was all about supporting those big porny photos; I know that now.

In my first few weeks at *Wine Spectator*, I took genuine delight in all the ordinary trappings of an early twenty-first century corporate media concern. I loved my new digital elevator pass, my email with the company's name in it, my telephone extension, my voicemail box. I loved the bad free coffee, the smell of microwave popcorn in the afternoon, the unfamiliar faces and names of colleagues I did not yet know. There was nothing actually special about any of it, but as compared to the ever-shrinking footprint of *Art Culinaire*, the staplers and the aggressive HVAC situation and all those levels of authority made *Wine Spectator* feel viable and legitimate and safe.

Also, there was the drinking. So much drinking! *Wine Spectator* is a magazine about alcohol, and, unsurprisingly, there was a lot of ambient and fully tolerated wine consumption in the office. We were technically "tasting," but actually *drinking*. At least I was.

There were frequent wine giveaways, in which we, the web editors, could claim up to three (3) bottles of Idaho Malbec and West Virginia NV Cuvée and whatever else had been rejected by the print magazine staff upstairs.

I quickly gleaned that I could open a bottle at my desk anytime after 11 a.m., as long as I shared it with at least one colleague, and made some effort to informally evaluate it before pouring myself a glass, so I could "see how the wine opened up over time," *haha*.

Working in the cubicle next to me was Rob, who soon became my office best friend and drinking buddy. He was a few years younger than me, a preppy NYU grad gone slightly to seed, with a bone-dry sense of humor and the ability to effortlessly draw hilarious and disgusting pictures inspired by *New York Post* headlines, which he would send to me in those inter-office envelopes with the waxy red string clasp. When I changed my mobile ringtone to the piano score from the revolting, viral "2 Girls 1 Cup" video, it was almost entirely for Rob's benefit. We were both very good at getting our work done, no matter how much we'd had to drink. We met our deadlines and our boss's expectations. We were a couple of high-functioning editors who kept a steady buzz at work each day.

Rob spent his lunch hours at a bar, drinking beer, and otherwise seemed to subsist on wine, Mountain Dew, cigarettes, and the occasional bag of potato chips. His hands shook in the morning; his hair was visibly dirty, and he frequently smelled like a terrible combination of bar rag and ashtray. He played several nights a week in a competitive dart league (his team was called Who Darted?). None of this indicated, to me, that Rob had a drinking problem, only that he was fun and cool and someone with whom I had a lot in common.

I noticed that Rob started drinking earlier in the day than me, and faster once he started. I would say that Rob's drinking made me feel better about my own, but I didn't feel at all bad about any of it. We had our professional mission—writing about wine—as a kind of respectability cloak, an alibi, and drinking all day was room tone. I had no idea that we were those metaphorical frogs who believed themselves to be just taking a bath in an ever-hotter stewpot.

As an associate web editor, I was responsible for cleaning up blog posts written by the magazine's senior editors. I got into frequent disagreements with one guy who had a revolting Humbert Humbertish way with wine descriptors. He would write that various bottles were "sexy babies" or "flirtatious teens" or "coquetteishly fuckable" (just kidding on that last one, but barely. This guy really wanted to stick it in a young Bordeaux.).

We were encouraged to pitch items to a weekly column called "Unfiltered," which was kind of a junkyard for light wine stories that didn't rise to the level of news. "Unfiltered" was edited by a guy named Jim who wore sunglasses on his head all day, made no secret of how much he wanted to be Anthony Bourdain, and was enamored of the fact that I'd worked on Tony's cookbook. When I first started, he had a lot of questions for me, the undercurrent of which was, always, "Bourdain, huh?"

Jim came by my desk one morning and asked me to write about an upcoming charity gala, involving some big food world people, for the "Unfiltered" column. He handed me a printed press release for the event, which was called "Mario Batali: Roasted, Battered and Fried." According to the text, the roasters would include Stanley Tucci, James Gandolfini, Sarah Silverman, Triumph the Insult Comic Dog, and Anthony Bourdain. I winced.

"No one will know you wrote it," said Jim, and it was true; all "Unfiltered" items were unattributed. "Try and get an original quote from someone involved."

I sent Tony an email, asking him what we could expect from the roast, and whether he was concerned about retaliation from Mario, and thanking him profusely for even considering a reply, and preemptively letting him off the hook if he was too busy, or traveling, or just didn't want to. Within ten minutes, he wrote back:

Every chef in New York has been waiting for an occasion where someone exposes the cloven hooves under those plastic clogs. You can expect jokes about lechery, drunkenness, fat jokes—you know, what he deserves. And I'm not afraid of retaliation, because one thing about Mario: he ain't moving anywhere too fast. I can outrun him.

    (Use as much or little of this as you like. Happy to help.)

TONY

chapter 16

The Narcissism of Small Differences

A few days before my wedding, my *Wine Spectator* coworkers organized a send-off dinner for me at a wine bar. It was a generous gesture, and I felt guilty and unworthy of it. I handled my feelings of discomfort by getting fucking shitfaced as quickly as possible. They'd chosen a place that focused on wines of the southern hemisphere—such a narrow focus was still possible in those innocent days before the world financial collapse of 2008—and I went hard on the New Zealand Sauvignon Blanc, redolent of green grass, grapefruit, and cat piss, and the South African Pinotage, with its bouquet of stewed cherries served in a bowl made of cow shit.

I pretty much ignored the scallop ceviche, kangaroo sliders, and slab of caramelized pork belly, all meant to be shared. I drank like I was fifteen years old and didn't know any better, which I really still somehow didn't. I drank no water.

I never once thought, "I want to hurt myself," but that was what I did, chugging wine through dinner and continuing on to a dank East Village bar with Rob until last call, drinking several vodka tonics before sliding home in a cab. After crawling up four flights of stairs, I was sick, kneeling in the bathroom, hard gray and blue granules of cat litter pressing into my bare knees.

Around 6 a.m., I tried to fall asleep on the couch, which worked only in micro-doses, five to ten minutes at a time, until my body woke me up again and again with the same bad news: *You are a dipshit who has knowingly overdosed on poison, which must be expelled.*

Alex and I had planned to start driving upstate around noon, arriving at my parents' house in time for cocktails and an early dinner, but at 11 a.m. I was still roiled with stomach cramps and retching bile.

I wondered, half in a panic, *What if I can't get better? What if I have to go to the hospital instead of getting married?*

I finally managed thirty consecutive minutes of sleep, and when I woke up, sweaty, I found to my relief that I could now at least keep a few sips of water down.

Alex moved around me in the bedroom, putting his undershirts and boxers and a razor into a duffel bag. I sincerely wished to be the cat—free of complex desires, happy and secure in the monotony of his future, dumb as a rock. Eventually I felt well enough to move into the living room, smoke some weed, descend the stairs and collapse into the front seat of our mostly reliable little red VW Golf.

When we stopped for gas at a Thruway rest stop outside of Albany, I walked to the far end of the parking lot and furtively smoked a little more weed. By the time we arrived at my parents' house, I was ready for a pre-dinner Manhattan, which I followed with a few glasses of my mom's "house wine," Carlo Rossi Chablis. My dad bought it by the jug.

The wedding weekend itself was big and fun. We were surrounded by people who cared about us, who had come from all over New York and New Jersey, and as far away as New Mexico, California, Arizona, England, Germany, and Israel. In lieu of a rehearsal dinner, we had a picnic at a state park pavilion, with some perfectly good grocery store sandwich platters and cookies, big bags of chips, watermelon, and coolers full of soda, beer, and wine. Everyone was invited, many came, and the weather was sunny and warm and just windy enough to sweep away the bugs and the weed smoke. Later that night, we convened with a bunch of our friends at a Cornell student bar, the Chapter House. Alex went a bit too hard with his high school buddies, but I wasn't really in a position to judge.

For the ceremony and reception, we had yellow school buses to get people from their hotels to the winery. That afternoon, ripped on potent homemade pot brownies, I stood alone in my wedding dress on the deck, watching the buses ramble up the unpaved driveway, dust clouds rippling around the open windows, I was reminded of the film adaptation of *Jesus Christ Superstar*, when the ominous brass and electric guitar notes of the overture kick in, and the cast comes roaring across the Judean Desert in a school bus with guns and crosses strapped to its roof, giddily preparing to worship and slay a sinewy blue-eyed Jesus.

For processional music, I'd wanted Cat Power's spooky, gorgeous version of "Sea of Love." Her vocals are pure and bright, though there's a pained raggedness in her delivery, and the spare instrumentation is so deliberately atonal as to sound like an indie horror anthem. Alex vetoed it as "too weird," so we used the Beatles' "All You Need is Love," with that nice bit of brassy pomp in the beginning, and a straightforward, wedding-appropriate message. My friend Jessica, who'd been with me in Atlantic City all those years ago, and was now a sex crimes prosecutor for the Manhattan DA's office, got website-ordained to perform our fast and resolutely nondenominational marriage ceremony.

When it was over, and Alex and I walked off the wooden platform as a married couple, the DJ playing "My Baby Just Cares for Me," by Nina Simone, I tried to beeline us to the bar, but was intercepted by my mother-in-law, who forced an excruciating receiving line. My own mother, though still capable of walking very short distances with a cane or walker, was being pushed around by my dad in a wheelchair for the day, and the rough outdoor terrain gave them both an enviable excuse to avoid the gauntlet of awkward hugs.

A childhood friend came through the line holding her infant

daughter, hugged me with one arm, then looked at my red dress and my soft body, and asked me if I was pregnant. Of all the conversations I had that day, that is one of the very few that I remember.

After a brief and relatively sexless honeymoon in Aruba, I was back in the office, working on *Wine Spectator*'s annual food issue, which featured cooking lessons from name-brand chefs: Daniel Boulud, Eric Ripert, Charlie Trotter, Emeril Lagasse, Alice Waters, and Mario Batali. Each chef provided a recipe, submitted to an interview, had their portrait taken, and participated in a cooking video for the website. The finished videos were short, maybe five minutes total, but the production team asked for two hours of each chef's time, for possible re-shoots, still photos, and a video interview.

Mario pushed back on the timing, saying he could only give an hour. I knew it would be tight, but I got the high-strung video director to reluctantly agree to it.

The day before his scheduled shoot, just before 5 p.m., I got a call from one of Mario's three (three!) assistants.

"I am so sorry," she said, "but Mario can only give you thirty minutes tomorrow."

"OK," I said, "but I don't know that we can actually do that."

"I'm so sorry," she said, again, and I could tell that she was. "I'm just quoting him here, but he said to tell you that if you can't get what you need in a half hour, that's your problem, not his."

Back when I was his assistant, I had made this same kind of call on Mario's behalf. He was paranoid about people wasting his time. I could almost hear him saying, *It's not an emotional issue,* but to be on the receiving end of a last-minute power flex sure fucking felt like one.

I told the video director, whose anxious reaction added to my general upset. I left the office, chugged rosé on the roof of my building until I vomited over the side and down into the air shaft, then went into my apartment, smoked some weed, and fell asleep on the couch, watching messy addicts disappoint their families on *Intervention*.

I woke up in pain and called in sick with a "migraine," skipping the shoot entirely and leaving supervisory duties to Owen, the features editor, who did his job like the mature professional that I couldn't force myself to be. I went back to bed, and woke up in the early afternoon, seized with anxiety that skipping the shoot might damage my relationship with Mario, my secret tormentor, who was almost certainly not thinking about me at all.

When the *Wine Spectator* food issue and cooking videos were released, I emailed to thank him for his contribution, and told him that his cooking demo "reminds me of the old Food Network, before they discovered boobs," a reference to the channel's new crop of attractive female hosts, and he wrote back, "You did a great job."

A few weeks after that, Tony Bourdain's assistant Beth called me. She was very pregnant, she said, and asked if I would fill in for her at Montana State University's opening football weekend, where Tony would be speaking and cooking a private dinner for some top alumni donors, at the head coach's house. Tony needed a sous chef. The pay was seven hundred dollars per day, including travel days, plus all of my expenses, and the recipes would be the easiest ones from the *Les Halles Cookbook*. I accepted, and used my last vacation day for the year.

The night before I left for Bozeman, I watched a new episode of *Top Chef* in which Tony, acting as a guest judge, said to one guy that his broccolini, burnt and drenched in mint-flavored oil, was unfit for even a prison meal tray. He told another that his overcooked lobster tail was like eating "doll head." Tony and I hadn't cooked together before; I was a little nervous.

My only obligation on the first night was to accompany Tony to a big dinner at which he was the guest of honor. "Just be a kind of human shield," said Beth. "The rabid super-freak fans tend to stand down when he's got someone next to him."

I hadn't seen Tony in person since that time in his Manhattan apartment, when we finished the cookbook edits and he gave me a big check. In the interim, he'd changed TV networks and published two new books. He'd also gotten divorced, remarried, and had a newborn daughter, all of which I knew from industry gossip and Page Six.

We met before the dinner in the fake-wood lobby of the Hilton

Garden Inn, which had a magnificent view of Home Depot, the Container Store, and an IHOP. Tony seemed quietly happy, and acted more glad to see me than I'd expected, given that we barely knew each other. He asked me how I was, congratulated me on my marriage, then went on at some length about the intoxicating quality of "new baby smell." He claimed to love all aspects of fatherhood, including changing diapers and being woken in the middle of the night by a hungry, squalling infant, and he seemed to mean it.

"Took out the earring, took off the thumb ring, threw 'em both in the Bosphorus Strait," he said, holding out his hands.

There was no reason for me to be anxious or unhappy that night, and though I enjoyed myself at dinner, I still drank too many gin and tonics, too quickly, didn't eat enough to compensate, and was ill. I stayed in bed till noon, ate some IHOP eggs and toast, and continued to rest till 3 p.m., which was go time.

The dinner at the football coach's home started with a canapé of steak tartare. Tony chopped the beef sirloin by hand and mixed it himself with mustard, ketchup, Tabasco, Worcestershire, capers, cornichons, and anchovies, then had me shape it into quenelles and transfer them onto rounds of baguette toast. We served an insanely rich lobster bisque ("You could never get away with using this much lobster in a commercial kitchen," said Tony, conspiratorial and proud), followed by mussels with chorizo and leeks, then daube of lamb Provençal with chive mashed potatoes and, finally, blueberries with lime sugar. The university rep told us that we'd be cooking for five of the wealthiest couples in the western United States—one guy owned all the Arby's franchises this side of the Mississippi, another was big in oil—and to a one, they were unassuming and polite. They drank very little of the host's wine, and the women insisted on clearing their own dishes, and their husbands,' too. Apart from the football coach's wife, none of them had read *Kitchen Confidential* or seen Tony on TV.

I stayed too busy to drink more than a single glass of white wine while we finished cleaning up. Back at the Hilton Garden Inn, I slept like a rock.

As autumn rolled on in New York, my in-office drinking remained steady and my nighttime and weekend drinking expanded to fill more and more space, like a giant spilled bowl of soup on the floor of my waking life. My true internal condition, experienced in brief passages between hangovers and drinking, was an eddying stream of irritation, dissatisfaction, and mild depression, exacerbated by the sharp sense that I was being such an ungrateful asshole for having these feelings. I was a gainfully employed newlywed with a rent-stabilized two-bedroom apartment in Manhattan. *What do you have to complain about? Look at all these fucking blessings, you piece of shit!* I thought, and then I would drink and smoke my way to the hollow oblivion that could sometimes feel like happiness.

One Saturday night, a few weeks after Christmas, Alex and I got dressed up and took a cab across town to a small black box theater, which my college acquaintance Ken had rented to throw himself a prom-themed thirty-third birthday party. I came at it with a bad attitude. Aggressively themed adult birthday parties, like grown-up kickball leagues and mud races and SantaCon, are annoying and embarrassing, the realm of people with too much time and disposable income. In addition to a DJ spinning funk and soul music, Ken's party held the promise/threat of Ken's band, a bunch of dudes who played earnest Grateful Dead covers. There was a big bowl of Everclear punch, and, if you knew the right guy and had cash, there was coke and mushrooms and ecstasy, which everyone had lately started calling Molly.

Ken was a math major in college, and now he was a coder who'd made a bunch of money in the first dot-com bubble of the late 90s. He talked frequently about how he was super-close with his parents and siblings, and about how they liked to rent houses in various fashionable rural areas for holiday skiing or camping trips, at which every member of the family played an instrument really well, and it was all just incredibly fun and cool. You know? Like one of those guys who just fucking *loved* summer camp and ultimate Frisbee?

He wasn't remotely a bad guy, but I could not relate, because I was jealous, though I couldn't articulate it at the time. I wanted a bigger cushion of financial security, and to make a lot more of my own money, using my own brain. I wanted to be surrounded by people who happily traveled to cool places together for holidays, people who didn't feel threatened by the way I held my silverware, or the fact that I'd shed my regional accent and moved away forever, and didn't call often enough.

My reaction to Ken was, at its heart, a petty resentment over relatively minor gradations within the American middle class; it's what some would call the narcissism of small differences. Ken's parents and grandparents had advanced degrees; my paternal grandparents both stopped school around eighth grade, and they met while working in a gun factory. My mom was a registered nurse, and her mother had been a public school secretary. In my family, the purchase of a new car was a long-term financial goal; in Ken's family, every child received a late model Volvo when they turned sixteen. Ken was raised in a secular Jewish family in the New York metropolitan area, and he seemed to believe that he was special, with no limits on what he could accomplish. I was raised Catholic, outside of Syracuse, and wasn't sure I deserved anything that I wanted.

My resentment and envy were myopic and unfair, but no less real to me for that as-yet-unearned knowledge. For all I knew, Ken hated himself, or was deeply depressed, or an addict in denial. What did I think the Kens of the world owed me? Should he have paid me, invited me into his family, or cut off a chunk of his apparent self-esteem and slapped it onto mine? I had so many advantages, just by virtue of being born a healthy white American at the end of the twentieth century, but to me, that was theoretical, because however much I had, I wanted more. Like an addict.

I wasn't thinking deeply about any of this at Ken's party; I was scanning the men in the room, some with and some without girlfriends or wives, clocking that they all seemed more socially at ease than Alex, who sat on a chair against the wall, holding a can of beer and talking to no one, just being his quiet and serious self. Why had he come? He never seemed to have any fun at these things. His inability to make small talk was a character asset, but I sometimes wanted the liability of bullshit, flirt, and banter.

I was angry with Alex for being himself. I felt lonely and unfulfilled, and fucking hated myself for it.

When I asked him if he wanted to leave, he replied, "Do *you* want to leave?" with an amused but annoyed edge in his voice, which made me feel defensive and frustrated and furious and insane.

He rarely just said what he meant, or what he wanted; I had to jiggle it out of him, though I could always tell by his tone and body language when something was bothering him. He hated to fight. On the rare occasion that I could goad him into finally really raising his voice at me, I would feel wildly exhilarated, and as far as I could tell, he would feel drained and defeated.

When we got home that night, he seemed tired, while I still had all that dangerous Everclear energy to be metabolized, my frustration and insecurity and disappointment whipped up by the tornado of my dumb blunt drunkenness, now contained in our cramped and dusty living room. I held out various pieces of junk mail and magazine pages to the cat, who stamped his teeth marks into each one.

"Look at what he's doing!" I said to Alex, who said, "Uh huh," and didn't look up from his book, which annoyed me. I took off one of my gold hoop earrings and stabbed it into his leg with the sharp post, through his trousers, just a quick in-out poke into the skin.

I think he yelled, "What the *fuck?!*", but the truth is, there's a kind of blank spot in my memory of exactly how he reacted. All I remember is my own feeling of immediate regret over having done such an obnoxious and shitty thing. I know that I apologized to him right away, went and grabbed rubbing alcohol and paper towels and told him to take off his pants so that I could tend to his wound, which offer he rejected, saying that he would do himself, later. This is mostly what I remember, that he retreated into himself, rather than tell me what an asshole I was.

I recall, too, that I tried to play it off as a joke, one that I was very anxious to get him in on; wasn't I funny, wild, out of control? Had the roles had been reversed, if he had drunkenly stabbed me with an earring, I would have lost my fucking mind. I was a monster.

I tried to go to bed soon after that, but once again I was sick all night and well into the next day, a dark and cold Sunday.

Right after the prom party, I went off the birth control pill and my antidepressant, spurred in part by my sister reminding me, "You're getting a little long in the tooth."

With reluctance, I visited my gynecologist for a baseline checkup and discussion of what I ought to be doing to prepare my body for human occupancy. She was a petite and well-preserved former professional ballerina, with photos of herself dancing onstage hung in the waiting and exam rooms, and a bedside manner like permafrost.

The doctor glanced at the height and weight numbers on my chart, then looked at me. "Your body mass index is far too high, almost clinically obese. You must lose some weight," she said, her voice heavy with contempt. "Also, don't eat raw fish, deli meats, or cheeses."

I joined Dolphin, the cheap gym in my neighborhood, and got easily talked into a year's worth of personal training sessions, which I couldn't really afford but put on my credit card anyway, reasoning weakly that maybe I'd write a book about the experience and make a lot of money. (Because, really, what's more interesting than a woman in her thirties trying to sensibly lose some weight, on the advice of her doctor?)

At the start of the first session, my assigned trainer, John, told me that I had to pose for a "before" picture, that we would then later compare to my smaller, better "after" body, sometime in the indefinite future. I was a born and bred pleaser, but this was my red line.

"No," I said, with more conviction than I had expressed to another human in my entire life. "I'm not doing that."

A week into the gym experiment, it occurred to me that my extremely regular period was a few days late. To date, Alex and I had embarked on exactly one round of unprotected intercourse, and I guessed that this hiccup was just my body adjusting to being off the pill. It took most people several months to get pregnant. Still, on my lunch hour, I bought a test from the Duane Reade, and peed on a stick in the single-use handicapped bathroom. The result was blazingly, immediately positive. I started to cry and went back to my desk, opened the interoffice messaging system, and wrote to my drinking buddy Rob:

"I'm fucking pregnant. This fucking sucks."

Then I called Alex and gave him the good news.

chapter 17
Black Death

Most nights during the first several weeks of my pregnancy, I had vivid dreams of inhaling huge bong hits, smoking cigarettes, and drinking gin and tonics by the bucket. I was suddenly sober, untethered from my antidepressant and the familiar hormones of the birth control pill, while awash in a flood of all-new hormones. They made me sleepy, depressed, and anxious, sure, but also predisposed me to fits of unhinged laughter over such minor provocations as learning, from a *New Yorker* profile, that the seemingly erudite George Clooney sprayed the leaves of his salad with something called Wish-Bone Balsamic Breeze.

"Party's over," I wrote in emails to various friends, when I was two months in, and felt it was safe to broadcast that I was *up the stick* and unavailable for our usual boozy good times. After sending birthday party regrets to my friend Sean, whom I'd known since high school, he wrote back, "Congratulations! I thought you hated children!"

"I think I do," I said, "but I am hoping to make an exception for this one."

I thought about getting fucked up all the time. I'd become so accustomed to blurring my anxieties and irritations with booze and weed, and now, every time it reflexively occurred to me to change the channel with a drink, I remembered that I just had to, like, feel things. It was so boring, and I fucking hated it.

After my first trimester, I allowed myself the occasional glass of wine or cocktail, which "everyone" (doctors, other parents, the literature) seemed to agree was just fine. The smell and the feel and the taste of alcohol brought a measure of color back into my dimmed world, and to my surprise, given the kamikaze nature of my pre-pregnancy drinking, one now felt like plenty enough.

I was still desperate for the specific effects of weed, and after finding a single, decades-old anecdotal study that indicated no ill effects on newborn babies whose mothers who used cannabis while pregnant, I resumed getting high, on a much-reduced schedule, a few times a week. I knew that no one would have condoned this, and thus it was my entirely private practice. It was essential for my mental health, I decided, and therefore good for my hypothetical baby, too.

I subscribed to an email newsletter that likened the growing embryo to a series of increasingly large foods: a grain of salt, a bean, a strawberry. I went on an exploratory visit to an East Village daycare and was alarmed to learn that leaving my kid there while I worked would cost about 60 percent of my salary, and also that all the spots were already spoken for, but I was welcome to put the little avocado on a waiting list.

We used Alex's savings and all our wedding gift money to put a down payment on an apartment in Jackson Heights, Queens, where real estate and childcare and groceries were cheaper, and we could have more space.

I read *What to Expect When You're Expecting*, peeked down the rabbit hole of pregnancy message boards, and learned that a baby's exit strategy (via sterile scheduled surgery, or in a horse trough at the

Manson Family Ranch while on a peyote trip, or anything in between) pretty much determined whether they would be a dim-witted school shooter with a water allergy or editor in chief of the *Harvard Law Review*.

What was *my* "birth plan"? *The Business of Being Born*, a documentary about the beauty of home birth and the evil of the surgical C-section, was released during my gestation period. Alex and I watched it, on the suggestion of his old high school buddy Vito, who lived in Wyoming, sold weed, and had a teenage daughter he saw once every two years.

"Vito can sit in a bathtub and press out a baby through his dick-hole with no drugs," I said to Alex as the credits rolled, "but I'm getting a *fucking* epidural, in a hospital, with a morphine chaser."

I went on maternity leave a week before my due date, which came and went without incident, leaving me free to float around our new, half-unpacked apartment, watching *Gossip Girl* and cooking lamb stew and chicken soup to stash in the freezer for the postpartum days. I could have stayed in that marvelous state of not-working, frequently napping bliss forever.

Eli was born just before Christmas, by the miraculous convenience of a C-section surgery. For my birth plan, I'd reluctantly chosen the classic front-door exit (while pharmaceutically numbed to the fucking sky!), but after twelve hours of unproductive induced labor and an epidural that did not take, Alex went out for a gyro and a seltzer just before the doctor came in and suggested a C-section, and I thought, *The sunroof it is!* and *Fuck you, Vito!*

During a C-section, you stay awake, but get the good good drugs. Under their spell, I found it very groovy and interesting to be strapped like Christ onto an operating table so that an auxiliary human could be removed from my body.

After several minutes of indeterminate surgical action, obscured behind a hanging sheet, the doctor said, "We're going to lift him out now." I heard his cry, they cleaned him up and wrapped him in a blanket, and Alex held him briefly near my face, into which he yelled without opening his eyes. Eli looked like a stranger, and also like a baby. I heard someone behind me say, "Hold on, what's in his mouth?" and someone else carried him away. I drifted off into a druggy half-sleep while someone stitched my body back together, then wheeled me and my bed into a recovery room and left me alone.

That one post-surgery hour, blitzed on a morphine cocktail and swaddled in warm flannel blankets, was the hands-down best part of the birth experience, and, as it turned out, the last time I'd feel relaxed for months. Once the morphine's softening effects dissipated, my abdomen throbbed and my arms and face were so itchy that more than ten minutes of consecutive sleep became impossible. The call button next to my bed didn't seem to work. Having just been sliced open and sewn back up, I couldn't hop out of bed and seek out a Benadryl (or more morphine, which was what I really wanted).

Around 6 a.m., a nurse brought Eli to me, so that we could attempt breastfeeding, using what she called the "c-clamp position" and the "football hold." It didn't go all that well; he wouldn't really close his mouth around the tap, and which itself was non-productive. "Your milk hasn't quite come in yet," she said. "We'll try again in a little while, and I can always give him some formula."

While I held him and scrutinized his red face, she topped up my beautiful, perfect drug I.V. and put Eli back in his plastic box on wheels.

"This is your last dose of morphine," she said. "We're switching you to Percocet." On the tray table in front of me, she placed what looked like a bong that was also a baby bottle, enclosed in a paper envelope with a plastic window.

"After surgery, your lungs need a little help recovering," she said, "so we have you practice on the incentive spirometer."

I ripped open the package and she showed me how to slowly breathe into the thing so as to keep a plastic ball afloat. Then she left with the baby, and I immediately fell asleep. Later, a doctor came in to tell me that Eli had a raisin-sized cyst growing out of the floor of his mouth, attached to the left side of his tongue. A specialist surgeon would come by later to discuss our options.

"It's not an emergency, but something to keep an eye on," he said.

I turned on the TV. Pat Kiernan, unflappable Canadian, read the news on NY1. Tears slid from my eyes. I wished I were Pat, a physically capable man with an intact abdomen, wearing actual clothing, not bleeding into a sanitary pad the size of a Costco sheet cake, with a cystic newborn baby. I felt like a very sad and useless empty suitcase.

Alex arrived later, freshly showered and cheerful. He seemed like he'd probably slept a good long fucking time in our bed, probably with the cat curled next to him, unencumbered by pain or anxiety. His parents came next, bearing an Edible Arrangement whose raw, sticky perishability and imminent fruit flies filled me with a nonsensical rage. I was so itchy, so tired.

The next time Eli was delivered to me, he was fully asleep, wrapped up tight in a standard-issue blue-and-pink-striped flannel blanket, wearing one of those dumb little caps. He had fat, pouty lips and enormous cheeks and he looked contented, if slightly judgmental. I took his cap off. His downy head was perfect.

In hospital captivity, I was forced to watch a state-produced video about how and why not to shake one's baby to death, along with some self-care advice for the postpartum period. On the screen, a young woman stood at the counter in a fluorescent-lit kitchen with bad cabinets, using a plastic-handled serrated knife to artlessly chop through an enormous pile of green and red bell peppers. What was she going to do with that many peppers? Why wasn't there an onion or some garlic? The camera cut to an infant on its stomach in a playpen, wearing a light blue terrycloth onesie. *Oh shit*, I thought. *This is my life now.* Alex didn't have to watch the video; he went out to lunch with his parents.

A young male surgeon visited my room in the late afternoon, after

Alex had returned with a chocolate chip cookie for me. The surgeon had on gray scrubs and expensive-looking running shoes and tiny socks. Why did these guys always look like they were on their way to Equinox?

"Hi, Mom, I'm here to talk about the cyst in your baby's mouth."

Wait, was everyone just going to call me *mom* now?

"We'll have to do some tests, but it looks like a ranula," the doctor continued.

"Ranula? I don't even know her!" I joked, then laughed alone until there were tears streaming down my face, which the doctor ignored, turning to tell Alex that the cyst had developed around a salivary gland, that it would have to be surgically removed, and that we should take the baby to see his colleague, a pediatric ENT surgeon with an office in midtown.

"We generally recommend waiting at least two months before scheduling the surgery, to give your baby the best chance of surviving the anesthesia," he said. I blinked. The men on one side of Alex's family were prone to weird benign cysts; they called it the family curse. *It's not my fault*, I told myself.

Two days later, we left the hospital with a bunch of paperwork, a package of diapers for Eli, some giant mesh panties and sixty Percocet tablets for me, and an infant for us. Alex drove us home in the very cool-looking but deeply unreliable 1979 Ford Bronco that he'd bought on a whim a few months before Eli was born. It was getting dark and snowing heavily; I sat in the backseat of the truck, one hand on the car seat, watching my son sleep, certain that we would somehow defy the guardrails and slide off the Queensboro Bridge and into the East River.

When we got home, the sky was black. Alex double-parked in front of the building, in the soft, wet snow, and together we wrestled the car seat out from the web of seatbelt straps. I was sweating, my incision throbbing; I could barely carry my own body up our building's three front steps.

"Let's get barbecue for dinner," said Alex. "I'm starving."

We were having two very different experiences. I was in pain, leaking the milk that had since come roaring in, and bleeding heavily from my intact birth canal, a phenomenon I did not expect or understand. My only concerns in the world involved the baby and my desperate desire to sleep, perhaps forever. Alex's most pressing issue seemed to be whether to order ribs, brisket, or chicken wings for dinner. He was giddy, talking about all the movies we could watch during his two weeks of paternity leave. I didn't know what to do or say to get what I wanted, and apart from unconsciousness, I didn't know what I wanted.

While Alex went to pick up our dinner, I sat on the couch in the darkened living room with Eli, mercifully, still asleep in the carrier. The cat approached, sniffed his face, then jumped and skittered away in dramatic terror, as if he'd just witnessed an explosion. This made me laugh, which sent a stabbing pain to the area of my tender abdominal incision.

After a fractured night of near-hourly wakings and feedings, I decided that I wanted go back to the hospital, where people would take care of everything, including me. In the lead-up to delivery, I'd been arrogant about not getting help—we wouldn't need it, we didn't want it, and anyway, we probably couldn't afford it—and now it was four days before Christmas and I thought, *Holy shit, we are fucked.* I called around to every postpartum doula service I could Google, but no one was available until a few weeks after the New Year. My mother's illness made her physically incapable of pitching in, and although Alex's mom would have been willing to come for a few days, we had nowhere for her to sleep, and anyway she was an anxious person and I knew that we would drive each other insane.

During that first full day at home with Eli, my upstairs neighbor Anya, herself the mother of a one-year-old, rang the doorbell to ask if we needed anything from the neighborhood pharmacy. I didn't know how badly I needed acknowledgment from someone who knew what I was going through until I got it from Anya. Later, she brought us a casserole of macaroni and cheese and a coffee cake. Standing in the kitchen, jamming warm cheesy pasta into my mouth, I felt taken care of. (If you know someone with a newborn, give them a casserole and a cake.)

Sleep remained elusive, for the obvious reason of the hungry newborn baby, but also because our direct upstairs neighbors were renovating their apartment, which meant near-constant daily demolition and construction noise. And, it turned out that Percocet, while great for the pain, exacerbated my insomnia, decimated my appetite, and contributed to some alarming hallucinations involving Paul McCartney and various McDonald's mascots.

In those early weeks, I felt that my entire life had been blown apart, and that I was just pieces of wreckage, entirely submerged in some very dark water. Everything was chaos, every hour seemed like a year, and a simple trip to the neighborhood pediatrician felt like an impossible logistical puzzle. I couldn't get the stupid baby sling to work. I became convinced that the dark streaks in the hardwood floor were evidence of black mold. I stopped brushing my hair, rarely flossed. I couldn't see more than a few minutes into the future. One evening, I convinced myself that a stranger would climb into the baby's window to harm him. I woke Alex up and insisted that he buy a handgun.

Horrible visions would come to mind, unbidden, just as I was dropping into sleep: I'd trip on the sidewalk while carrying the baby and he would go flying out of my arms and into the path of oncoming traffic, or we'd be in a car on the highway and get sideswiped by a tractor trailer and go tumbling off the side of the road in a fireball.

My obstetrician, Joan the therapist, and a college friend who was now a doctor all urged me to get back on antidepressants. "There aren't that many conclusive studies about the effects on a nursing baby," my friend said, "but I think the benefits outweigh the risks."

I chose instead to treat my dark feelings with weed, which I concluded, after some scattershot research, was no worse than a pharmaceutical for a big, healthy breastfeeding baby, with the added bonus of getting to check the fuck out for an hour or so at a time. When Eli napped, I'd smoke a little weed and drift into the kitchen to cook something simple, like a puréed vegetable soup or a pasta. Chopping garlic and moving it around a pan while listening to music, I'd feel good for a half hour or so, until his waking cries activated my nervous system like a mild electric shock, shunting me back into a state of panic that would slowly dissolve into guilt about having smoked weed, and despair over my diminished capacity to cook full meals.

Through our neighborhood listserv, I joined a "baby group" of other mothers of newborns who would meet out for walks or gather in someone's apartment to compare notes on such diverse topics as cradle cap (gross) and postpartum blow jobs (gross). We laughed at ourselves and each other and at our ridiculously cute and sometimes maddening babies. We shared stories about baffled spouses and clueless in-laws and jealous pets, being peed and vomited and shat on, and the absurdity of trying to move around New York City with leaking breasts and tiny helpless creatures and all the stuff they required to stay fed and asleep and alive.

Everyone was on maternity leave, at least for a little while. Among us were a federal prosecutor and an architect, a journalist and a union organizer. One mom, Christen, was an artist with a newborn and a five-year-old. She had a pair of intriguing abstract color photos hung on her living room wall, which she was quick to explain were interior self-portraits of her own cervix. She told us that after her first child was born, she'd written and performed a one-woman show about breastfeeding, masturbation, and the FedEx guy. I liked her right away.

When Eli was six weeks old, the little raisin-sized cyst in his mouth suddenly swelled up into an angry grape. It got so big that he couldn't close his mouth around my breast, though he could still take a bottle. I took him to be examined by the ENT surgeon, who told me that the cyst was infected, and scheduled an emergency surgery for the next day.

"Don't worry, mom. He'll heal quickly," said the doctor. "Babies are like starfish."

I took Eli home and I pumped. The motor on the machine made a droning, repetitive noise that sounded like the words "black death."

I'd been instructed not to feed him anything but water after midnight, to prevent him from aspirating milk into his tiny lungs while under anesthesia. At 4:30 a.m., before we left for the hospital, I offered him a bottle filled with cool water. He took one long pull and exploded into hungry, betrayed sobs. My boobs were very full; I had to pump before we got in the car.

"Black death," said the breast pump. "Black death."

Eli and I were both crying when I handed him over to the anesthesiologist, another very fit-looking dude in fancy sneakers. The chance of fatality was one in 300,000; one was more than zero. A few hours later, the surgeon handed him back to me, alive and furiously angry, in a big recovery room full of wailing babies and toddlers. A kind nurse led me to a rocking chair, and encouraged me to try nursing him.

"He might be a little sore, but he's probably very hungry," she said, and within a minute he was latched on, like nothing had ever been wrong. He and I spent one night in the hospital, and Alex drove us home the next morning.

I soon went back to *Wine Spectator*, four days a week, with Wednesdays off, for which arrangement I'd forfeited my health insurance and 20 percent of my salary, though I was still doing 100 percent of the work I'd done previously. In the morning, I dropped Eli off with an older woman named Jennifer who looked after five infants in her home every day. She never took them outdoors, and the gigantic TV in her living room was always on, but my baby was safe, for only $700 a month. Jennifer loved Eli like she loved all the children in her care. One day when I came to pick him up, she said, in her lilting Caribbean accent, "He has such a serious face, he looks like he's gonna be a judge."

Going back to work gave me a new freedom from obsessively monitoring the baby's every whimper and smile, though it was exhausting in a whole new way. Our overnights were a minefield of unpredictable wakings. Even when Eli slept well, I was too easily disturbed by Alex's snoring and shifting, and often moved to the couch. I started taking shots of brown liquor anywhere from 2 a.m. to 7 a.m., to settle my nerves. At work, I regularly slipped out of the office and onto the street to smoke weed, which made me feel guilty but thrilled to have a transgressive secret.

I was often so tired by the end of each workday that I'd forget the logic of traffic and crossing lights. One time I called a locksmith in a panic, because I couldn't get my keys to work, and Eli was wailing in his stroller. At 6:05 p.m., technically "after hours," a guy came and sprayed some WD-40 in the lock and opened the door with my keys and I realized that I'd been turning them in the wrong direction. That cost me $200.

When I'd been back at work for a few months, one of my colleagues got pregnant, and, in trying to strategize her own post-maternity leave return, she asked for the same part-time deal that I had, at which point management pulled the plug on my four days a week situation, and said I could either work full-time or not at all.

"The company doesn't want to set a precedent," my boss explained. She looked miserable and embarrassed. She herself was recently married, and thinking about a baby. "We're not a family-friendly company."

I returned to a full-time schedule and put the word out that I was looking for a part-time job. I heard from exactly one person, Tony Bourdain, who emailed me back within a few hours. "My assistant Beth is leaving. Would you ever consider working for me?" Once again, incredibly, I was in the right place at the right time. I said yes to Tony, and gave *Wine Spectator* my notice the next day.

chapter 18
I'm Your Assistant

"I'm back on the bottom!" I said, every time I told someone that I'd left *Wine Spectator* to become Tony Bourdain's assistant. I was only half to three-quarters joking.

On the one hand, working from home relieved me of my daily struggles with the clock, clean clothes, the breast pump, and all the human and mechanical obstacles presented by the New York City subway system. On the other hand, I knew that it was a weird backward move, to downgrade from full-time editor to part-time remote assistant, so I reflexively insulted my choice, beating everyone else to the punch. I didn't yet know that almost no one gives a shit about a change in your career, up or down the ladder, unless they are personally impacted by it.

I replaced Tony's assistant Beth, for whom I'd covered in Montana. Beth had worked for Tony for six or seven years, since his media career took him away from the kitchen and out onto the endless road. Tony wrote about Beth as a take-no-shit line cook in *Kitchen Confidential*, giving her the nickname "Grill Bitch," which she embraced. She had accompanied Tony on book tours and produced his live cooking demos at various festivals. She helped out behind the scenes on local episodes of his docu-travel series *No Reservations* and occa-sionally showed up on screen. She even had her own sideline business, selling T-shirts printed with Tony's illustration of a skull gripping a chef's knife in its teeth.

My version of the job would be much more low-key, Tony said when he hired me, with no travel required. The biggest responsibil-ity would be to constantly collate and update all the information in his complex calendar. Just before I started, he sent me an email with the ominous subject line, "Bourdain: The Gathering Storm," with his schedule for the next several months attached.

It seemed exciting but brutal. *No Reservations* had three Emmy nominations that year, so he'd go to LA for the award ceremony and pack in about a dozen meetings while he was there. He'd then shoot TV in Prague for a week, followed by three days at home, full of meetings, interviews, doctor appointments, two public appearances, and a hair-cut. There was a quick overnight in New Orleans to meet with direc-tor David Simon about a writing job on his series *Treme*, followed by a weeklong shoot in coastal Ecuador. After two days at home, there was a geographically nonsensical string of speaking engagements in Des Moines, Miami, Ann Arbor, Chicago, Washington DC, Schenectady, Denver, Rochester, and Cleveland, followed directly by a two-week TV shoot in Harbin, China. Seven weeks, twenty-six flights.

"This should be fairly easy, as I'm booked solid," he said, "so you'll get to diplomatically say 'no' to almost everything new."

The other big part of the job was handling a deluge of daily que-ries, proposals, interview requests, cold calls, and urgent decisions to be made. These came from TV producers, his book publisher, literary and lecture agencies, network publicists, fellow chefs, former colleagues, charities, non-profits, schools, fans, old friends, and the occasional sociopathic stalker.

"Do you prefer to fly out of JFK or Newark?" I'd ask him. "Four Seasons or Ritz-Carlton? Would you like to endorse this line of knives, this spice blend, this brand of chicken feed? Any interest in blurbing this new book? Please write a letter to the government on behalf of this line cook seeking US citizenship. Want to open a restaurant in Las Vegas, Los Angeles, or Philly? Please contribute a recipe to this cookbook for an Alzheimer's charity. Can you please speak to the leading daily newspaper in Bogotá? You're invited to be a featured guest on a cruise down the Danube. Please sign this stack of photos for a fan in Macedonia. Want to accept an honorary degree from this unaccredited university? You're invited to officiate a stranger's wedding in Delaware."

Every other Tuesday, right after therapy with Joan, I'd go by Les Halles restaurant and the TV production office, to pick up shopping bags full of mail for Tony, which I would then sort through, recycling the junk and dropping the rest with his doorman.

Among the huge amount of correspondence he received were like and love letters, dislike and hate letters. There were self-published memoirs, illustrations, and entreaties to come and film his TV show wherever the writer lived. There was a marriage proposal, which included a women's cubic zirconia ring and a lock of hair. A teenage girl from New Jersey sent an impressively detailed list of sexual favors that she'd gladly perform for/with/on him and a friend of his choosing. People sent Tony photos and descriptions of their own travels, recipes for the food they cooked, pictures of the tattoos of his face that they'd committed to various body parts. They wanted his attention and his approval. They wanted him to know that he had made an impression.

I was responsible, too, for making his restaurant reservations and doctor appointments, booking his cars, and ordering and sending gifts of smoked fish or fancy fruit to directors, producers, and editors whom he wanted to thank for a job particularly well done.

Tony treated me like a person with inherent value and paid me on time. It was a good arrangement all around, and I felt lucky and glad.

More than six months passed before I saw him in person, at a poetry reading organized to honor his longtime editor and publisher, Dan Halpern, himself a poet. Among the other presenters were Joyce Carol Oates, John Ashbery, and Richard Ford. I had no official function there; I had asked for a ticket because I wanted to attend, because it seemed like kind of a big deal to get all these writers together in a room.

Shortly before the reading started, I spotted Tony, entering the auditorium from the back. As I approached him, and he saw me, I saw in the slightly defensive set of his face and body language that he didn't recognize me. He had probably met thousands of new people in the three years since we'd cooked dinner together in that football coach's kitchen in Bozeman.

"Hi, I'm your assistant, Laurie Woolever," I said, holding out my hand to shake his. He looked startled and then laughed, his face now slightly sheepish.

Tony was the first reader to say a few words about Dan. He began: "Authors, in my experience, are often bitter, unhappy people, envious, with many complaints. I'm a happy man," said Tony, "and my happiness is largely due to the fact that I've been published by Dan Halpern.

"I don't really know about this poetry stuff. I'm way too crude and too stupid to understand such things," he said. This bit of hyperbolic self-deprecation was pure schtick, I knew, but still, a little whisper of sympathetic denial rippled through the audience, and something pinged hard inside me. I was slightly stunned that Tony would abase himself in order to get there first.

He read aloud Dan's poem "How to Eat Alone," in which are embedded the instructions for preparing a roast lamb dinner for one. The poem begins:

> *While it's still light out*
> *Set the table for one:*
> *a red linen tablecloth,*
> *one white plate, a bowl*
> *for the salad*
> *and the proper silverware.*

And concludes:

Before you begin to eat,
raise your glass in honor
of yourself.
The company is the best you'll ever have.

At home, matters of motherhood seemed to be slowly improving. My postpartum misery lost its dangerous edge after we undertook the process of "sleep training," during which I let Eli cry in his crib at bedtime, until he gave up and fell asleep. Sleep training is either a harmless and efficient way to teach a baby to sleep through the night, for everyone's well-being, or it's an unspeakably cruel and selfish torture that destroys a baby's ability to form a trusting relationship with other humans. The truth depends on the order in which Google serves you your answers and your level of personal desperation. In the middle of our first night of sleep training, as Eli screamed alone in his crib after a 2 a.m. wakeup, my online search for validation led me to a support group for adults who'd been "permanently injured by sleep training," about whom I had many unkind thoughts. Anyway, after three nights of training, Eli slept like a diaper-clad log.

Another victory: breastfeeding, which had turned out to be an unbelievable calorie furnace for my body. I was always hungry, and all the pregnancy pounds, and more, slid off with zero effort. I knew it would have to end at some point, but I didn't want it to. Would it be super-weird to become a wet nurse for the purpose of maintaining my new smaller size? Probably, yeah.

When he was almost a year old, Eli suddenly refused the tit at naptime, and then again at bedtime, and I put it away, feeling suddenly like a creep and knowing it was the end of the unbothered daily milk-shake and chicken parm sandwich era.

I planned a big first birthday party for Eli at our apartment and invited all of our new neighborhood friends, our single and/or childless friends scattered throughout Manhattan and Brooklyn, my sister and her family, and all of Alex's relatives in New Jersey—surely too many people for the size of our apartment, but I didn't care. I wanted a big, messy gathering, for my own enjoyment.

New York was hit with a state-of-emergency-level blizzard in the early-morning hours before the party. Only the locals showed up, which saved us from having to host the overwhelming shitshow it would have otherwise been. The night before the party and again in the morning, I spent some truly happy hours caramelizing pounds of onions for grilled cheese sandwiches and baking the same chocolate blackout cake that my friend Margaret Braun had made for our wedding cake, the recipe for which is in her book, *Cakewalk*.

"The secret is buttermilk (which keeps the cake moist) and a little extra salt (which adds a wonderful sharpness to chocolate flavors)," she wrote in the recipe's headnote, to which I would add that it's got cocoa powder, so you don't have to fuss with melting chocolate, and it's fortified with strong coffee, which I just love on principle.

Eli enjoyed the cake, of course, and after he played his part, eating it by the grubby fistful, I put him down for a nap, and all the guests drifted away, with the exception of Rob, my *Wine Spectator* buddy, who stuck around to guzzle two bottles of Champagne and several bong hits with me. We stood in front of the living room window, blowing out the smoke, mesmerized by the building's porter as he pushed a snowblower around the courtyard, clearing a path. Drunk and stoned, with a stack of dishes to wash and half a leftover cake on the counter, I felt more like my old self than I had since first discovering that I was pregnant.

That winter, as Eli began to walk and talk, my neighbor Anya, she of the lifesaving postpartum mac and cheese and coffee cake, invited me to be part of a four-family dinner co-op. Every Sunday evening, we'd get together in someone's apartment and exchange Pyrex containers full of the food we'd cooked for each other: lasagna, chicken adobo, muffaletta sandwiches, aloo gobi—stuff that tasted good and would hold well for a few days and made dinnertime less of a scramble, with fewer resentments and less takeout. I loved the whole process, from planning my meal, shopping for it, the cooking, and packaging, writing out the reheating or assembly instructions, and discovering what everyone else had made to share. It felt good to be taken care of in this mutually beneficial way. I wrote a feature about our co-op, and others, for the *New York Times*, which resulted in a brief, gratifying wave of attention and validation, followed by a frustrating, fruitless scramble to cook up more food trend pieces for the paper of record.

chapter 19

It's Not a Metaphor

A few months before Eli turned two, he developed a marvelous interest in television and videos, first Elmo, and soon after *Thomas the Tank Engine*, a show about the British class system and the colonial rape of resources, and *Yo Gabba Gabba!*, a music-based show made for children whose parents smoke weed.

The more I could start to carve out time alone to write or cook (or, to be honest, take a nap or masturbate or get blazing high and stare out the window), the more I could recognize that having a baby made life better: more purposeful and predictable, and often funnier, cuter, more tender, simpler.

Also: way more gross!

Like a true and normal baby, Eli had roseola and diarrhea, peed in the bath, had diaper rash, and some revoltingly goopy ear infections. Around the same time he discovered the eye-rolling ecstasy of Nutella, Eli developed a big zit under his chin, the kind of thing that I didn't expect to see on his face until adolescence.

I thought if I ignored it, it might resolve on its own, but it didn't: the age-inappropriate blemish continually flared up and subsided, flared up and subsided. I avoided the temptation to squeeze it, because I didn't want to hurt him, but then one day I gave in and pressed down gently on either side of it. The volume of stuff that came coiling out of that little open pore under his doughy baby face was truly disgusting in a way that I couldn't stop thinking about, but eventually the blemish healed and disappeared, because babies are like starfish, and I forgot about it.

Months later, I was drunk on white wine on a Monday afternoon, sitting on my living room floor with two other neighborhood moms and our respective children, who were now squishy, ridiculous, adorable toddlers. On Mondays, I'd keep Eli home from daycare and our little group would get together in a park or at someone's place, to ride out the interminable daytime hours together. A bougie wine store had just opened in our neighborhood, and most Mondays I'd buy and open a bottle or two of $10 vinho verde and drink more than my share of it while the kids pushed around toys, and sometimes each other.

"I'm just really bored with my life right now," I said to one of the moms. "Everything feels so predictable and small. I'd love for something interesting to happen and kind of push things off the track."

I don't believe in any of that manifesting bullshit, but that night, Eli took an unusually long time to settle in his crib at bedtime, and woke up crying two more times. We were off the track, in a bad way. The sleep disruption ground my nerves into a powder, which made me feel awfully sorry for myself, which was excuse enough to belt a few shots of the whiskey my parents had given us for Christmas, at 1 and 3 a.m. At 5 a.m., I sat on the couch with my laptop, in the dark, with a third shot already poured, trying to find an answer to this specific problem. Among the possibilities I found were:

Two-year-olds cry—it's normal! Invest in noise-canceling
    headphones. Here's a link.
A growth spurt, probably. His brain development is
    happening so fast, it sometimes jolts his body awake. Like a
    taser.
He's angry because you sleep trained him too early.

Let him cry. Cry when the baby cries.

Get him tested for ADHD.

Get him tested for celiac disease.

Get him tested for a gifted and talented preschool.

Bring him into your bed.

Do not under any circumstances bring him into your bed.

Two days later, after two more intermittently sleepless nights, Eli woke up at 6:30 a.m., cheerful and oblivious to the grotesquely swollen bump that had blown up under his chin. It was the size of half a quail egg, and it was in the exact spot where that epic zit had been.

The bump wasn't hot or red, and he didn't have a fever. For breakfast, he ate as much toast with Nutella and banana chunks as usual, and drained his milk cup. In a state of confused exhaustion, I decided that he could still go to daycare, instead of going straight to the doctor.

Jennifer gave me the side-eye about the bump, then said, "OK, I'll take him, but stay by your phone." (As if I were ever not by my phone.)

When I picked him up from daycare and took him to the grubby neighborhood pediatric practice the next afternoon, the doctor felt Eli's bump briefly and said, "This is very likely an infected cyst. Why didn't you bring him in earlier? He needs to go to the emergency room."

Oh shit. Why *didn't* I bring him in earlier? I couldn't explain it, really, except to say that there's a calculus that you do as the parent of a maybe-sick young child, taking into account your own intuition, the demands on your time, what you've managed to find out via Google, and your relationship with your child's doctor. Ours was an old-school, elderly male pediatrician, and in my need to be a "good" patient who didn't waste anyone's time, I'd waited, guessing or hoping that he would've said, "This is nothing; it will go away on its own."

But: did I actually think that an unexplained bump under my baby's chin was nothing? Was I that deep in denial about the way things work, about how things have to be examined and dealt with? *It's not a metaphor*, I said to myself in the cab to the hospital, while Eli dozed off in the portable car seat, sucking his thumb, *and it's probably not a tumor.*

It was a chaotic Friday night in a New York City hospital emergency room, and a baby with a bump was low-priority. Alex came from his office to join us, and we three waited four hours for a doctor to examine him. Eli ate three chewy granola bars from a vending machine, and messily drank his first can of uncut apple juice. We read books and took micro-walks and watched people, and he toggled back and forth between our laps.

When we finally got Eli a cot with a curtain around it, and saw a distracted young ER doctor, he did a quick exam and said, "No fever, no tenderness, vital signs all normal. This isn't an emergency. Go home, and see an ENT specialist on Monday."

Eli fell deeply asleep in the taxi back to Jackson Heights, and Alex handed me his phone, on which was displayed the menu of a neighborhood Thai restaurant that delivered till midnight. After a long evening in an ER with a sick (but not yet sick enough!) toddler, I found my husband's fixation on dinner so fucking annoying, an absolute outrage of selfishness.

From the moment the pediatrician had said "emergency room," I experienced a kind of tunnel vision, the world rapidly shrinking so that it only included his body and mine, and whatever or whoever could help us solve the problem of his face, that cyst. Nothing mattered but resolution. I couldn't allow myself to enjoy food or sleep or entertainment, and I felt threatened by any incursion on my dwindling reserves of attention and concern. I did not know how to ask for or accept help, not even from my husband, who was simply hungry for dinner, and I knew it was unfair of me to be so bothered, but I found it hard to care about two things at once, especially when one thing was my toddler on the brink of sepsis (or not?) and the other thing was spicy squid salad. I just wanted to scramble some eggs with a pinch of grated cheese and call it a night. He ordered jungle curry, sweet sausage salad, and sticky rice, and I went right to bed before it arrived.

We spent an uneventful but cranky weekend sequestered at home, and after a Monday morning specialist visit, Eli was directly admitted to Weill Cornell, where he and I stayed for the next seven nights.

Eli was a true champion at hospital living, just crushing the competition in the toddler division, with his baffling acceptance of almost all of it (the exception being the moment he was pierced through the forearm with a wide-gauge needle for an IV antibiotic port). He seemed far more intrigued by than afraid of the hospital experience, and he greeted every person and situation, even an objectively scary CT scan, with some combination of cheerful curiosity and passive indifference. He was super-pumped about the nonstop TV and movies and the thrice-daily desserts, delivered on a tray: pudding cups, red Jell-O, vanilla ice cream.

A few hours after he emerged from his second of two surgeries, there was a visiting musician in the playroom, doing a kid-oriented drum performance, and when Eli heard it from the hallway, he went strut-dancing into the room as if leading a second line at a New Orleans jazz funeral, while I trailed behind him, pushing his IV stand.

Unlike my joyfully oblivious toddler son, I was suspicious, irritable, and self-pitying, despite knowing that an infected cyst was a relative paper cut on a pediatric unit housing multiple cancer patients, a baby with a gnarly bone deformity, and a kid with cystic fibrosis. Still, I cried several times per day, because I was exhausted and scared and I hated spending days and nights in the hospital, surrounded by other people's noises and smells and worries. I cried when we watched an episode of *Yo Gabba Gabba!* in which Tony Bourdain appeared as the kindly "Dr. Tony," an appearance I'd helped to arrange, for the benefit of his own young child, who hated doctors and loved TV. Tony had told me not to worry about work, that nothing was more important than my kid, but the hours were long and I had an iPhone, so I was able to keep up, and grateful for the distraction.

I felt responsible for Eli's infection. I had squeezed the blemish, and wished for drama, and so my penance was a week on a vinyl-covered cot, next to a hospital crib that was basically a cage on wheels, in a room that we shared with an extremely dramatic four-year-old girl who'd just been diagnosed with diabetes, and whose mother made long, loud phone calls to relatives in Eastern Europe.

It's not accurate to say that I completely lost my mind, but it felt chaotically mislaid. I ate fistfuls of M&M's in lieu of dinner, and when Alex came to see Eli in the evenings after work, I'd take off for the closest bar and drink as many vodka tonics as I could manage in the span of two hours.

I just wanted to retreat selfishly into my own head, to get stoned and check all the way the fuck out, in silence, *alone*.

After we were finally discharged, Eli and I spent the next several days recovering on the couch, watching TV and eating snacks and reading books. He was tender and tired, some mornings falling asleep before lunch, sitting up, thumb in mouth.

Within an hour of dropping him at daycare for the first time in weeks, I had this overwhelming desire to do something self-indulgent that would make up for all the misery of the hospital experience.

I sent a text to my old friend Greg, the married photographer, "just saying hi," which quickly and predictably became sexting, over the course of a few weeks, after which we met at the Grand Central Oyster Bar, having jointly invented the flimsiest of work-based pretexts ("let's collaborate on some kind of project") to justify it.

We had gin and tonics and eighteen oysters and a bottle of Grüner Veltliner that smelled like grapefruit and parsley. I opened and slowly devoured the floury little crackers from the plastic package while we talked about our home lives and our work, the places we'd been and the places we wanted to go.

Our goodbye hug at the end of the evening melted into a sloppy sidewalk make-out that set my entire mind and body on fire. *I deserve this*, I thought. *This is fine.*

After several of the best minutes I'd had in recent memory, open-mouth kissing a relative stranger while wearing my wedding ring, we pulled apart and walked away from each other. Where would we go? There was nowhere to go, and we both had to get back to our families.

I took an expensive taxi home, texting with Greg about the things we wished we could be doing as I crossed the Queensboro Bridge. Alex was on the couch when I walked in, feeling exquisitely uninhibited, and invited him to join me in bed, immediately.

I could be onto something, I thought later that night, while he snored next to me. *Start my engine out in the world, and finish the race at home. Everyone wins?* Only in the morning did I feel the full weight of guilty self-loathing, compounded by a hangover, sitting on my chest, like an overweight cat with halitosis.

I didn't go back on the pill after Eli was born, out of laziness and a half-baked notion that there was something admirable about being entirely free of prescription drugs. (Was it also an easy excuse not to have sex?) Because I'd gotten pregnant so quickly with Eli, I'd never spent a minute worrying about ovulation windows. It turns out, you can have a bachelor's degree in science, and have suffered a bout of postpartum depression that turns you entirely off the notion of a second kid, and you can still be so incredibly careless that you accidentally get pregnant anyway.

After another unmistakably positive pee stick result, I beelined from the bathroom to my laptop and Googled "herbal abortion." Could I just handle it at home, with, like, calendula or licorice root? Because I knew that I could not and would not carry this little bit of activated sourdough starter to term.

I told Alex both parts of it that night after dinner: that I was pregnant, and that I planned to terminate as soon as possible. He was quietly disappointed, but didn't fight me on it. I just couldn't bear another round of postpartum depression atop the competing demands of a toddler and a newborn, I said. I felt that we were a complete family unit. When other people I knew said they were having their second kid, I only ever thought that they must be insane. If I had another baby, I joked to Alex, with some measure of seriousness, it would end in a murder-suicide. I also didn't want to get sober, but this I kept to myself.

My abortion wasn't traumatic. I was relaxed, thanks to my friend Christen, the neighborhood mom with the cervix photos, who gave me two Ativan pills. The doctor who did the procedure was my age, more or less, with a great head of curly reddish hair. She was friendly, and chatted with me throughout the procedure.

"What kind of work do you do?" she asked, after administering the local anesthesia.

"Have you heard of Anthony Bourdain?" I said.

She laughed. "Um, yes. His face is all over the buses and subways right now," she said, and it was true; the network was going hard to promote a new season of *No Reservations*.

"I'm his assistant," I said, "and I also do as much freelance writing as I can."

"That's *amazing*. You're going to feel a pinch now," she said as she introduced the suction tube into my uterus. "What's he like? He seems like a great guy. The episode in Kurdistan was incredible. I really admire him."

"He's a great boss," I said. This was weird.

"I'm going to begin the vacuum aspiration now," she said.

Alex had taken a half-day off work. When it was all done, we picked up a huge order of shawarma and falafel and pitas and baba ganouj from a nearby place that he liked a lot. Back at home, I got into bed and fell asleep right away. At 5 p.m., Alex went to pick up Eli from daycare, and told him that I was sick, but that I would be all better in the morning. I woke up when Eli opened the bedroom door. He climbed up onto the bed and snuggled in next to me and sucked his thumb, and we watched a DVR'ed episode of *Yo Gabba Gabba!* while Alex got his dinner together. He had the most beautiful hair, thick and silky, in variegated shades of honey blond that would have been difficult and expensive to replicate in a salon. There were a few smeary bits of avocado in it. I put my hand on his head, and he turned to look at me and I could see the little dark pink scar, the width of a dime, under his chin, where the cyst had been. I felt breathlessly in love with him, and happy to be his mother.

chapter 20

Sexless Separates

John handed me a boxing glove and said, "I mean, everyone can believe in whatever god they want, as long as they accept Christ as their savior."

"Uh huh," I said.

John was my personal trainer. He had a lot of opinions, many of them pertaining to the endangered equal rights of men. He didn't trust Hillary Clinton; there was "something about her face." He believed in keeping an open mind about religion, but was immoveable on the aforementioned Jesus caveat.

That I disagreed with almost everything he said was irrelevant, since he asked me no questions and gave me no opportunity to weigh in. Was the world full of guys like this? I didn't really want to know.

John had been my trainer at the gym I went to before Eli was born, the one who tried to get me to do a "before" photo shoot. Back then, when I told him I was moving to Queens, he gave me his number and said that he lived in Queens, too, and was willing to train me at home for only $25 per session, with every sixth session thrown in for free, so here we were, a few years later, in my living room. Today I would punch and kick the pads he held up. Other times he had me doing weight-lifting sets or pulling on stretchy cables. I got blazing high before each session.

John had a super-intense, long-lingering personal scent with insistent top notes of sweat and drugstore body spray, with a base of vintage mutton and freshly ground white peppercorns. Unlike with Noah the cook all those years ago, I did not find it sexually compelling to smell John; it was just a cost of doing business. He asked me to recommend his services to my neighborhood friends, and I thought about whether any of them would tolerate his combination of body odor and beliefs, then told him that, alas, no one I knew was in the market for a trainer.

To his credit, John never charged me for my last-minute cancellations, of which there were many, because I'd be trying to make a deadline, or Eli would be sick, or I just couldn't bear to see him on a particular day.

After a few months of training, I felt relatively stronger but hadn't lost any of the weight I'd packed back on in the post-breastfeeding era. My twentieth high school reunion was looming, which felt like as good an excuse as any to grasp the nettle and join goddamn motherfucking WeightWatchers.

Dieting according to its strict program was boring and infantilizing, and at first, the limitations felt like an absolute outrage: the point-counting (even for alcohol!), and the food-weighing, and the recalibrating of my ideas about hunger and fullness. Ultimately, of course, it worked, because I took in fewer calories than I burned. In a quest to find a modicum of daily joy, I bought sugar-free tonic water (which tasted awful, but slightly better with gin) and powdered peanut butter (which gave me hilarious, apocalyptic gas).

Thanks to many helpful therapeutic discussions with Joan, I recognized this self-improvement phase as a response to my no-big-deal, very much my choice abortion, which nonetheless left me feeling alienated from my body and disinterested in sex of any kind with any person, even myself. After the abortion, all the suggestive texts from Greg the married photographer went unanswered, and eventually he stopped trying.

Feeling (and being) overweight had been a hurdle to intimacy, so maybe whittling down the size of my body would solve what I saw as the fundamental problem in my marriage, which was still a lack of sex, and my guilt about it.

Over many months of dieting, the pounds slipped away and my interest in sex did return, though it was only theoretical, with the signal coming from far outside the house, in the form of hot TV men: specifically, the many illicit conquests of Jon Hamm's Don Draper on *Mad Men*, along with those of horny alcoholic novelist Hank Moody, played by David Duchovny on *Californication*. On Sunday nights, on the couch with Alex, I found myself turned on by watching these fictional men have boozy encounters with intriguing and beautiful strangers, women whom they easily seduced with minimal dialogue, every scene shot through with the excitement and tension of the forbidden.

As an act of faith and protection, I got a copper IUD. I chose some internet porn for me and Alex to watch together (which we found mildly funny but deeply embarrassing, and turned off after fewer than five minutes). I shaved off all my pubic hair. I made sure that we both had impeccable breath and body odor. None of this, however, changed the fundamental truth that, most of the time, I just didn't want to be doing this, and by *this*, I meant *be naked and vulnerable with my spouse*.

On the rare occasions when I relaxed and we would kiss and it felt OK or even interesting, I was afraid to keep it going, because what if he got into it and I got cold feet? How could I extricate and explain myself without hurting his feelings? Or: what if I *did* like it? How could I reconcile an interest in marital sex with the ways I had already transgressed?

I wondered how much passive battering our relationship could take. I knew from extensive reading and lots of conversations with other married women that this was "normal," that "things ebb and flow," that "you've got to work at it to make a marriage last," but none of that made me feel better.

I had a small handful of married women friends with whom I'd commiserate over feeling bored, frustrated, and guilty about a common desire to act out various fantasies with people other than our spouses. This was all I wanted to talk about; I'd try to speed us through the kid updates and work complaints so that we could get to the good stuff. I was compelled to confess my sins to someone other than my therapist, someone who wasn't professionally obligated to play it cool. I wanted to shock my audience; I wanted their attention and admiration and approval, and I wanted them to help me justify my past and future bad behavior to myself.

Independently, two of these friends sent me a link to an essay by novelist Amy Sohn, published on *The Awl*, called "The 40 Year Reversion." In it, she inventoried the ways that she and her mom friends indulged in the same kinds of behavior I'd been indulging in and/or fantasizing about: heavy drinking, dabbling in drugs, staying out late, cheating. She theorized that all this acting out was pushback against the dull and immutable obligations and rigidity of managing a family with young children. It was adolescent-style rebellion in women who should have outgrown the need for it, and while this was nothing *truly* new—see Anna Karenina, Lady Chatterley, Erica Jong—we now had smartphones and independent credit cards, for greater privacy, and drug dealers who delivered to our homes.

> *... we're masturbating excessively, cheating on good people, doing coke in newly price-inflated townhouses, and sexting compulsively—though rarely with our partners. . . . we are avoiding the big questions—Should I quit my job? Have another child? Divorce?—by behaving like a bunch of crazy twentysomething hipsters. Call us the Regressives. . . . there is a wild, life-craving, narcissistic, oblivious madness to it that reminds me of Don Draper and pals in the mid-sixties. These women are the men their mothers divorced.*

It was both terrifying and comforting to know that I was hardly alone in my discontent and desire. To see a description of my feelings and behavior in published form made it more real, and harder to ignore, but some boring better angel in me believed in denying my urge for chaos and abandon.

"I want to give my marriage a chance," I said to Joan.

How I would do this, I decided, would be to force myself into the shape of a serene, cerebral, mothering woman and wife, achieving whatever modest success I could find time for, while providing the best possible home environment for my husband and son. I associated all of this with a uniform of drapey, sexless Eileen Fisher separates, which I could not actually afford, so I approximated this look with pieces from the new Gap Factory store in my neighborhood.

As befits such a mature thinking woman, I spent many months pitching, researching, reporting, and writing a wonky feature for *Dissent* magazine about the labor issues faced by restaurant workers. I was proud of the piece, which called out the National Restaurant Association for suppressing the tipped minimum wage for decades, and called out the ownership class for underpaying undocumented workers, exploiting their immigration status.

I was also ashamed of the piece, because I'd studiously ignored one of the biggest labor stories of that moment, in which several of Mario Batali's employees filed a huge class-action lawsuit around misappropriation of tips. It wasn't a secret, but I feared that calling further attention to it in my own reporting would be seen by Mario as disloyal, and possibly a blackballing offense.

That spring, Eli and Alex and I went to Las Vegas, New Mexico, to visit some of Alex's family who lived there. Unlike the other Las Vegas, the New Mexico version doesn't have much in the way of built-in entertainment, apart from a series of functional hot springs, a relic of a nineteenth-century hotel that's now part of a college campus. Alex wasn't interested in a soak, so I talked his super-cool uncle, a retired statistician, into driving me over there in his elderly

BMW, which had held up for decades in the desert air. He parked the car on the side of highway, pointed me to the trail, and pulled his *New York Times* from its plastic delivery sleeve. He would wait and read while I soaked.

I made my way down to the trail to the first set of pools, all of which were small and thoroughly occupied, so I kept going to a second set of pools, where there were only a few people. A middle-aged woman with no top on bathed happily in a very small pool, her face turned up to the sun, the bottoms of her smooth black braids floating alongside her boobs. A man soaked alone in another, much larger pool, where there was room for at least three or more bodies. He smiled up at me and I asked politely if it was OK for me to join.

"Yeah, sure, come on in," he said. It was a mid-spring day, not more than 50 degrees Fahrenheit. I wiggled out of my sweatpants and fleece jacket, under which I wore a very modest one-piece black bathing suit. It felt great to slip into the hot water from the cold air. I just sat there for a few minutes, eyes closed, slightly self-conscious but enjoying the sensation and the novelty of it all.

"Where do you live?" asked the man. I opened my eyes. He was maybe ten years older than me, with long gray-and-white hair in a ponytail and a few mottled-looking tattoos on his chest and upper arms.

"Oh, I, uh, New York," I said. I didn't really want to talk, but what was I supposed to do?

"Never been there," he said. "Wanna fuck?" I noticed then that he had his hard dick in his hand, sticking out of the waistband of his gray shorts, just below the steaming surface of the water.

"Oh, um, ha ha, no, thanks. My uncle is waiting for me," I said, motioning vaguely toward the trail, as if I needed a legitimate excuse to not fuck a stranger in an outdoor hot spring.

"Come on. You can just come over here and sit on my dick. No one will see," he said, stroking himself, not breaking eye contact.

Did I want to fuck? I did not, not him, not there, but still, a small part of me thought, *WeightWatchers worked!* and *Will I regret turning down this singular and weird opportunity?*

"Thank you so much, but no," I said. "I'm actually married. I've got to go." I hoisted my theoretically fuckable self out of the water, picked up my clothes, and jammed my wet feet half into my sneakers, with the socks balled up and jammed into the toe box. I walked down the trail to the next set of pools, but they were all occupied by one or more men. I turned around and walked back to the car, past the "wanna fuck?" guy, without looking to see whether he was jerking off or what.

I didn't tell Alex's uncle, but I did tell Alex, later, as a funny story, no harm no foul, right? Can you believe how crazy people are out here in the desert?

B y the weekend of my twentieth high school reunion, held in a pavilion on the southern shore of Oneida Lake on a warm Saturday afternoon in mid-July, I'd reduced my way to a once-unthinkable size eight. The childhood friend who came to my wedding and asked if I was pregnant was there; she pulled me aside to congratulate me on losing weight. Truly, I might have been doing it all for that one moment of acknowledgment.

The reunion itself was not very well attended. There were 140 people in our graduating class, only about 35 of whom showed up, but among them was Dave Mirra, BMX bike legend and an early pioneer of the sport. Dave went pro while we were still in high school, and eventually set a record for winning the most medals in BMX Freestyle at the X Games.

Despite his big success, Dave didn't seem to have become a douchebag. I'd interviewed him a few years back, for a celebrity feature in *Wine Spectator*, and I could still hear his distinctive up-state accent when we spoke on the phone about his collection of California Cabernets, and now here he was at the reunion, being gracious and cool to everyone who wanted to talk to him, which was pretty much everyone. I saw how deferential we all were toward him; our reaction to his fame had created a closed weather system of respect and awe. The place we grew up was Podunk epitomized, and there was something sweet about the pride everyone took in Dave's success and fame.

Orbiting Dave and his beautiful young wife were three guys who'd been his good friends in school, since kindergarten. There was Bert, always a class clown, frequently in trouble, but fundamentally gentle and misunderstood, his antics a cover for some learning difficulties. He seemed to be doing OK; I hoped he was doing OK.

There were two others, Curtis and Daryl, who did not seem OK. They had been legendary in high school, and now both their faces looked so much older than everyone else's, their neglected teeth the color of milky coffee, their dead eyes almost entirely black. I had been around plenty of people on all kinds of drugs, but seeing the shape of these two gave me an unfamiliar chill.

Still, I made small talk with Curtis, who told me that he was on permanent disability after getting injured at his factory job. Curtis had been the drunk driver in a bad car accident shortly after our high school graduation. His passenger, a nice girl in a grade below ours, died in the crash. I think he did a little jail time, then apparently resumed his life and, it would seem, his habits.

When I said hi to Daryl, he smiled and nodded, but seemed too fucked up to form words.

(A few years after that night, Daryl would be charged with sexual assault of a minor, and Curtis would kill his girlfriend and himself, inside their house, with a long rifle, after what the cops and the local papers called a "domestic dispute.")

Someone made a joke, or maybe just an accurate observation, about the joys of Oxycontin abuse, and someone else suggested that we might ought to keep the party going into the night, at a bar in town.

Alex and I didn't go. He'd done well, finding a few like-minded spouses with whom to sit and soberly observe the action, and I'd had enough of this night. On the way back to my parents' house, I had him take us through the drive-through window at Wendy's, where I got a big sloppy burger, which I ate in the car, only briefly lamenting its enormous WeightWatchers point value.

chapter 21

This Is Nowhere

"*God, I love Twitter. You should* join Twitter," said Tony, while scrolling Twitter. We were waiting together at the counter of an AT&T store on the Upper East Side, so that he could buy an iPhone, to replace the geriatric StarTAC flip phone I'd inherited from Beth.

I didn't really want to join Twitter. I already used Facebook for frequent hits of electronic validation, posting cute photos of Eli or regularly performing some bit of self-effacing cleverness for the benefit of my carefully selected echo chamber. I didn't understand Twitter; I had been generally slow to really understand the value of social media at all. Shortly after I started working at *Wine Spectator*, my boss, who managed the magazine's website, explained to me the then-fledgling concept of "social media."

"People create and join networks online," she said, "and then they can post updates about what they're doing, share photos or videos, and start discussions with other users."

And I thought, "That sounds so fucking juvenile and lame. What kind of loser adults are gonna waste their time on *that* bullshit?"

Standing there in the phone store that day with Tony, having of course gotten stoned before leaving my apartment, I was anxious about running out of compelling small talk, so I put the onus on him.

"How do you know what to write on Twitter?" I asked. "And, like, how do you decide what to actually respond to?"

"You ignore the stupid shit and respond to what interests you," he said.

"Right, OK. How's things going with *Lucky Peach*?" I asked. *Lucky Peach* was a new food magazine, for which he'd been writing essays about food and film, with titles like "Eat, Drink, Fuck, Die." Media critic David Carr had just devoted most of his weekly *New York Times* column to singing its praises, and all the food bros and cool kids loved it.

"It's great. Do you want to write for them? You should write for them," Tony said, pulling out his own phone. "I'm going to email those guys right now, tell them to connect with you, give you some work, and then you can pitch them some ideas before we leave for Vietnam."

"Thanks," I said, pleased and a little stunned. I'd lobbed him a question out of fear of dead air between us, and Tony had casually whisked me past the gatekeepers. I sent the editor, Peter Meehan, a handful of ideas about our upcoming travel, and he told me to focus on soups, and to take a lot of photos.

About a month later, in March of 2014, we were in the central Vietnamese city of Hue, the onetime capital that's still known as the Imperial City. This was my first time traveling on a shoot with Tony and the crew, and my first time on the ground in Asia. I had no responsibility to the production; this was just a generous perk.

On our first full day in Hue, I rode behind Tony on his motor scooter for the short distance between our hotel and Dong Ba, the city's central market. It was crammed with hundreds of stalls full of jewelry, fresh and dried fish, all manner of cookware and dishes, hot soup, umbrellas, shrimp paste, calamansi, fresh and dried herbs, spices, plastic toys, fishing gear, sandals, meat, big bags of rice, cosmetics, and much more. The crew were already there, set up to capture Tony's arrival at the market. When the director saw that I was on the back of Tony's bike, he made a slashing motion across his neck.

"Whoops," said Tony to me, laughing. "He's *pissed*." He pulled the bike over and I awkwardly dismounted. He circled the block and made his approach again, this time solo, for the camera operators, who followed him through the congested lanes of the market as he searched for his target: soup merchant Kim Chau.

I stood by as they shot the scene, Tony lapping up a bowl of Chau's bún bò Hue while talking about the long effects of the war with Nguyen Qui Duc, a onetime refugee who'd returned to Vietnam a few years prior, to open an artists' and musicians' salon. After that, Tony waved me over and ordered me a loaded bowl of bún bò Hue, which he'd just called "the greatest soup in the world," and in that moment, with the complex heat and acidity, deep beefy and porky meatiness, the iron tang of the pork blood cubes and the sweet crunch of banana blossoms combined in one astounding spoonful, sweat pooling behind my knees and ears and between my breasts, I was inclined to agree.

Back in New York, I took Tony's suggestion and joined Twitter, so that I could keep up with the food and media worlds, maybe direct a few more eyeballs to my freelance articles. One evening soon after, drunk and a little punchy from a cocktail-heavy dinner with some neighborhood parents and their kids, I sat on the couch, half watching a cartoon with five-year-old Eli, then picked up my phone and tweeted what was in my heart:

"People need to stop fucking enabling Curious George."

Tony almost immediately retweeted it, and within an hour, I had thousands of new followers. I knew that it was an absurd, meaningless thing to get excited about, but still, I was awed by the easy effort-to-validation ratio.

A few weeks later, I read an online news item about the West 8th Street branch of Gray's Papaya suddenly closing. I retweeted the link and included a few nostalgic words about Mario Batali having taken me to Gray's for a hot dog on my first day as his assistant. Within minutes, I got a DM from John Bennet, a *New Yorker* editor who, based on that tweet, invited me to his office, to discuss any food-related stories I might have. I showed up dead sober, with clean hair and a list of a dozen ideas.

"Write up one of these pitches, about eight hundred words, send it to me, and if we like it, we'll use it for the web," Bennet said. "We pay $250 per piece."

If we like it, we'll use it. This was no guarantee, just encouragement to try, but being singled out by a *New Yorker* editor already felt like a win. Even if it was because of a tweet. Even if it was because I'd invoked that great door-opening name, *Mario Batali*. Even if they only paid 31 cents per word, if anything at all.

For my first attempt at the *New Yorker*, I wrote about an all-day cooking class taught by a retired nurse named Despina, who had immigrated to New York from Greece in 1972. Despina was now teaching people, up to a dozen at a time, to cook Greek dishes in her modest East Elmhurst, Queens, apartment, under the auspices of League of Kitchens, a fledgling mobile cooking school that hired immigrant women as instructors.

Early in the day, Despina demonstrated her method for making a Greek pudding cake called *halva* (not to be confused with the sweetened sesame paste of the same name). She gently shook coarse semolina into a pool of olive oil shimmering at the bottom of a tall-sided pasta pot. While a plane headed toward nearby LaGuardia Airport flew over, very low, and very loud, she poured whole milk and sugar into a second pot. The fellow student standing next to me asked whether the dish could be made with skim milk. Despina didn't look up from her work.

"You can use it, but it will taste bad. And, this *skim milk* is not good for you," she practically growled. "Dr. Oz says so."

When the sweetened (whole!) milk had simmered to her satis-faction, Despina removed it from the stove, then ran a black plastic slotted spoon through it, again and again, to retrieve the seven cloves and three cinnamon sticks steeping within, counting each one out as it was captured. She whisked the hot milk into the toasted semolina, then poured the whole thing into a light blue Tupperware ring mold that she said she'd had for thirty years, and left it on the countertop to cool.

Next, she cooked white gigante beans and tomatoes in a little vegetable stock and a huge quantity of Greek olive oil. We all made tiropita, savory phyllo hand pies stuffed with ricotta and feta cheese. We coarsely chopped onions and garlic and celery and carrots for a Greek lentil soup called *fakes*, pronounced like "fuck yes."

Toward the end of the day, we sat and ate our dishes together around Despina's dining room table. These were rather humble recipes, using basic ingredients, nothing terribly fancy, but perhaps because it was all homemade and hot, and because we had done it ourselves, under Despina's expert eye, it all tasted fresher and brighter, deeper and richer and altogether more delicious than I'd expected. As we were finishing up and starting to clear our plates, Despina's husband called home, on the landline.

"He didn't want to bother us," she said, after speaking to him briefly in Greek. "He went to see the George Clooney movie about statues, and ate dinner at McDonald's."

That little *bonk* of fast food's brief intrusion into our slow food afternoon was such a fucking *New Yorker* kicker that they would have to accept my story, I thought. I wrote it up during the first few days of a cheap-o vacation in a pirate-themed motel with Alex and Eli in Lauderdale-by-the-Sea, Florida, where the Wi-Fi was iffy and the pool was too cold. I crossed my fingers and sent the piece off to John.

A few days later, he emailed to say, "The piece didn't go, and I'm sorry it took so long to come to a regrettable decision. I hope you'll shop it elsewhere, and I hope you have success with it. I'd be DELIGHTED to read or consider anything you send."

I was crushed, but kept going. My next spec piece was about *Fed Up*, an anti-sugar documentary produced by Katie Couric, who reminisced about the weird dietary innovations of the 90s at a press conference, saying, "I mean, peanut butter, mayonnaise, you name it: if it said low-fat, I grabbed it."

From the film *Fed Up*, I learned that some people are what doctors call "TOFI": thin on the outside, fat on the inside, their internal organs smothered in adipose tissue, increasing their risk of chronic illness and death, despite their outward health and hotness. I also learned that, in a study of forty-three cocaine-addicted lab rats, forty of them chose sugar water over cocaine.

"Great piece," said John, "but we're already running something about sugar in the *New Yorker* this week. Sorry."

Frustrated but undeterred, I decided next to write about the annual Oz festival in my hometown of Chittenango, which was also the birthplace of L. Frank Baum, author of *The Wonderful Wizard of Oz*.

L. Frank Baum's connection to Chittenango could best be described as *tenuous*; his family left the village and set out for the Midwestern prairies in 1857, six months after his birth. Still, fame is fame, and, more than a century later, in the 1970s, Chittenango started to celebrate Baum, first by installing yellow brick sidewalks in the commercial district, and then establishing the first Wizard of Oz festival, to mark the author's May 15 birthday. Soon, a number of locals gave their old or new businesses Oz-themed names: Over the Rainbow Crafts, Aunty Em's Diner, Toto's Bar & Grill, Emerald City Bowling Lanes.

The Wizard of Oz festival grew annually, and for a brief, shining period in the 1990s, some of the actors who'd portrayed Munchkins in the film came to Chittenango, dressed in replica costumes. This group always included Meinhardt Raabe, the Munchkin Coroner, who each year in the parade would recite his famous lines about the Wicked Witch of the East being "not only nearly dead" but "really most sincerely dead."

To a kid in an isolated small town, the Oz festival was a big deal, the biggest. Our houses were built on land that had very recently been grazed by dairy cattle. We had classmates who got up at 4 a.m. to milk cows, and others who skipped school on the opening days of deer hunting and trout fishing seasons.

As an eight-year-old, I marched in the Oz parade with my Brownie troop. As a twelve-year-old, I went to the festival to eat handfuls of sticky cotton candy from a plastic bag, and to be part of a pack of horny adolescents flitting around, basically suckin' on a chili dog outside the Tastee Freez. We wore training bras and tight tank tops and so much surreptitiously applied foundation and eyeliner and lipstick that when my mother came to pick me up in the late afternoon, she told me that I looked "like a hooker."

As a forty-year-old in pursuit of a *New Yorker* byline, I spent a few days in Chittenango, observing and asking questions, taking photos and notes.

The theme that year was "Timeless Oz," and in some ways it fit: the barrel-chested Rotary Club dads were still selling hot dogs and soda out of their solid wooden chuck wagon. There were still children slurping soft-serve and blue ices. Local politicians and business owners still waved from the seats of modest convertibles and tricked-out pickup trucks. The yellow brick sidewalk still lined both sides of Genesee Street.

But time is also relentless, and there were some new developments, including festival food truck operators from who-knows-where, selling hunks of deep-fried mac and cheese, Hawaiian shave ice, and whoopie pies, "stuffed to the gills with fluffy white filling," which seemed like a *Penthouse* letters outtake, and a subtle admission that the "filling" was made with Crisco.

Time had been relentless, too, with the Munchkins, most of whom were now (really most sincerely) dead, save for Jerry Maren, a member of the three-man Lollipop Guild, who'd also played the Hamburglar in McDonald's TV ads. In 2010, Maren appeared in the genre-busting film *Dahmer vs. Gacy*, as a mime who gets strangled to death by John Wayne Gacy.

Having a career actor like Maren at the festival every year had conferred an intoxicating connection between us (Chittenango) and them (Hollywood), but that was over now. He was now ninety-five, and justifiably retired from appearing anywhere outside his home.

In this post-Munchkin era, the parade's organizers sought fresh relevance by attempting to break the Guinness world record for the largest gathering of people dressed as *Wizard of Oz* characters. This feat would require 447 Wicked Witches, Glindas, Scarecrows, Cowardly Lions, Tin Men, and Dorothys—roughly ten percent of the village population—to stand together and be counted.

The day was hot and sunny, and the high school football field was crisply divided into three rows that would each accommodate up to a thousand costumed record-breakers. A Guinness videographer, witnesses, and stewards were on hand to enforce the rules (no live animals, no high heels) and collect the five-dollar per person entry fee. I stood by with my tape recorder and my camera, watching as they double-checked wristbands and counted and corralled participants onto a small section of the field. In Chittenango, five dollars was a not-insignificant sum of money, especially if you multiplied it by a couple of kids and an adult or two. The regular old Oz costume contest, a much-loved tradition, had always been free to enter.

While waiting for the official count to begin, I spoke with a tall, slender man in his thirties named Albert, who said that he was dressed as Dorothy Gale, in short blue gingham overalls and sneakers with red sequins. He'd come to Chittenango all the way from Southern California to attend the International Wizard of Oz Club (IWOC) annual convention, which was being held in the village, concurrent with the festival. He told me that he found the place "super adorable," but also disclosed that he'd been called "faggot" a few times as he'd wandered Genesee Street.

I wanted to apologize to Albert, on behalf of Chittenango, but I hadn't disclosed that it was my hometown. To my knowledge, there were exactly zero out gay people in Chittenango when I was growing up; it wasn't safe then, and it sounded like it wasn't safe now.

We chatted a bit about the Munchkin actors. "I once met Jerry Maren at a toilet-recycling event in El Segundo," Albert told me. "He was dressed up as a Santa's elf."

I thanked Albert for his time and walked to the edge of the field, to get a head count on the number of people dressed as Oz characters. It didn't look good.

It . . . wasn't good. At noon, the official cutoff time, only 247 costumed entrants were present, just over half as many as would have broken the record. The Dorothys et al. stood together for a group photo, then dispersed, without much outward expression of disappointment or sadness, to take in the rest of the festival. It was as if, collectively, they'd never expected to win.

I watched the parade, then returned to my parents' house. They had invited their friends Pam and Joe to join us for an early dinner of grilled hot dogs, Syracuse salt potatoes, cucumber spears, and a blueberry pie that they'd made together that morning.

My mom had been making pie crust the same way since 1969, when she was a newlywed, and took a compulsory lesson from her new mother-in-law. Now that she was fully wheelchair-bound and losing motor control in her hands, she'd had to teach my dad to make the crust, the way his mother had once taught her.

We all hovered out around the kitchen island, drinking wine and eating slices of cheddar cheese on Triscuits, my parents and their friends catching each other up on health concerns and summer plans. I seasoned three pounds of 80/20 ground beef with salt and black pepper and onion powder, then formed it into patties, which I laid out on a heavy Pfaltzgraff platter, white with blue flowers.

I peeled and cut the cucumbers, gently salted them, and arranged them on a smaller plate, also Pfaltzgraff. The potatoes simmered in their oceanic bath on the electric stovetop. I went to the fridge and pulled out what my dad called "the good butter," made and sold in small quantities at a high cost by a local dairy farm, which he jealously guarded, making sure it was used only for garnishing salt potatoes and sweet corn in summer and baked potatoes in winter.

A nearly empty bottle of Finger Lakes Riesling sat on the counter, wrapped in a foil chilling jacket, and there were two more bottles in the fridge. I was very thirsty, and our wineglasses were rather small, with chunky, dishwasher-safe stems. I uncorked the bottle and gave myself what I thought was a subtle third refill. Joe caught my eye as I turned back to the butter, now melting gently in a small copper-bottomed pot. He said, "Boy, you sure can put it away," pointing at his own nearly full glass.

"Sure can," I said, smiling at Joe, who had always been something of a judgmental cunt.

I slept like shit that night, drunk and dehydrated and full of pie. I went home in the morning, wrote the Oz piece, and sent it off to John Bennet at the *New Yorker* that evening.

A few days of silence followed, and then John wrote to say, "Not for us, sorry. The fact that they failed to break the record was kind of a downer." Three days after that, 1,093 people *did* break the record, at another Oz festival, in Judy Garland's hometown of Grand Rapids, Minnesota.

Three rejections in a row left me feeling frustrated and embarrassed, and I decided to give it a rest for a while. Taking advantage of the sway that Tony had over *Lucky Peach* editor Peter Meehan, I sold him a reframed version of the Oz story, for the magazine's upcoming "Fantasy" issue. I didn't know whether Peter thought the story was actually any good or was just afraid to say no out of deference to Tony, but anyway, I was happy to place it, and to get paid for it.

I called the story "Everybody Knows This Is Munchkinland," swapping out the word "Nowhere" from the title of the Neil Young song. It wasn't until years later, when I took the time to listen to the lyrics, that I realized the *nowhere* Neil complained about was Los Angeles, not some rural backwater.

J ust as I started thinking again about writing another spec piece for the *New Yorker*, Tony recruited me to coauthor a new cookbook with him, in which we would document, in recipes and short essays, his transition from restaurant chef to world-traveling family man.

We met one morning at the TV production office and had a long discussion about the book, how the work would go, and what recipes we could add to the short list he'd already started.

"Matzo ball soup?" I asked.

"No. I hate matzo ball soup," said Tony. I crossed it off my list.

"OK, how about chicken noodle?" I said.

"Ech, no. Too nurturing," he said, "but I do want to do a cream of tomato soup. We're looking for Campbell's Soup; that's the ideal. Basically, it's onion, carrot, and celery, sautéed to light brown, then we throw in canned plum tomato, fresh plum tomato, chicken stock, bay leaf. Simmer, purée, add cream, adjust. As I remember, I put a little caraway seed in this thing. OK, clambake."

He sighed, looked out the window, laced his fingers together and cracked his knuckles. "Clambake is more about *theory*. What I want to make the case for is that the whole *idea* of a clambake is a terrible one. Everything should be cooked separately, because clams, potatoes, corn, sausages, they all have different cooking times. You know what? Fuck it: Let's cut it."

"OK," I said. "Shrimp cocktail?"

"Yeah, we just need a good cocktail sauce. If there's some way to add a violent note, great," he said. *Violence*, I scribbled.

"Sausage gravy and biscuits?"

"Oh yeah. Have you ever seen a dog try to eat a grape?" he asked.

"Um, I think so?" I said, unsure where this was going.

"The way they roll it around in their mouth—should I spit it out? Is it a toy? Is it food? That's what it's like when people try sausage gravy for the first time. Is it sauce? Is it edible? White gravy is kind of horrifying. Let's give people some actual chunks of sausage in our version," he said.

"Hot brown sandwich?" I continued. Tony paused for a while.

"Yeah, no, I'm not gonna pretend I'm into hot browns." I drew a line through this one, with relief. The scatological jokes would have been a tough needle to thread in a cookbook.

"OK, let's go through the pastas," I said.

"Top priority, must-include, is linguine with white clam sauce," he said, and I could see from his posture and hear in his tone that he was starting to get warmed up and enjoy himself. "It's classic, super classic. What I do, though, I steam the littlenecks, take them out of the shell, maybe I have at 'em with a knife, pepper flakes, lots of garlic. So, into that pan with the white wine, I'll throw in a shitload of completely shucked shelled clams ready to go, and then I'll throw in a few clams in the shell for garnish. And I'll roll my pasta around in there, throw in parsley, little bit of shellfish stock, clam broth, and, most important: finish it with butter." He looked as satisfied as if he'd just actually cooked and eaten the dish.

"Any cheese to finish?"

"No cheese. Absolutely not," he said.

It went on like this, Tony talking himself into and out of ideas, me suggesting things and asking questions and taking notes. He already had a bunch of deeply weird and funny ideas for photos. This was going to be fun.

I still wanted a *New Yorker* byline, as long as I had a connection to someone there who believed in me, but the next time I reached out to John Bennet with an idea for a story, the email bounced back; he'd retired from the magazine, and left no forwarding address, so I put my time and ambition into writing a book with Tony, which he had decided to call *Appetites: A Cookbook*.

chapter 22

Brian

"I have some bad news," my mother said when I answered the phone. "Brian's dead."

Brian, my cousin, was four years younger than me, and had always been wild. His mother, my aunt, had babied her first three kids. She couldn't bear to let them go out into the world, and she held them back an extra year before they started kindergarten. Brian was the fourth kid, born after a six-year gap, and he started school right on time.

He was funny and outgoing, forever on the move, seeking attention, frequently breaking something, getting injured, creating chaos. To me he seemed fearless, always doing whatever he felt like doing, with no apparent thought about consequences. One Christmas afternoon when he was about five years old, he found a tiny hole in the front room couch cushion, used his little hands to make it much bigger, pulled out wads of the stuffing, and made a frantic attempt to chew and swallow it, quietly goaded on by his two older brothers until my uncle, a largely silent Old School Dad, walked in and hauled Brian off for what I assumed was a swift spanking. He came back red-faced and sniffling, but was quickly distracted by a cup of ginger ale.

As a high school student, Brian transformed from a husky adolescent to an alarmingly thin teenager, then bulked up, shaved his head, joined the army, and seemed to find some structure, but later went AWOL. For a while after that, he was estranged from his parents, living with his sister, and then with my grandfather. Brian stayed local, within a few miles of where he grew up.

He worked in restaurants for a while, then got a steady job as a meat cutter in a grocery store, met a nice local girl who worked as a radiologist, took up fishing and hunting, bought a truck, hunting gear, and a house with an extra fridge in the garage, just for beer. My parents told me a story of once going to Brian's for a barbecue, and how he made a big show of drinking a whole twelve-pack of PBR while expertly grilling hot dogs and venison burgers.

Brian and his girlfriend got married on a warm August afternoon in her mom's backyard, with a reception at the VFW hall, which I recall being heavy on beer and blended whiskey, poured into translucent plastic cups, and light on food. Their first dance as a couple was to "Kung Fu Fighting," by Carl Douglas. They declared their intention to remain child-free, devoting their time and money to leisure pursuits and their dogs, but after a few years, they had a baby boy anyway, and shortly after that was the last time I saw Brian alive, at my own wedding, proudly carrying around his toddler son.

That day, standing on the deck of the winery, Brian asked me how I could stand to live in New York City, and told me about his one visit there. The traffic and masses of people, the subway and the tall buildings had all terrified him; he insisted that he only really felt safe in the woods, or out on a boat. He didn't seem especially shitfaced that day, but there was an open bar, so he might have been drunk. I certainly was.

A year or so later, Brian got his first DWI, then another one, both reported in the local paper, of which petty crime was its beating heart. The weekly police blotter, full of domestic assaults and pot busts and meth lab discoveries, accounted for at least two full pages in every issue.

Brian lost his truck, my mom told me, and then his driver license. He lost his job. He got divorced and had no custodial rights to his son. From there, it was a spiral of rehabs, arrests, halfway houses, jobs secured and swiftly lost or abandoned, and many heroic and fruitless efforts from his family to help him get and stay sober.

A few years into all this, Brian was arrested at a Walmart, for trying to shoplift a portable radio and a bottle of rubbing alcohol. The local newspaper ran that story on the front page, no more than a few sentences, but with a cruelly large color reproduction of his mugshot, which is the only photo I can still find of him online. In it, he looks wall-eyed, his pupils enormous, the lights behind his stare blown out completely, like a fish on a hook whose minutes to live are few. His mouth is downturned in some odd combination of boredom, defiance, and resignation, his cheeks are mottled, his shoulders slumped. It's only by virtue of his beard, shaped almost like the Batman logo and covering his jawline and chin, that you can see he was taking care of one part of himself, a hint that he had access to running water, a mirror, and a razor at least some of the time.

After that, Brian moved up north, to a bay on the south shore of Lake Ontario. Whether it was better or worse for him up there, whether it made any difference in his bottomless thirst for alcohol and the oblivion and trouble it provided, I had no idea.

There was no news after that, until someone found him dead in a reclining chair in his home. That's all I knew: Brian was an alcoholic, and no intervention or rehab or jail or halfway house or 12-step program had worked for him. He drank himself to death, which is impressive, in its way. You've got to go at it pretty hard to be dead from drinking at thirty-seven.

"You don't have to come to the funeral, but anyway it's happening this Wednesday," my mom said. Her voice wobbled, and I could tell that she was crying. She had been Brian's godmother and was present at his birth, back when she was working as a labor and delivery nurse. I know that she had a special affection for him, because of his funny and wild spirit. When he was about four years old, Brian had handed her the sheet of stickers from the new toy car track he'd just gotten for Christmas, and, perhaps a little tipsy, she'd affixed ones that said "crash" and "dash" onto her sweater, right over each of her boobs, then went around showing everyone, lapping up their laughs.

I got off the phone, poured myself a tumbler of day-old rosé from the fridge, and booked a flight to Syracuse and a rental car. I wanted to know what it looked like when someone died young, and I wanted to bear first-person witness to the latest in what I believed was an unusually long line of tragedies in my family.

Just before departing, I sent a short email to Tony:

I'll be offline this afternoon and evening at a funeral, as it seems my young cousin has managed to drink himself to death.

I was self-consciously art-directing my dispatch of this sad news, trying to be slightly detached and slyly entertaining, for the amusement of my boss, a man who constantly joked about death. When he wrote back, "I'm sorry for your loss," I felt embarrassed. I'd failed to properly convey my nuanced message, and I hadn't put enough distance between myself and my family's grief. I didn't feel entitled to sympathy; I just wanted him to know that, although I might not immediately respond to his requests, I was fine, completely unaffected, still very much on the job.

A few years before Brian died, when our grandfather was still alive but already in his own long alcoholic decline, I visited him, grudgingly, in the Tin Tunnel, which is what my mother called the trailer where he lived alone, consuming a 1.75-liter bottle of Black Velvet every few days, and eating mostly canned soup. He spent his days watching syndicated sitcom reruns and daytime talk shows. He had been especially fond of *Ellen*, until my mom told him that Ellen was gay.

I made this visit with my mom, Alex, and Eli, who was then a toddler, dressed in a blue Mets onesie and gray shorts with an elastic waist. He cruised around the small space, peering at various eye-level objects and photographs. When Eli stopped at a faded portrait of a preteen boy with a familiar moony face, my grandfather snatched it up, tilted the image toward Alex, and started in.

"This is my son Dennis," he said. "Dennis had three surgeries in his brain. He had a brain tumor that was shaped like a *hannnnnd*," this last word said in his drinky voice, kind of sliding into the "n" sound and holding it too long before ending on a slightly wet "d," while he held up one of his own *hannnnnds*. I gave Eli a saltine from an open packet on the coffee table in front of us, and pulled him onto my lap.

"After Dennis's first surgery, when he was twelve years old, I was right beside him when he woke up, and he couldn't move half his body, and he just looked at me as if to say, 'Why?' After the last surgery, the doctor said there were parts of the tumor they just couldn't get. They would've had to take the whole *brainnnn*. He died when he was fourteen years old."

"And while all this was happening, my daughter Patricia," he said, nodding over at my mother, her face an obsequious mask, "she was in her first year at Saint Mary's School of Nursing, in Rochester, eighteen years old, and she passed out, on a *city bus*. Someone called an ambulance, and she was hospitalized; she was in a coma for a long time, and when she came out of it, she was diagnosed with mul-dibble sclerosis. Mmm-hmm. And then, about ten years later, my beloved wife, Nellie, fell down a set of stairs and broke her back, and spent the rest of her life in agony, and never walked again."

My mother rolled her eyes at me, out of view of my grandfather, who held his eye contact with Alex, even as he took a large sip of his large Manhattan. Alex, meanwhile, did all the right things: he nodded, shook his head, made little noises of disbelief, and for this, I was grateful. My grandfather hadn't come to our wedding, because we didn't have a Catholic wedding mass, and because Alex, though never bar mitzvahed, is "culturally Jewish."

He took another pull from the glass and set it back down hard onto the soggy paper coaster.

While my grandfather's story of family death and disease was one that he had every right to share, his monologue roused in me an acute desire to level his entire trailer park with a flame-throwing machine gun attached to a bulldozer. It wasn't so much his frank recitation of sorrows; it was the *way* he recited them that felt like a bludgeoning accusation, an indictment of everyone else's softness. He operated on a scarcity model in which there was only enough empathy in the world for his pain. And, as he calcified into an increasingly drunk, self-pitying, judgmental hypocrite, I found it impossible to spare him any empathy of my own.

According to my mother, his pious suffering had always been the prevailing family weather. There was no state of illness, short of a terminal brain tumor, that would excuse his children from Sunday mass. As a kid, my mother was forbidden from celebrating her own birthday, because it was December 7, Pearl Harbor Day. The day she turned sixteen, she came to the family dinner table wearing lipstick for the first time, and her father told her to go wash her face, that she looked like a whore, and how dare she, today of all days?

My grandfather was proud of having flown forty-eight combat missions in a B-24 bomber jet over the South Pacific in World War II, missions which resulted in thousands of injuries and deaths; that's the reality of war. He earned a Purple Heart, but never disclosed his qualifying injury, or anything else about that experience, only the number of missions, the model of his plane, and the fact of the medal, now framed over a dark green felt background and hung among the family photos. I filled in the blanks myself, projected onto him a simple karmic equation of responsibility for the deaths of innocent people in a time of war.

Here is a list of the postwar tragedies that I know about: my grandfather's younger brother Thomas was an army sergeant in the Korean War, who died in an accidental gas stove explosion. There was Dennis, the baby of the family, dead of brain cancer at age fourteen. There was my mother with multiple sclerosis, a glacier-paced tragedy that would slowly erode her nervous system and cause it to attack itself, dooming her to a life of increasing pain, immobility, and isolation.

My great aunt Harriet had a son whom she named Thomas, in honor of the uncle he'd never met, and this Thomas also died young, only nineteen years old, in a car accident.

And now, here was my cousin Brian, the latest tragedy, who drank himself to death, leaving behind a child and two parents who had tried their best to save him.

How much grief is normal in a family, and what does it mean if you experience more than your share? Are these acts of a vengeful god, a bad genetic Bingo card, the machinery of war, or simply a long run of bad luck? I wanted to find meaning in it, though of course it would make no difference; all these deaths were random, tragic, and final.

A few hours before Brian's service, my dad asked me to call ahead to the funeral home, to confirm that there was a ramp at the entrance to accommodate my mother in her wheelchair. The service wasn't a mass, but a Catholic priest led a prayer and said a few ceremonially comforting things for the two dozen or so friends and family who had gathered in the heavily carpeted and wood-paneled room. Brian's white casket was open, and he looked pretty much like he had in his mugshot, sad and downcast, only dressed in a button-down shirt and a suit jacket instead of a sweatshirt, his eyes closed, his hands folded over his chest.

Later, my parents and I went to Hamilton, about twenty minutes away by deep country roads, to eat spicy chicken wings and drink beer at Ray's, a very good barbecue restaurant. We talked a little about Brian, and also about Dave Mirra, my high school classmate and BMX champion, who had recently taken his own life, using a shotgun he kept in the glove compartment of his truck. Dave was the first action sport athlete to be posthumously diagnosed with chronic traumatic encephalopathy (CTE), the result of multiple on-the-job concussions, compounded by having been being hit by a car and fracturing his skull as a teenager. This was what passed for dinner gossip: injury, illness, addiction, and death.

Back at their house, I opened a bottle of the expensive aged whiskey that Tony was paid to endorse, and made myself a generous pour. The company had sent me four bottles, one of which I'd passed along to my parents. I made my mother a long pour, too, and sat with her in the living room. She handed me some photos she'd pulled from albums, from when my cousins and I were all little kids. There were my sister and me in matching red Christmas jumpers with white turtlenecks underneath, the cousins with orange soda mustaches, piles of crumpled wrapping paper, a maroon sofa, a dark green rug, the edges of a scrawny pine tree hung with silver string.

Another photo, this time a summer evening: a bunch of us in the back of a light blue motorboat, strapped into puffy orange life vests, with sunburned noses and bare legs, and my uncle backing the boat away from the dock, holding a can of PBR, not smiling, never smiling. Then, Brian's tenth-grade school picture, with the bleached hair and the dark roots, his face drawn, mouth downturned, but his eyes still alive.

After a while, my dad came over to the side of my mother's electric wheelchair and asked if she was ready to go to bed, which she was. He wheeled the manual wheelchair up alongside the electric one, pressed down on the rubber brake, and spotted her as she shakily held herself up on her skinny arms, to pivot and transfer from one chair to the other. He gently removed her sneakers and socks. They both said good night, and he wheeled her down the hall, to their bedroom. Once I heard the door *thunk* shut, I quietly removed the whiskey from the cabinet and poured myself a second glass.

With the television off and my parents tucked away, full-body fatigue dropped wetly over me, like a tent collapsing in a rainstorm. Taxidermied moose and elk and deer mounts, trophies from my dad's hunting adventures, loomed above, mute and serene. Brian had once or twice brought his young son over to see this impressive collection of dead animals, before his shit went off the rails.

I drained the glass, slow and steady, my head already inflamed by tomorrow's hangover. How far away was my circumstance from Brian's? I'd gone to college, for one thing. I'd moved to New York, and mostly kept it together. I was alive, drinking high-quality whiskey that my famous boss had given me. Brian was cold and dead and alone, a few miles away, in a suit, in a box, in a refrigerator.

E arly the next morning, I drove back to the airport squinting, with a pounding headache and a hot, sour hole in my guts. I started to think about defrosting some boneless chicken breasts for dinner, and whether I could fit in a double workout before Eli got home from school, to make up for the handfuls of sour gummy worms I'd eaten before passing out, and the leg day I'd missed. I was getting my photo taken in two weeks, for possible inclusion in the pages of *Appetites*, and I wanted to look thin.

chapter 23

Vortex

I ran into my friend Elena in the Foodtown dairy aisle, in the slim margin of time between doing a workout in my living room and picking Eli up from his afterschool program. Elena was an attorney with an impressive government job, two kids, a loving husband, and an enviably slim figure.

"Did you join the neighborhood fitness cult?" she asked.

I was in yoga pants and a denim work shirt over a hot pink sports bra, flushed and unshowered, hefting a black plastic shopping basket that contained a half gallon of almond milk, a cardboard carton of eggs, a bunch of kale, a bunch of spinach, vacuum-sealed chicken breasts, and a bag of keto "thin" bread, which is to real bread as toilet paper is to a bath towel.

I had indeed joined the neighborhood fitness cult, driven by my need to be photographed as the smallest possible version of myself for *Appetites: A Cookbook*. My imperfect face and body, and photographic renderings of same, had been a source of shame and self-loathing since middle school, and I wanted to try to like (or at least not hate) the way I looked in the book.

The fitness cult wasn't really a cult; it was a pyramid scheme built on expensive protein powder smoothies, harsh calorie restriction, and the extremely renewable resource of women's body anxiety. There were online accountability groups, with daily exhortations to post photos of our flexed biceps, our dwindling waistlines, our sad flavor hacks for our tragic protein shakes. This shit made WeightWatchers seem like a sewing circle.

My "coach" was a stay-at-home mom whose child rode the school bus with Eli. She was sweet and disarming, with a gift for separating affluent middle-aged women from their money, convincing us that shrinking our bodies was the key to improving, maintaining, or leaving our marriages and/or careers. The more of us she attracted to the program with promises of lost pounds and inches, the bigger her commission on all that protein powder.

The pyramid scheme starter kit came with color-coded portion control boxes into which I would jam a quarter of an avocado (tiny blue box, for "fats"), a half-cup of cooked quinoa (slightly bigger yellow "carb" box) or cubes of tofu (red "protein" box). There were intense workout videos led by former bikini fitness models who'd sooner eat a silicone breast implant than a white potato. If I "went off-course" (ate normally) for a few days, I'd spend close to $100 on a "three-day cleanse," consisting of nine packets of an extra-bad-tasting variety of protein powder, three fiber laxative drink mixes, and a workbook in which to document my misery, regret and raw vegetable "snacks."

I lost several pounds and entirely stopped getting my period, and both of these things felt like victory. Right before cookbook photography began, I briefly saw the face of god (a number on the scale that I hadn't seen since seventh grade). A few people told me that my own face was "starting to look weird" and my mother expressed concern that I was getting "too thin," which I don't think was, like, *medically* true—I was still within the guidelines of a "normal" BMI—but that observation, from the woman who tracked my weight like a wheelchair-bound George Balanchine, meant more to me than any intentional words of praise.

Did this reflect a disordered relationship with food, my body, and my mother? Absolutely. Was I a willing participant in a misogynistic, toxically capitalist enterprise that betrayed my feminist principles and took a toll on my health? Obviously, yes, fuck yes, but I did it, willingly, because I could not stand the prospect of looking fat in full-color, high-gloss print.

After all the dieting and sweaty self-denial, one single photo of me appears in *Appetites: A Cookbook*, in which I pretend to eat a roast beef po boy sandwich, dripping with loosened mayonnaise. My (thin!) face bears an expression of deeply self-conscious discomfort, and my hair, which was on day five of an expensive professional blowout, looks dull and greasy, but my waist is narrow, my shoulders toned, and I am wearing a pair of "slim fit" orange Gap khakis in a once-inconceivable size six.

In my obsessive pursuit of "health," I was not alone: my participation in the fitness cult overlapped with the period of his life in which Tony Bourdain got deeply involved in Brazilian jiu-jitsu, sometimes forgoing everything but unsalted poached chicken breasts and steamed cauliflower in order to make weight for tournaments.

Tony's obsession with the sport became almost as well-documented as his televised eating and drinking adventures, because he dropped references to jiu-jitsu in every interview—and this was a man who was obligated to give a lot of interviews. He posted on Instagram and Twitter about pendulum sweeps, arm bars, and rear naked chokes. He shared pictures of his post-training meat feasts. He composed long captions about earning a new stripe, a blue belt, a gruesome groin injury that briefly landed him in the hospital. At a press junket for his whiskey endorsement, he was photographed with a huge yellow bandage attached to his ear; it looked like a cartoon hunk of Swiss cheese. He wrote about jiu-jitsu as a family affair for the headnote of the açai bowl recipe in *Appetites*.

When Tony traveled, I found for him suitable jiu-jitsu academies, in places as varied as Houston, Glasgow, Seoul, Tbilisi, Dakar, Pittsburgh, Antarctica, and Rome. I'd then have to tell his frustrated producers and directors that their planned early-morning hunting or fishing or wet market scenes would be in direct conflict with Tony's need to get nearly choked out before sunrise by hulking strangers in windowless rooms that smelled, at best, like feet.

It mattered to him not at all whether a person had any interest in or understanding of what he was saying; he talked about jiu-jitsu to anyone within earshot. He was evangelical about it. He got a half dozen of the TV crew to start training at his preferred academy, which was a block away from the production office, and they would all train together on the road.

When I mentioned to Tony that I was also getting serious about fitness, and he started the hard sell on me doing jiu-jitsu, I discovered my limit. It might have been a savvy career move to play along, but I was simply not made for a full-contact grappling sport with a high possibility of staph infections, broken bones, and prolonged exposure to strangers' sweaty armpits, crotches, and ass cracks.

That being said, I *was* willing to enroll Eli, age seven, in a kids' jiu-jitsu class, at the academy in Astoria where Tony's daughter occasionally trained. It cost three times as much as the karate classes he took in our neighborhood, and it wasn't a resounding success by any metric. Eli didn't like the way his jiu jitsu *gi* fit him, and he complained of a stomachache before nearly every class. I told myself that putting him in jiu-jitsu was about building his confidence and coordination, about helping him learn self-defense and discipline, but I knew it was really about further endearing myself to Tony, who in all likelihood didn't give a shit one way or the other. (We quietly pulled the plug after five months.)

So yeah, I was aware that I wanted to please Tony, but increasingly, I also kind of wanted to *be* Tony, or at least the parts of Tony that were public-facing.

I mean, didn't everyone want to be Tony? There seemed to be no limit to the world's fascination with his origin story, what he'd made of himself and how he spent his days and nights. When it came time to promote a new season of TV, a book, or the whiskey, I'd work with publicists to schedule his interviews with magazine and newspaper journalists who would meet him in Borneo or some dank midtown dive bar. They would all write more or less the same story, heavy on local color and the thrill of shadowing the man, and padded out with slight variations on the superficially shocking answers and anecdotes they'd come for. "What's the craziest thing you've ever eaten?" they'd ask, and "What would your last meal be?"

Wannabe travel TV hosts, some young and some old but almost all of them men, would find their way to me, looking to replicate Tony's formula for success, as if it were a recipe. They wanted him to see the YouTube pilots they'd shot in Saigon or Bangkok, read their manuscripts, put in a good word for them with the production company or the network. They wanted to hit the jackpot just like he had, creating something resonant and real and brand-new that would catapult them out of obscurity and into a higher tax bracket, a better class of airline seat, a professional mandate to eat at the best sushi counters and tapas bars and noodle stands, everywhere in the world. No one seemed willing to admit that Tony was one of one, a unique phenomenon.

I wanted some of what he had, too—the explosive writing success and the attendant income boost—and I also wanted what I saw as his unchecked freedom to indulge every one of his desires.

From my vantage point, Tony could say and write about whatever he wanted. He was encouraged to be himself. His *brand* was "himself," with pleasure and romance and the impractical but passionate pursuit of art as his guiding principles. He chose where to travel for TV, and with whom, and had a huge amount of control over the end product. He was cavalier about money, spending whatever necessary to live in comfort and avoid thinking for an extra minute about the boring logistical details of real life. This, especially, I found dangerously, enormously appealing.

Perhaps most enviable of all, Tony had just neatly and amicably disentangled himself from his marriage, and was now free to be wildly and openly in love with someone new.

n the spring, I went to Japan with Tony and the *Parts Unknown* crew. We started in Kanazawa, a small city on the northern coast of the mainland. Kanazwa's relative isolation saved it from being leveled by Allied bombing campaigns in World War II, leaving its centuries-old districts of breathtaking Edo-era architecture largely intact and well-preserved.

In recent years, Kanazawa had begun to attract western tourists, thanks in part to a new spur of the Shinkansen bullet train, built in the run-up to the 1998 Winter Olympics in Nagano, which connected the city to Tokyo by rail. Even more recent was a seductive *New York Times* travel feature, "In Search of Japan's Hidden Culinary Revolution," which included rhapsodic descriptions of the Kanazawan way with all the edible creatures in the Sea of Japan. The writer of the piece, Eli Gottlieb, took a little swipe at Tony, explaining:

> *The trip there last winter was to be the climax of my weeklong attempt to find the hidden culinary truth of Japan, beyond the reach of guidebooks or the well-intentioned efforts of such celebrity investigators as Anthony Bourdain.*

(Did Gottlieb also want to be Tony? It seemed likely.)

I spent most of my few days in Kanazawa alone, eating chicken katsu and raw squid salads and egg salad sandwiches from convenience stores. I had two spectacular meals of raw and lightly cooked scallops and clams and oysters and fish, one at the big Omicho Market, the other at Yamashita, a diminutive restaurant highlighted in Gottlieb's article. I joined the TV crew (sans Tony) for a ramen lunch near the train station, and I watched them shoot an elaborate kaiseki dinner scene at a fancy ryokan. I knew it was such a privilege to be on that set, yet I was always slightly uncomfortable there, feeling aimless and unnecessary.

When the Kanazawa portion of the shoot was done, Tony and I rode a late-morning Shinkansen together to Tokyo, while the crew took the camera gear across the mainland in a large passenger van.

Before we left, the field producer met us in the hotel lobby and gave us our paper train tickets. We rolled our suitcases across a short walkway to the entrance of Kanazawa Station, where we passed under a soaring glass dome supported by two pillars that resembled a loose bunch of mahogany matchsticks. The effect was both impressive and kitschy, like a middling burlesque performance.

The escalator deposited us onto the outdoor platform, and Tony was excited to spot a vending machine stocked with dozens of varieties of hot and cold canned coffee drinks, some yards away. He took off toward it, pulling his suitcase with one hand and digging for coins in his jacket pocket with the other. He was so consumed with his desire for the novelty of Japanese canned coffee, heated to order, that his paper train ticket fluttered entirely unnoticed from his pocket to the cement platform floor, dancing sickeningly close to the edge of the tracks in the early spring breeze. This was a man with millions of frequent flyer miles, famous for his travel expertise; I couldn't believe that he'd made the rookie mistake of carelessly stashing such a valuable ticket in his side pocket.

What would have happened if we'd missed the train because of Tony's semi-ironic lust for a tinny beverage in a can bearing the face of Tommy Lee Jones? Fortunately, we were both quick on our feet—him to the machine, me to chase down his flyaway ticket—and we didn't have to find out.

Once on board, I was charmed by the bento box lunch and dazzled by the scenery roaring past while Tony slept. Three hours later, the train slid to a gentle stop inside Tokyo Station. A man in a neat, dark suit appeared outside the door closest to our seats, holding a small hand-lettered sign that said BOURDAIN-SAN.

We followed him through the labyrinthine station and out into a waiting Bentley. He piloted the immaculate vehicle through the city and up to the front entrance of the Park Hyatt, where the hotel's general manager, executive chef, and head concierge were already assembled, standing up straight and equidistant from each other, like chess pieces, with another row of managers standing behind them.

It occurred to me, looking at their faces, what funny things we humans do and arrange to impress each other, to reflect our respect for accomplishments and perceived prestige.

Inside, the hotel itself looked and felt like some combination of the New York Public Library and Versailles and Wes Anderson and Bergdorf Goodman and many more references for which I had no reference. Up in my room, I could see a vast swath of Tokyo from my window ledge, where I sat and ate a snack from the minibar that was just slivered almonds and tiny dried whole anchovies. Struck by a predictable desperation to show off to everyone I knew that I was in this place, this fucking *incredible place*, I went hard on a series of Instagram posts with self-conscious captions.

The crew wouldn't arrive for another few hours, and there was no evening shoot scheduled. Tony sent a text, suggesting an early outing for yakitori and beer in Shinjuku.

We took a cab from the hotel to the brightest and most jangly intersection in Shinjuku and walked into the first yakitori spot we saw. We happily ate all the smoky grilled parts of the chicken's body, dripping with golden fat. We drank beer and Tony talked about how things had gone in Kanazawa, and what was coming up in Tokyo, and into the rest of the season.

"So, big news for the Hanoi shoot, I just found out," he said, "and this is like, tell no one, *no one*," at which I nodded soberly, and he continued. "We're gonna shoot a scene with Obama. We've been talking to the White House for over a year already. They suggested shooting on Air Force One, but you know, fuck that. Then we're carrying water for the administration. We're gonna do it in Hanoi, in a local noodle place, street level, relaxed."

Tony paid the check and we crossed the street for round two, big bowls of ramen in an opaque porky broth. I wasn't hungry, but was unwilling to say no and let the opportunity pass. Incredibly, given his height and his striking appearance, he went largely unnoticed amid the chaos of Shinjuku, and was only approached once, by a pair of young American men who simply said hello and kept it moving. We wandered through the tiny, crooked streets of the Golden Gai, while he pointed out the Albatross, a microscopic bar where he'd had big drinking adventures in the earliest days of his television career.

After that, I was on my own in Tokyo. Tony was shooting just a few scenes, in tiny ramen joints and sushi counters, where there was no room for an extra body. The production then moved on to a rural mountain town, and I stayed back to report an assignment, for Eater dot com, about Rosemary's, a popular New York Italian restaurant on the cusp of opening a second location inside a brand-new Tokyo shopping mall. The kitchen was being supervised by Wade, a comrade from the Babbo days who was hilariously profane and irreverent while remaining respectful and kind.

Before reporting this story, I'd only ever heard about how masterful Japanese cooks were at replicating the cuisines of other cultures, but this wasn't turning out to be the case at Rosemary's Tokyo, despite the enormous amount of effort that Wade had expended training them. The food was good but bore little resemblance to its New York counterpart; the flavors were subtle where they were meant to be bold. The hand-cut Japanese version of Wade's normally silky signature octopus salame, which in New York was portioned on an electric slicer, gave my jaw a vigorous workout. The resolutely Italian focaccia that Wade developed in New York was structured and chewy, tasting strongly of olive oil and herbs; in the hands of the Tokyo cooks, it was pure, fluffy, flavorless milk bread. Rather than dwell on these differences, I turned the article into a superficial think piece about the necessity of authenticity, and vowed not to write about friends' businesses again.

On the morning of my forty-second birthday, I ordered the full Park Hyatt Japanese breakfast: grilled mackerel with grated daikon, a bowl of polished white rice, an austere miso soup, pickled greens and carrots, a silky sweet chawanmushi, and roasted green tea. I swam laps in the pool, and took a long nap in the exquisite bed with its crisp and flawless white linens. I ate lunch at a cheerful kaiten-zushi restaurant in which a conveyor belt circled the busy sushi bar. That night, Tony and a few crew members joined me for a steak and Bordeaux dinner at the hotel. Tamara, the field producer, told me that this was Tony's idea, to rally a little party so that I wouldn't be alone for my birthday dinner, and although we made a jovial evening of it, I couldn't shake the worry that everyone was tired and would probably rather be decompressing, alone.

When I returned to my room after dinner, there was a bottle of Veuve Clicquot on the coffee table, nestled into an ice bucket, and on the couch, inside a stiff paper gift bag, an elegant moss-green cotton yukata from the hotel gift shop, with a note that said, "Happy birthday from Tony and the crew."

On my last night in Tokyo, I went to the Park Hyatt's famous New York bar, carrying the oddly shaped hotel version of the *New York Times* that was left outside my door each morning. A six-piece jazz band, fronted by a female vocalist, was in the middle of a set of familiar English-language standards about love and heartbreak.

Sitting at a communal table in the center of the room, I ordered a negroni, and looked around for anyone who might be worth talking to. I was trying to make something happen, putting myself in the way of adventure, in the company of English-speaking men.

I read the paper and drank my cocktail quickly, and as soon as the glass was drained, leaving just a single perfect sphere of ice, the waiter set down a fresh negroni in front of me.

"This is from the gentleman at the corner seat at the bar," he said, subtly indicating with his head in the direction of my benefactor, who looked like a better-preserved Jack Nicholson. Hmmm. *Thank you*, I mouthed toward him, and smiled, and looked back down at my newspaper. What was the etiquette? I didn't know, but I was thirsty, and my drink cost the equivalent of twenty-five American dollars.

The waiter was still standing next to me.

"He has asked if he may join you?"

"Yes, thank you," I said, and within a few minutes the stranger was seated in the chair next to me, with a tumbler of whiskey, leaning in, asking me questions about myself, my work, why I was there.

"I'd love to meet Bourdain, have a drink with him," he said. "I think we've got a lot in common." I nodded and smiled. *If I had a negroni for every time a man said that to me.*

He kept gently touching my arm, testing my boundaries, and I relaxed into it. He told me about his career as pilot and about his Japanese wife who hated him and was out of town visiting her family, about how he liked to come here to the Park Hyatt and talk to other Americans.

We each had two more drinks before the bar closed, at midnight. He settled the check, and we drifted out toward the elevators, still talking. It was my last night in Japan, and no one needed anything from me. I invited him upstairs to my room. He took off his shoes at the door and sat in the club chair and I sat on the foot of the bed. He asked my permission to give me a foot massage. I had never been a foot person, but he seemed to know what he was doing, and whatever that was felt incredible. The cocktails made me feel pliable and willing, the foot massage creating synergy as he worked his hands up my body, pulling garments off as he went.

"Let's just take care of you," he said. "I'm far too old to take my pants off with a stranger."

I laughed at him and looked around the expensive room, with its black lacquer chairs and serious fabrics and seamless silence and I thought, *This is really something,* and *I've forgotten his name* and *old guys sometimes know what they're doing* and *this is* Lost in Translation *fanfic.*

My breasts had become small and unremarkable from all the dieting, but he was interested in them nonetheless. He put my left nipple in his mouth and, just before making me come with his hand, he bit it so hard it drew blood.

I got out from under him and went for the robe that I'd left lying across the sofa. I opened the room-temperature Veuve Clicquot and poured us both a glass, and after he finished his, I suggested that he leave, which he did. I took a bath, then got into bed and watched CNN International until the sun started to come up, at which point I drew the smooth electric window shades and slept deeply for a few hours.

I woke feeling sour and wrong, on the verge of tears for no specific reason, a little after 9 a.m. I had four hours before I had to board a shuttle bus to Narita. My breast was sore and when I looked down, I remembered that an elderly stranger had bitten it. I dressed and went to the nearest pharmacy, looking in vain for hydrogen peroxide or bacitracin, anything to stop my nipple from becoming infected by some rando's disgusting saliva germs. I eventually found alcohol wipes and a package of oddly shaped little Japanese Band-Aids. How would I explain this to Alex? I'd have to be careful to keep myself covered up around him.

I've always hated running, because I am very bad at it, but when I got back from Tokyo, I started training to run a 5K. "Running away from myself" feels like too obvious a metaphor for what I was actually doing, though I suppose it's apt enough. My menstrual period had made a reappearance in April after I'd gained a few pounds, which I blamed on all the ramen and okonomiyaki and fried snacks I'd eaten in Kanazawa and Tokyo. I hoped that taking up running might shut my system down again.

I registered for a Father's Day race on Roosevelt Island, where Eli attended elementary school, and told lots of people that I was training for a 5K, to hold myself accountable. Though I remained a slow runner and didn't have anything like proper form, I could feel myself getting marginally better week by week, more able to run longer distances without stopping, while I listened to a bizarre playlist of *Hamilton* soundtrack bangers, some exceptionally filthy Run the Jewels songs, and PJ Harvey's most ragged tracks. It all felt pretty good.

Concurrently, it seemed that, whatever regrets I had, my experience with the old man in Tokyo had opened a nihilistic vortex in me, a kind of manic greed for consecutive nights of blackout drinking, and a hunger for the sense of triumph I felt in the immediate before and after a sexual transgression. "Life is short," I'd say to myself, or to one of the very few friends I'd confide in. "I want to be happy." I avoided talking about this feeling of endless need in therapy with Joan, because I didn't want to examine it, or be therapeutically encouraged to make better choices. I wanted to keep pushing, see how weird and dark it could get.

Two weeks before running the 5K, I attended a charity fundraising dinner, "co-hosted" by Tony and Mario, at which the catering staff prepared appetizers from the forthcoming *Appetites*: deviled quail eggs with caviar, and shrimp cocktail with a fiery sambal cocktail sauce (the "violent note" Tony had suggested when we'd started developing recipes for the book).

I spent weeks negotiating the details of Tony's participation with the organizers, who were loath to accept that his name couldn't appear on any promotional materials featuring the vodka sponsor, for fear of violating his whiskey endorsement contract. They wanted two separate speeches but settled for a single round of remarks during the cocktail hour, in which he would still hit the major talking points about the cause, then comically shame and hector the deep-pocketed guests into making large donations.

The event was held downtown, on a high floor of a postmodern office building that had once been called Two World Financial Center but was rebranded after 9/11 as 225 Liberty Street. It was just a few blocks from Ground Zero, with a wall of windows facing west, over the Hudson.

The prospect of being together at a party with both Mario and Tony gave me a queasy feeling, like the anticipation of introducing high school friends to college friends, or an ex-boyfriend to my husband. (Such was the nature of my delusional self-centeredness, this expectation that anyone at all, let alone the evening's headliners, would think about me even a fraction as much as I was thinking about them, or myself.)

Mario had been the face of the charity for several years. Every time I saw some mention about this in the press or social media, I remembered him once saying, "Woolie, I don't have a charitable bone in my body," as honest and respectable an admission as I'd ever heard. In the interim, he must have figured out that aligning himself with a major charity was great (free) PR, and would give him better access to the rock stars and politicians who'd reached the same conclusion.

The other chefs on the roster that night were all cool kids whom I could tell had been hand-picked by Mario, captain of the kickball team. There were some guys he liked to party with, east and west coast versions. There were two young women, accomplished chefs who also happened to be extremely attractive, and there was superstar pastry chef Dominique Ansel, because unlimited access to Cronuts was exactly what this crowd wanted. The whole roster made good sense, stocked full of the right names to attract the right type of moneyed young people who could be groomed into becoming lifelong donors to the cause.

I predictably drank too many cocktails and glasses of wine, too fast, and barely ate anything, jacked up as I was on the dense fog of social climber energy and the power of being seated with Tony, the evening's most sought-after celebrity guest. Some friends of Jonathan Cheban, an extremely minor reality TV celebrity who called himself "Foodgod," kept coming by the table to ask if Tony would be willing to meet him, and Tony kept brushing them off.

I didn't cross paths with Mario until after the end of the night, when everyone converged just outside the lobby door to search for their respective chauffeured SUVs.

He said, "Hi, Woolie!" He was with his wife, Susi, whom I hadn't seen since before leaving the job fourteen years earlier. She acted happy and surprised to see me, hugged me, and looked me up and down, and said, "You're all grown up now," about which I had no idea how to feel.

Everyone said their good nights and got into their cars and I started walking toward the E train, only then feeling fully wasted and unwilling to descend into the station. My tank was full, and I was all alone. Shouldn't I do something with this freedom, this good hair and flattering outfit, before resuming the role of married Queens mom?

I had a kind of backward logic going: *I am too drunk to go home, so I'd better stay out and keep drinking.* I got a cab to Jimmy's Corner in midtown, sat at the half-empty bar, ordered a vodka tonic, and squinted at the old fight posters and framed photos of boxers and celebrities. Within a few minutes, a man who seemed more or less my age sat next to me and introduced himself. He was friendly and low-key, and soon I was telling him all about my feelings of inadequacy and frustration and boredom, of not really knowing what to do with my perfectly good life as a forty-two-year-old assistant and wife and mother, that I was a bad person who had been doing bad things. He was a good listener, and kept asking questions, and I kept ordering and drinking vodka tonics that he kept paying for, and I do not blame him, or anyone else, for what happened next, which is that we started kissing in the bar and ended up in his office, in a tall building across the street, where we had blurry but consensual intercourse on a couch next to his desk, after which I asked him about the long scar on his chest, but did not or could not listen while he explained it. And then he flagged and ushered me into a cab and I went home. It was about 2 a.m. I fell asleep on the couch, and when I woke up at 7 a.m., Alex was standing over me, his face amused but also a little sad.

He said, "What time did you get in?"

"Ugh, probably about two? I stayed out and got really drunk with Mario's assistants after the dinner," I said.

"I just had a dream that we got divorced, and it really sucked," he said. Was he trying to tell me that he knew something? I couldn't read him.

He went to wake Eli up for school, and I hauled myself off the couch, wondering how bad I smelled. I toasted two frozen waffles for Eli, scraped a buttered knife across the crispy squares, drizzled the maple syrup, folded up two slices of fancy nitrate-free deli ham, poured a glass of whole milk, which was, somewhat bafflingly, Eli's beverage of choice at every meal. I filled the moka pot with water and packed espresso into the filter, which made just enough coffee for me and Alex to each have a cup, and turned on the gas flame.

They both left the apartment for the day, and I sat on the couch and thought, *Is this my rock bottom?* I didn't look for a 12-step meeting or reach out to anyone who might have encouraged me to do so. I took a scalding shower, slept, smoked some weed, answered emails, ate leftover pasta. At about 4 p.m., I walked to the local wine store and picked out a couple of rosés to open with the moms in our building's courtyard, while the kids ran the length of the sidewalk down its center, over and over.

I lived. Nothing bad happened—the kind stranger with the mysterious scar didn't kill me or give me so much as an unexplained scratch, and Alex didn't find out. And so, I kept looking for something new that would help me disappear from myself.

chapter 24

Jack

In mid-July, I went on a Sunday lunch date with Jack, a successful novelist who occasionally slummed it as a food writer. We'd crossed paths a half dozen times, at press dinners and restaurant opening parties in my early freelance days. He spoke softly and he didn't drink, which had irritated me when we first met. I could detect no hint of relatable vulnerability in him, just a kind of guarded nonchalance. In conversation, he made self-consciously oblique references to a childhood home in Wales, his MFA in fiction, and his outdoorsy adventures in Central and South America.

Around the start of Obama's first term, when social media began to populate our screens with all our most consequential and tangential connections, Facebook suggested that I make Jack my "friend." I hadn't seen or thought about him in a long time, but now our thin thread of common acquaintances had put him back on my radar.

For all his cultivated mystery, Jack was an active social media user, sharing artful photos and descriptions of exquisite objects: a vase, a painting, a daybed in moody lighting. He wrote and posted capsule reviews of films both beautifully foreign and violently domestic, subtly if purposefully showcasing his own cleverness. He frequently ate at high-end restaurants, in the company of women whom he did not name but described with a kind of breathless amusement, their beauty positioned to flatter him, the lone beholder, and his pictures revealing only a pleasing neck and clavicle, an elegant hand holding a Christofle sliver-plate fork. He wrote extensively about the food, of course, and his reviews were often funny and irreverent and even slightly profane, while reflecting a deep knowledge of the subject.

One night shortly after Jack posted to Instagram a black and white party photo of a slim woman in just her bra and underpants, wearing a full-head deer mask with antlers, I had a pleasant sex dream about him. Drunk and stoned the next day, which was Thanksgiving, I snuck away from my in-laws' crowded table and sent him a direct message, saying only that I'd dreamt of him. His tersely incurious reply ("Interesting!") made me regret having said anything, and I put the whole thing out of my mind as best I could.

But then, about a year after that, he sent me another message.

"I know you're probably very busy, being a married mother and all," Jack wrote, "but I really enjoy what you post online, and I was wondering if I could take you to lunch?"

It pleased my ego to be flattered by a man who peacocked his own good taste, though I assumed that he was merely networking when I accepted Jack's invitation.

"He's kind of old," I said to Alex, "and kind of weird. He writes about food. I think he probably wants a piece of Tony, like everyone else who tries to be my new friend."

We met in the dark lobby of the NoMad hotel. Jack kissed me on my right cheek and then led the way back to the dining room, where the host and bartender both greeted him like a sea captain just home from a long voyage, and he did kind of sail through that room, wearing a cornflower-blue linen shirt, unbuttoned rather daringly low, and lightweight linen trousers. He had a full head of loosely curly hair, light brown and slightly gray, and a salt and pepper mustache and beard.

When the host walked away, he said, "I'm a regular," and he sounded so pleased with himself that I couldn't tell if it was a joke.

I ordered a salad composed mostly of carrots and pistachios with a dab of whipped ricotta and a slice of sourdough toast that I ignored. I drank two glasses of rosé and wanted but did not dare order a third. Jack ate a burger with bacon and cheddar and long, crunchy-looking golden fries served in a cast-iron pot with a tiny bale jar of coarse salt nestled in among them. After his first sip of Coke, he said to me, "I don't drink alcohol. Never started, actually," and I let my face assume an expression of mild surprise; I didn't want to let on that I remembered this fact or anything at all about him from our brief, years-ago interactions. "I've never been drunk," he continued. "I don't enjoy the feeling of being out of control."

"I do," I said.

We gossiped about the few people we knew in common, and I told him about the imminent *Appetites: A Cookbook*. He asked about Tony, in a measured, unimpressed way, as if he considered him a peer. I asked Jack about his novels, which I hadn't read, though I'd gleaned enough from Facebook to know that they were both about gruesome crimes, wrapped around unconventional love stories. He told me that the second one, set in Aruba, had proved surprisingly popular in Dutch translation.

For his entertainment, I made fun of the neighborhood fitness cult and the 5K I had run, which turned out to be a fundraiser for testicular cancer research. I told him about the person wearing a hairy scrotum costume, who gave each runner a high five as they crossed the finish line.

He talked about his diet, which involved eating only meat, fish, eggs, nuts, and beans for six days in a row, followed by one day of extreme carb indulgence, to somehow reignite his metabolism and stave off total kidney overload. Today, he said, was his carb day, and he'd already had the better part of a baguette from Balthazar and an apricot and toasted almond Cronut.

"I even managed to stick to my diet at Junoon the other day, though I'm suspecting there was jaggery in the lobster mulligatawny," he said, looking suddenly serious and concerned, and I thought, *This is a fucking ridiculous man.*

"Honestly, that sounds like something that Dame Maggie Smith might utter to her crime-solving cat," I said, and then held my breath. Could he take a jab? He laughed. I exhaled.

"What have you got on there—a romper?" he said, in a mocking tone.

I'd worn what I thought was a very cute outfit: a lightweight sleeveless jumpsuit, printed with an abstract navy-and-white tropical leaf motif that showcased my clavicle and shoulders.

"It's a jumpsuit."

"Isn't that rather difficult to navigate while using the ladies' room?" he asked. I shrugged my shoulders and kind of squinted noncommittally, unwilling to discuss toilet matters. "I don't understand this current vogue for women's *onesies* in New York. Personally, I prefer skirts," he continued, though I hadn't asked.

He'd put me on the defensive, but there was a weird pleasure in being the target of Jack's teasing, his close observation and critique, his suggestion for how to course-correct, so as to please him.

When lunch was done, Jack picked up the check, and as we walked out of the hotel and into the late afternoon shadow that fell over Broadway, he suggested I might like to read one of his favorite graphic novels, which I ordered on my phone while riding the R train back to Jackson Heights. Later that evening, I sent him a DM to thank him for lunch and report that I'd ordered the book. He wrote back: "Give me your email address, so that we can correspond like adults."

We began an exchange of long and frequent letters, delivered instantly. Jack's focused interest in me, his questions and his intelligence and flashes of bone-dry humor, lit up all my greedy pleasure centers. We wrote to each other about what we were eating, reading, looking at, working on, thinking about. We expressed mutual disbelief over the presidential candidacy of Donald Trump, who had just declared, at the Republican National Convention, "I have no patience for injustice, no tolerance for government incompetence, no sympathy for leaders who fail their citizens."

I told him that I wasn't happy being married.

"My husband and I are a lot alike, in our insecurities and sadness and the ways we seek comfort," I wrote, "only, he's a good, solid and loyal person, and I think I might not be. Something has felt *off* for a long time, and I'm often lonely, but my fear of being totally alone and unloved has kept me stuck in place."

My admission read like a letter to an advice columnist, only he didn't offer any advice; he crowed about the exquisite soaps and lotions he'd just picked up at Aesop, described the niche Japanese porn he liked to watch, gestured toward the kinds of encounters he'd had with other women. We wrote about what we liked in bed, and what we might do if we found ourselves together in one. He made it clear that he had "other irons in the fire," but that those were strictly casual arrangements. "I think I want something more sustainable with you," he said.

Several weeks into our digital friendship, drunk at home on the couch while Alex watched a zombie show in our bedroom and Eli slept in his, I typed out for Jack a self-conscious account of having spent that night in Tokyo with an elderly stranger, casting myself in my boozy little mind film as a glamorous seductress who woke with regrets but would surely do it again anyway. I sent it and held my breath until he replied:

"I think that the shame people feel about sex is something that really turns up the heat. I love people who want forbidden things. I love that you're ashamed of what you desire. That being said, I don't care for this Tokyo story. Though sincere, it reads as performative."

God, *fuck you*, I thought, first feeling foolish and wounded, and then desperate to redeem myself in his eyes. I adjusted my approach, presenting what I hoped was a more natural version of myself, one that appeared not to give a fuck about what he thought, which of course was an utter lie. A person with a will to self-preservation might have chosen that moment to back away from Jack, but to me cutting off our correspondence now seemed neither desirable nor possible, because, when I wasn't getting my feelings hurt, it felt so fucking good, the hazy prospect of intense real-life physical intimacy, and the actual daily intimacy of exchanging stories and ideas and feelings. He knew how to seduce with words, and how to withhold in a way that made me want to beg. He expertly inflicted subtle pain that made its eventual recession its own form of pleasure.

And it was so easy to keep this thing hidden from Alex. We rarely discussed anything deeper than groceries, laundry, the school bus, the cat, our upcoming visits to one side of the family or another. We kept ourselves benevolently isolated from each other with our increasingly asynchronous sleep schedules and domestic routines, our ubiquitous smartphones and our laptops.

I was, truly, super-busy on Tony's behalf, which gave me a reason to be online, all the time. The promotional machinery for *Appetites: A Cookbook* had started. Tony had some new books on his imprint that he was obligated to talk up, plus there was an imminent season premiere of *Parts Unknown*, concurrent with shoots for the next season, and an empty new apartment to be furnished. I was constantly parceling out chunks of his time, confirming and reconfirming interviews, pre-interviews, live radio and podcasts and late night and early morning television hits, pick-ups and drop-offs, face-to-face meetings, flights, voiceover sessions, and multiple fittings for the custom Tom Ford tuxedo he'd wear to the Emmys, while coordinating the ordering and delivery and installation of furniture and art and televisions and carpets and custom window treatments to his new home on the sixty-fourth floor of a west side high-rise apartment building.

One afternoon, I met Tony and a small CNN crew at a smoky, masculine Japanese beef restaurant called Takashi, to make promotional videos for *Parts Unknown*. Tony described the highlights of each forthcoming episode, over plates of grilled cow parts deliberately chosen to elicit the biggest response from his interviewer, Anderson Cooper, who'd once made the mistake of admitting to Tony that he had the palate of a five-year-old.

Between set-ups, while Anderson recovered from an upsetting mouthful of calf's liver, Tony stepped outside for a cigarette. I followed, to see if he needed anything, and to act as buffer and timekeeper, in the ever-more-likely event that he was clocked by an enthusiastic fan with a story to tell.

He lit and drew hard on a Marlboro Red, and I told him that the *Today Show* had just agreed to have him on to promote *Appetites* on publication day.

"You should go on with me," he said. "It's as much your book as it is mine. I mean, if you want to be on the *Today Show*, you should be on the *Today Show*."

Did I want to be on the *Today Show*? I knew it was something that I was supposed to want, and I knew that Tony's easy encouragement was a reflection of his generosity, and his security with his own place atop the world. I knew that to demur would be to leave something on the table.

What I didn't yet know was that Tony's encouragement didn't matter to the people who actually ran things, who said that I couldn't be on the *Today Show* unless I had a reel to prove that I was very good on live TV (which I didn't, couldn't, and surely wasn't). There was so much that I didn't know, including what the fuck a reel even was; including the very fact of how much I didn't know.

For figuring it all out, a literary agent would have been helpful, but I'd decided against having one. The chance to write a book with Tony had essentially fallen from the sky, without my having asked for it, so why would I give someone 15 percent off the top? I mean, I would never negotiate against Tony, who was directly paying me what seemed like a very fair amount of money for my work, so what would be the point?

The point, as I would later learn, was that without an agent, there was no one guiding me throughout the whole complex process of creating a book with a very famous coauthor. This was a different thing than ghostwriting recipes for Mario's books or editing and testing recipes for the *Les Halles Cookbook*. I didn't know what was reasonable to expect, or how I might best capitalize on the situation, to further my own goals (had I even been thinking about things like goals, which I wasn't. I was thinking about what to say next to Jack).

Without an agent, I had no advocate, and little awareness of situations in which I should advocate for myself.

For example: several of the big-box stores objected to the grotesque but beautiful *Appetites* cover art by Ralph Steadman, and they refused to stock the book until the publisher designed a neutral paper cover for the massive number of copies these Walmarts and Costcos intended to order. My name, which was on the Steadman cover, got left off the new one. Though the publisher said that it was just an oversight, nothing personal, it was humiliating. No one had consulted me about the neutral cover design, because, to them, without an agent, I wasn't really a separate entity; I was an extension of Tony.

This was the downside of working hard in the shadow of an important man. I should have known better, because I'd spent almost my entire career working in such shadows—Mario's, Hector's, all the big chefs I interviewed for *Art Culinaire*, everyone with power at *Wine Spectator*, and now Tony. Very few people are curious about the unknown women who prop up the work of important men. Without the Tonys and Marios and Hectors of the world, there would have been no book or TV show or magazine work for me. The flip side of this, that the end products, credited solely to the marquee men, wouldn't exist without the work of women like me, was both a maddening riddle and a colossal "no shit."

And meanwhile, on publication day, in the greenroom at the *Today Show*, with Tom Hanks and Derek Jeter chatting a few feet away, Tony said to me, shortly before his live segment, "This is excruciating. I hate this so much. I would give any amount of money to not be doing this right now."

At the dinner table, the night before school started, Eli asked, "Did you know that Daddy's cheating on you?"

At seven years old, he had a sly, surprising sense of humor, and had been lately showing an Oedipal interest in trying to turn me against Alex. I played along a bit, and then we all had a little laugh, and I said, "I know that's not true, Eli; I pretty much know where Daddy is all the time, and he's just not that kind of guy," and then Alex murmured something to indicate concurrence, adding, "I'm old-school," which sort of made me want to die.

The next morning, I missed sending Eli off to his first day of third grade, because I was on a 7 a.m. flight to Los Angeles, to supervise a *People* magazine photo shoot with Tony. The shoot had been strategically scheduled to promote both *Appetites* and the new season of *Parts Unknown*. Tony was already in LA, to attend the Emmys and then shoot an episode of the series. He was staying at the Chateau Marmont, so I stayed there, too, patching together reimbursements from the publisher and the network to cover the outrageous expense of doing so.

While I waited to check in at the hotel's dimly lit front desk, the heavyset man in front of me barked a series of short commands and responses at the young clerk. His gravelly, New York–accented voice sounded familiar, and when he snatched up his room key and turned toward the elevator, I got a brief look at his profile and recognized him as film producer Harvey Weinstein, who'd somewhat recently urged Tony (via email, via me) to watch the chef drama *Burnt*, a DVD of which an assistant had hand-delivered to his building. Weinstein asked Tony to say positive things about the film on Twitter, just before its theatrical release. In exchange for this favor, he said, he'd throw Tony a great party in New York, anyplace he wanted, the next time he had something to promote. I don't know if Tony ever watched the film, but he asked me to decline the offer on his behalf. (*Burnt*, in which Bradley Cooper's character drunkenly attempts suicide via sous vide is, objectively, a piece of shit.)

A bellman carried my suitcase to my little bungalow, which was shaded by a small forest of dark green waxy-leafed trees and had a full kitchen with vintage fixtures. I texted Tony, who said that I should come join him on the pool deck. Though it was a hot and sunny early September afternoon, he was completely alone out there, sitting at an umbrella-shaded table with a margarita, a pack of Marlboros, and his iPad in front of him.

"Harvey Weinstein's here," I said, sitting down. "He was checking in ahead of me. Seems like kind of a dick."

"Yeah, he's actually a fucking monster," said Tony. He took a long pull on his drink, then extracted a cigarette from the pack and lit it from a book of hotel matches. It seemed like he had more to say about Weinstein, but he just dragged athletically on the Marlboro, blew out the smoke and said, "Let's see if we can get an early table at Park's in K-Town tonight. Don't eat lunch if you can help it; they're gonna murder us with meat."

Back in my bungalow, I made the dinner reservation by phone, then called room service for a pot of coffee, and smoked a few of my own cigarettes, which habit I had recently picked up in pursuit of keeping both appetite and anxiety suppressed. It was incredible to me that the hotel allowed smoking indoors. The resolutely uncool old furnishings and the heavy stained glass windows, the ashtrays and the iron sink, my hunger and fatigue and a slight nicotine buzz all made me feel that I was on another planet. I caught up on some emails, put on the hotel robe and took a restless nap.

Later, I waited for Tony on a black leather–upholstered armchair, opposite the hotel garage. The only way to be on time for a planned meeting with him was to be absurdly early, so that you never kept him waiting. I passed fifteen minutes on my phone, writing an email to Jack, describing the hotel, and Weinstein, and telling him that I wished that he were there. In the middle of this, Alex texted me a short video of Eli standing outside our apartment building, waiting for the school bus with his blue backpack at his feet, looking sleepy, absentmindedly scratching the side of his head while he smiled wide for what he thought was a still photo. He had a little ketchup on one side of his mouth. He was guileless and perfect.

Tony arrived then, and we waited silently while a valet pulled his rented black Dodge Challenger out of the garage, then held the door open for him while I went around to the other side. The interior smelled, not unpleasantly, of cigarette smoke, and there was an empty In-N-Out bag on the passenger seat, which he swatted onto the floor. We drifted down the steep driveway, the vehicle's underside making brief scraping contact with the pavement before Tony turned the car hard onto Sunset Boulevard, the engine emitting a wholly American growl.

"I love a rental," he said.

At the restaurant, the host immediately recognized Tony. She ushered us to a much larger table than seemed necessary, until the dozens of little plates of banchan and then the various cuts of meat piled up in front of us—galbi, tongue, short ribs, rib eye—and as we worked through it, I did feel, as he'd as predicted, a slow beef-based homicide being perpetrated. On the drive back to the hotel, we stopped at a liquor store, where Tony bought a bottle of Casa Dragones sipping tequila for $269, and handed me the receipt, saying, "I'm gonna use this on tomorrow's shoot, so let's get someone to reimburse me for it."

Early the next morning, while Tony grappled with strangers at a West Hollywood jiu-jitsu academy, I let about two dozen people— still and video camera crews, food stylists, prop stylists, an editor, a writer, a publicist—into his suite, to set up for the *People* shoot, an endeavor that began to strike me as fairly ridiculous. In order to sell two products—a book and a TV show—we were all working to create the illusion that Tony himself had cooked sausage-and-pepper heroes in his hotel room for his LA-based buddies chef Roy Choi and musician Josh Homme. We'd included that specific sandwich recipe in *Appetites* so that Tony could write a headnote about his "addiction" to the terrible New York street fair version, which inevitably resulted in explosive diarrhea. The photo in the book shows him eating the hero while sitting on his own home toilet. That, to me, was power: making a poop joke in a cookbook while showing off your expensive Japanese plumbing.

The photographer's three assistants unpacked lights and stands and battery packs while the food styling team set up cutting boards and bowls and sheet trays, and I stared at my phone, feeling conspicuously superfluous. It had been the same with Mario on the set of his show *Molto Mario*, and the same again on the set of *Parts Unknown*, where everyone around me had a defined purpose—operating cameras, cooking food—while I just hung out in the orbit of the star, trying to look busy and stay out of the way while paying close enough attention to spring into action if needed. I drifted from the living room to the kitchen to the balcony, looked again at my phone, sat on the couch and thumbed through the galley of the book. It was a thrilling relief when Tony texted me a list of ingredients he wanted delivered from the hotel bar to the room so that he could make a pitcher of what he called "Corvette Summer cocktails" for Josh and Roy, who were expected at 10 a.m.

I got the tequila last night, but I'm gonna need 2 qt fresh-squeezed grapefruit juice, 6 limes, 2 qt tonic, 1 pt simple syrup, ice in bucket with scoop, pitcher, long-handled cocktail spoon, paring knife, 2x Marlboro Reds. Ask the bar to put the whole thing on a rolling cart.

After tax and gratuity, this cost just under $300, charged to Tony's room, to be sorted out later with the publisher and the network, neither of whom I guessed would be thrilled to pay for Tony's cigarettes, billed at $15 per pack, twice their California street value.

Hours into the day, after the interview and the still photos, the sandwiches and the mixing and drinking of multiple pitchers of cocktails, the smoking of so many Marlboros, Tony said goodbye to Roy and Josh, then sat on the celery-green velvet sectional

sofa in his suite, to submit to a video interview. A man barely out
of his teens asked him what was his go-to hangover cure, his guilty
pleasure fast food, which TV shows he hated. Tony was so good at
this kind of thing, and the young crew members seemed genuinely
enchanted by the answers I had heard him give many, many times
before (Coca-Cola, a joint, and kung pao chicken; Popeye's mac and
cheese; *Friends*).

Later, we had dinner at the Thai restaurant Night + Market, and
again we were murdered with food, about twice as much as what we
had ordered, and almost all of it spicy in a way that inflicted pain
that then gave way to an endorphin rush of pleasure. We drank Thai
beer to wash down crisp fried pig tails, braised and chewy, coated
with a sauce that was at once sweet, fiery, sour, fishy, pungent. We
ate Chiang Rai–style pork larb with a mind-blowing spectrum of
flavors that included plenty of heat, brown sugar, and the salty funk
of fermented shrimp paste, plus green herbal notes from mint, cilantro, sawtooth, and rau ram, tempered with raw and fried garlic,
tingly Sichuan peppercorns, and the unmistakable mineral tang of
pork blood. A soft mound of jasmine rice, draped with glistening
uni, salmon roe, and scallions, gave us temporary reprieve from
other dishes' relentless fire. I took a few photos of him with all
the food, to be used for the *New York* magazine Grub Street Diet,
which he'd tried to get out of writing, suggesting (unsuccessfully)
to the editor that I should do it instead.

After dinner, as he shifted the rumbling Challenger into park outside the hotel garage, Tony said, "Thanks for the company," which
startled me.

I said, "Oh, of course." I'd assumed that Tony took me to dinner
out of a sense of professional obligation, and that he would always
rather be alone, given his slight but enduring awkwardness in unstructured social situations. That he would prefer company to being
alone at dinner was new information.

I flew home the next day but didn't land until after midnight.

Missing Eli's first few days of school made me feel like a shitty mom, even as I knew he'd been just fine with Alex. In the morning, a Saturday, we sat together on the couch, watching an episode of *Uncle Grandpa*, a cartoon about pizza and farts.

Eli said, "My head really itches," while scratching his scalp, and before I lifted a lock of his gorgeous long hair, I knew that I'd find lice. Alex's mom had taken him on some kind of pirate-themed boat ride at the Jersey shore earlier in the week, from which she'd texted a photo of him wearing an eye patch and a skull and crossbones-emblazoned black felt tricorne hat that had probably been on dozens of buggy little heads that very day.

I did what the internet told me to do, saturating Eli's dry hair with Pantene conditioner to trap and smother the insects and loosen their eggs, before combing it all out. It was tiresome but weirdly satisfying, this primate grooming behavior, the accumulation of tiny animal corpses and egg sacs transferred from scalp to comb to paper towel.

Alex stripped Eli's bed and laundered everything at super-high temps. In between trips to the basement machines, he suggested that we look at some paint samples and cabinets online.

We were doing a full kitchen renovation, putting in new floors and having the whole place painted, a project that was entirely Alex's idea, financed with a home equity loan. He'd solicited my input dozens of times, but I couldn't focus on it. We were married, and it was my home, too, but I felt disconnected from the whole notion of home ownership, and unwilling to participate in a project that represented hope for a shared future.

Every time Alex opened his laptop to show me floor plans and photos of cabinets and tiles, I'd stare listlessly out the dining room window onto the street, wondering about what the other neighborhood moms were doing. Were they happy? Were they free? After dinner, I'd lean hard into drinking, first wine and then Scotch, to steady and extend the distance between me and the dissatisfaction of my actual life.

Alex and I had moved into the apartment when I was a month away from giving birth, and I wasn't able to do much of the packing or unpacking. Pregnant, I couldn't carry heavy stuff, and as a new mom, I was hobbled by surgery and flattened by depression. Alex did as much of the dismantling and setup as he could, but we still had stacks of boxes that we'd never unpacked, which we'd ignored for years, and which became a problem again as we emptied the apartment for renovation. I would look at those boxes with their seven or eight years of accumulated dust and think, *This is just the most obvious fucking metaphor for this marriage.*

What was even in those boxes? Cables and cords, old keyboards and monitors and motherboards, a DVD burner, manuals, floppy disks. Every time we would start a conversation about unpacking the boxes and getting rid of shit, Alex would suggest some vague but grandiose plan about floating shelves or off-site storage. It sounded expensive and complicated, and I would get overwhelmed and frustrated and dismissive. We couldn't deal with our actual physical shit, nor acknowledge or interrogate our anemic sex life, our lack of connection, the way we sometimes seemed like polite acquaintances enduring an accidental shared commute.

Jack and I met again for lunch shortly after I returned from LA, at L'Amico, another expensive hotel restaurant where he was an apparent regular. Though I was excited to see him again, I found it hard to relax and talk about myself, instead launching into the nerve-racking news of my workday, which was: at the insistence of his new girlfriend, Tony had leaked to the *New York Post* that he and his wife were separating, sending the CNN publicist into a panic and calling into question the promotional angle for *Appetites: A Cookbook*, which relied heavily on the concept of Tony as contented family man. Coincidentally, Brad Pitt and Angelina Jolie chose the same day to announce their divorce, and their A-list news neatly eclipsed the end of Tony's marriage.

I ate a radicchio salad and drank two glasses of vermentino; Jack had veal meatballs and a Coke, and we split a dish of fior di latte gelato and the check, then went our separate ways, without so much as a handshake. I walked to the train feeling dazed and disappointed. After all the heat of our written correspondence, sitting next to each other in real life, we'd both been awkwardly polite and entirely chaste. I said as much in an email to Jack that night:

> *There is something bizarre about the difference between what I've been willing to type to you, and how reserved I felt in your actual human presence. I suppose it's not so unusual, this online versus IRL schism, but strange to me nonetheless.*

His reply came quickly.

> *I don't think it was that you were being reserved so much as it was that I had set out some limits. Had I sat down next to you and immediately put my hand between your legs, you wouldn't have moved it, I don't think.*
> *I don't know what, if anything, I actually want from you. I worry about your anger, your frustration, your depression, and that you see me as a solution to those challenges, which I am not.*

I tried my best to telegraph my utter emotional independence from him, and to mask how important our flourishing friendship had already become to me. That act seemed to work: Jack invited me to spend a weekday in bed with him, in his apartment, while Alex worked and Eli was in school.

He instructed me to wear a skirt or dress, and black panties and bra, and to bring something to drink with me, so that I'd be relaxed. I wore a black crepe sheath, and bought three little airplane bottles of gin at a nearby liquor store. He lived in a studio on the third floor of an elegant nineteenth-century midtown building, a former dormitory for bachelors. The lobby walls were painted with a floridly Orientalist mural. I walked up a wide wooden staircase to the third floor, and when I turned into the hall, he was standing in the open doorway of his apartment.

"Hi," I said.

"Show me your cunt," he said.

"I'm not doing that out here," I said. He moved aside, waved me in with a small smile.

I could see over his shoulder the heavy gold velvet drapes drawn across a single wide window so that the apartment was mostly dark, with a sliver of autumnal sunlight edging through. An optimistic but melancholy piano melody with vague electronic undertones played from a soundbar beneath the TV screen, which itself was fixed upon a stand in front of a marble fireplace, showing an aerial nighttime shot of Hong Kong.

I put my shoulder bag down next to the door, took off my shoes, and pulled the gin out of my bag. He pointed to a small stainless steel pet dish on the floor, next to the bed.

"Put the gin into the bowl," he said, "but first, take off your dress."

I disrobed as directed, then unscrewed the tiny metal caps on each of the three bottles and emptied the contents into the bowl. I felt self-conscious and skeptical, but anyway, here I was. I sat on the floor and looked up at him.

"Now, get on your hands and knees and drink the gin, like a dog," he said. I considered his request for a moment while I tried hard to keep my stomach in, shoulders pulled back, my legs folded prettily underneath me.

"I don't think this whole thing is for me." I felt the weather change around us. Jack sighed and sat on the edge of his bed.

"Well, then, get yourself a glass and some ice," he said, waving toward the tidy kitchenette. I poured the gin from the bowl into a glass tumbler, and made myself a rather wanting cocktail, topping it off with some tap water and a glug of maple syrup from a small bottle in the fridge, so as not to drink just straight gin at 10 a.m. in a relative stranger's apartment, in my underwear. I stirred it with a teaspoon and took a huge gulp.

"Now get into the bed," said Jack, and that's what I did and where I stayed, for the next hour or so, sitting up to occasionally sip my drink. We spoke no words of any consequence, only to direct or redirect the immediate goings-on.

When I took a moment to lie back and stretch my arms above my head and look at the ceiling, drunk on satiated desire and watery sweet gin, he said, "This is no way for you to live."

"What do you mean?"

"Well, first of all, I can tell that you drink too much, and you smoke too much pot. You lie to your husband. You lie to yourself. You're parceling yourself out to too many people, so that no one gets too much. So no one has any claim on you."

"Hmm," I said. I didn't want to hear this, didn't want have any part of this conversation, so I said the thing that I hoped would end it: "You're right."

I stayed a few more hours, painfully conscious of the minutes ticking down, how soon I'd have to get dressed, go home, shower, dress in yoga pants or jeans to meet the school bus, make dinner and be a wife and a mother.

I didn't hear from him that night, which made me feel sick and jittery. Late the next morning, he sent an email that speared me like a fishhook, and would drag me along behind his boat for a very long time.

Wish you were here, because I would like to brush the back of my wrist softly on your bare hip, and to apologize. I understand, now, that shaming you is not particularly helpful. You surely know that the way you're living isn't ideal, but I understand that you're doing what you need to do, to squeeze out some modicum of happiness or satisfaction.

And, yes, I'm a hypocrite: judging you for cheating, while holding you naked and soft against me in my bed. Worrying about your drinking, and making you bring your own gin, so that you're suitably pliant with me.

Yesterday was odd and dysfunctional, but at the end of the day I kind of adore you, and I loved having you draped naked and languorous across me, soft and open. I want you in my life, to the extent that you want to be in it.

chapter 25

Class Act

It was January 2017. *I'd been* offered a seat on a bus from Queens to the Women's March in DC, but I couldn't bear the prospect of captivity among an earnest group of moms for so many hours, so I stayed home to attend the New York version.

Alex and Eli were away, skiing in the Catskills, and I had a plan: first the march, then an early dinner in Brooklyn with my friend Stefanie, after which I'd take advantage of Alex's absence to spend the night with Jack.

I packed a glass pipe full of weed, lit it, and inhaled a huge hit while standing on the closed toilet lid, then blew the smoke out the high, narrow window and onto the street, trying not to aim it directly at the woman striding by on the sidewalk, pushing a swaddled infant in a complicated stroller.

A friend of a friend had recently passed through town, selling high-quality homegrown weed at friend-of-a-friend prices. I bought a full ounce and hid it in an old blue-and-white-striped canvas duffel bag, along with THC-laced chocolates, gummies, lozenges and mints, vape pens and cartridges, all gifts from another friend, in Colorado.

The ritual of pulling out the stash bag and selecting something to fuck me up still gave me a small, reliable thrill.

Appetites: A Cookbook had now been out in the world for almost three months. It hit the *Times* best-seller list in its first week, and sales remained brisk, and the reviews were generally quite positive, but now the validating cycle of publicity and attention had come to its inevitable end. I wasn't sure what I had to look forward to, apart from boozy weeknight dinners with the neighbors, the occasional assignation with Jack, and that first high of the day.

By then, I was getting high before I left the apartment for any reason, even a quick run to Foodtown or the post office. Smoking weed had once created a soft buffer between me and all my difficult feelings, a way to separate myself from the aggravation and chaos of the outside world, but now, being high just brought a sharper focus to the imperfections inside me, and out there: the maddening slowness of the people walking two or three abreast in front of me. The drivers who didn't use a blinker before turning into a cross-walk. People who didn't pick up their dog's shit, or who purposely dropped their trash on the ground. The neuron-grinding wail of car horns and alarms. The deep, slushy puddles at nearly every street corner. The way the insides of my thighs still rubbed together when I walked, wearing holes into the fabric of my pants, regardless of how much I dieted and exercised.

Weed didn't work for me the way it once had, but sometimes, if I layered in another coping mechanism—a drink, a cigarette, a filthy text sent or received, a hard hit of sugar—in just the right order, for the right amount of time—I could still enjoy twenty to forty minutes of relative peace before the world seeped back in.

Anyway, the alternative—just soberly feeling whatever I was feeling, unmitigated by any illicit substance—seemed boring and awful and frankly unnecessary, especially now that I had a duffel bag full of drugs.

I shed the robe and put on the fancy black bra and underpants that I'd bought before that first visit to Jack's, then heavy tights, for protection against the bitter cold, and my most flattering pair of jeans, which were alarmingly snug after a Christmas season of bourbon-laced eggnog and Champagne and gravy.

I brushed and flossed and rinsed, stuffed one more pinch of weed into the pipe, lit and quickly inhaled, exhaled, then tucked a full-strength gummy into an empty pill bottle, for later. Heavy wool sweater, boots, parka, hat, scarf, gloves. On the way out, I took a photo of the cover of Tocqueville's *Democracy in America*, which Alex had bought a few years prior. I hadn't read it and had no intention of reading it, but it made for a timely and relevant Instagram post that attracted hundreds of likes over the course of the day.

While walking to the subway, I listened to a track from the new Tribe Called Quest album, whose optimistic reference to the first female US president was already outdated; Trump had just been inaugurated.

Those of us who were shocked by the election result, and who were then further shocked when confronted with evidence of our own privileged naiveté, were now awash in hysterical dread and engaging in what Joan called "acting-out behaviors." It felt insane, surreal. I had nothing to compare it to, this slow-motion anticipation of disaster.

As a coping mechanism, I was getting more fucked-up than ever, persisting in my affair with Jack, and dissociating around my family. Still, I thought I was probably doing better than the two neighborhood moms who told me separately and without irony about their plans to kill themselves with their children when the inevitable nuclear/civil/water war began.

On the other hand, I maybe wasn't doing quite as well as the people who were making big showy commitments to "working groups" and "resistance" and "the long fight," all of which seemed like the right actions, but so fucking exhausting to even witness, let alone participate in or attempt to sustain for the next four years.

Further, the women's march felt galvanizing, energizing, et cetera, while also looking like a performance, a gigantic photo op, and maybe too much of a party. In front of the UN and later on Fifth Avenue, I took a bunch of the same photos that everyone was taking: funny signs, a mass of humanity, an ominous line of helmeted, shield-clutching cops in front of Trump Tower.

Later, I drank the bulk of two bottles of white wine while Stefanie and I caught up on work and family matters over ceviche and salads. Stefanie was a video artist whom I'd met while working at *Wine Spectator*, and by coincidence, her husband was the post-production supervisor on *Parts Unknown*, so we always had a lot to discuss.

"Are you OK?" she asked after we paid the check. "You don't seem happy."

"I'm fine." I wanted to tell Stefanie that I was on my way to spend the night with a man who didn't love me and wasn't my husband, and that I was pretty sure I was a terrible mother and just generally kind of a loser, but she was fond of Alex, and I didn't want to burden her with the knowledge of what I was up to. "I'm fine."

I got to Jack's apartment, he let me in, and when I started artlessly shedding my clothes, he said, "You might as well leave them on. I'm not feeling up to it, and anyway, I can see that you're quite drunk." I felt as if I'd been punched in the stomach. I started to cry, and he chuckled.

"God, you're being melodramatic. You're not going to change my mind with this playacting at being wounded," he said. "You're welcome to say, but we're not going to fool around tonight." I stayed anyway. Of course I stayed.

Within a week of the inauguration, Mario Batali gave an interview to *People* magazine, in which he called Trump's immigration ban on people from majority-Muslim countries "stupid" and "a thinly veiled fear move," and offered his support to those actively protesting. When I saw the positive pickup that his

quote got in food and entertainment publications, I wrote Mario a
quick email:

*You are the best for speaking up early and often about all of
this, potentially putting yourself and your business in the line
of fire. Bravo. I hope many more follow suit and that there's not
a friendly seat left in Manhattan or elsewhere for the fear- and
hate-mongers.*

He wrote back, thanking me for the note and congratulating me
on the success of *Appetites* ". . . and just everything you have become.
You are a class act with a solid core of genius, and I always knew it."
It's crazy how much this dashed-off bit of praise meant to me.

In early February, Tony asked me to coauthor a new book with
him, which would be a kind of travel guide to the whole world, based
on everywhere he'd gone for television. Here was something to look
forward to.

Eli had a week of winter break from school at the end of February.
Tony had given me a very generous bonus for setting up his
new apartment, and for the work I did on *Appetites*, so I used a
big chunk of it to pay for a week in a resort in Cancun for me, Alex,
and Eli. It seemed promising: a high-end hotel on the beach with
a dozen different restaurants, swim-up bars in some of the pools,
and as much booze as you wanted to drink. There was a kids' club,
which would solve the problem we'd had on other vacations, during
which Eli became inevitably bored and lonely. Only, when we arrived at the resort, the first thing we saw was a group of school-aged
kids wearing ratty yellow pinafores over their bathing suits, being
death-marched across the pool deck by an indifferent-looking young
woman.

"That's the kids' club kids!" I said to Eli, but I knew my kid; the
vibes were bad, and we were sunk.

"Yeah, I don't want to do that," he said. "I just want to stay with you guys."

The next morning, after breakfast at a massive, chaotic buffet, I took a taxi alone into the nearest town, found a pharmacy, and bought over-the-counter boxes of Xanax and codeine, hoping maybe I could just keep myself in a state of pilled-out numbness all week, in the absence of weed, which I did not bring and did not know how to procure, or where I would even smoke it if I could find it. Back at the hotel, lounging with Alex in a palapa-topped cabana while Eli swam nearby, I washed down a Xanax with a rum and Coke. Within a few minutes, I fell into a coma-like sleep that lasted about forty minutes. When I woke up, I was already crying, for no reason that I could articulate. After that, I stuck to codeine and little shots of vodka.

Tony called midweek, asking me to handle a situation with the *New York Post*. An Italian tabloid had just published a story about Tony and his new girlfriend, Asia Argento, complete with a Roman street canoodle photo, and the *Post* wanted to be first with the story in the US.

"Verbally confirm with the reporter that it's true, nothing more, and don't leave any fingerprints that this info came from our camp," he said.

Successfully managing this bit of business was probably the highlight of my week, as it gave me an excuse to be alone in our room, away from the other guests, all those wet bodies and towels and voices, all that open-mouthed chewing of pool deck cheeseburgers while everyone, including me, stared at their fucking phones.

Shortly after returning from Mexico, I was off again, to a culinary conference in Louisville, Kentucky, where I would speak on two panels, one about cookbook coauthorship, and one about food feature writing.

The night before I left, we had a boozy chicken dinner with my friend and neighbor Alison and her family, during which the kids played Minecraft on their iPads and the adults drained several bottles of wine. Alison, my most steadfast neighborhood drinking buddy, worked for the James Beard Foundation, and would also be in Louisville for the conference. Later that night, I drunkenly sexted with Jack, while lying in bed next to the sleeping Alex.

In the morning, I got Eli on the bus to school, then smoked a joint, packed for the weekend, and Ubered to LaGuardia. The plane was very small. I put on my headphones and stared out the window, listening to a podcast about the *Real Housewives of Beverly Hills*. A middle-aged man sat down in the seat next to me, buckled his seatbelt, and touched my thigh.

When I removed my headphones and looked at him, he said, "Are you going home?" I could smell his stale coffee breath.

"Nope, I live here," I said, and then for the entirety of the two-hour flight, he talked to me about his family, his church, his hunting exploits, and how he liked to cook every cut of every type of meat he had ever eaten. He gave me a smiling hard sell on visiting the Creation Museum and the life-sized Noah's Ark, both in Kentucky. He punctuated his many points by touching me again and again, on my arm, my leg, my hand. I was hungover and stoned and lacked the wherewithal to do much more than nod and smile.

My first panel was in the evening, in a small conference room at the host hotel. I drank enough wine at dinner to steady the ship, and sipped bourbon throughout the one-hour program, during which I felt dull and inarticulate. I struggled to keep my voice steady and I couldn't get warm, despite wearing a thermal shirt, a sweater, and a big scarf. I refilled my plastic cup with bourbon before returning to my room, where I lay in bed, texting Jack, brittle and lonely. He told me that he'd just finished up a "visit" with a "playmate." Knowing that he fooled around with other women made me insane with jealousy, which I couldn't hide from him.

"I've no margin to deal with your hurt feelings," Jack texted. "You've got exactly zero legs to stand on here, married person."

Later in the conversation, when I told him that I didn't care for the word *cum*, he replied, "I look forward to hearing your explanation why, which will no doubt be entertainingly facile."

"Sometimes you can be a real dick," I wrote back. I finished the bourbon and went to sleep. When I woke up at 7 a.m. and reached for my phone, my right hand was shaking.

"Sometimes you can be too sensitive," Jack had texted back, and it took me a few minutes to remember what had made me mad, and then I was mad again. *Facile* was a pretentious asshole's way of calling me *stupid*.

I met Alison and Anya, (the neighbor who brought me cake and casserole after Eli was born, who was now an editor at Epicurious), for an early lunch at a casual restaurant, where I drank more than half of a bottle of rosé before our fried chicken sandwiches hit the table. It was 11 a.m., plenty late enough to drink away a hangover. The wine warmed my veins, but still my hands shook as I laboriously sawed through the soft potato bun, the pickles, and the crisp thigh with an allegedly compostable plastic knife.

"I think I drink too much," I said to my friends.

"Do you . . . think it might be time to quit?" Anya said, in the same voice I'd heard her use with her five-year-old daughter. I didn't feel condescended to; I felt taken care of. It was a question I'd asked myself so many times lately.

I said, "Yeah, I think so," my eyes filling with tears. I started to laugh at myself, and poured the rest of the rosé into my tumbler.

I power-drank my way through a bourbon-tasting seminar, a boozy book party, a cocktail party, dinner in a restaurant. I drank a glass of prosecco the next morning, before my panel. I slept all afternoon and then drank wine and cocktails at the awards ceremony and a walk-around after-party. At the after-after party, hosted by a local chef's restaurant, I drank bourbon and engaged in a silly, flirtatious conversation with an important editor, whom I merrily and for what reason I cannot recall, told to go fuck himself. Back at the hotel bar,

I got mouthy to some strangers about Trump, and the bartender politely asked me to go to my room. I set my alarm for 4:30 a.m., enough time, I figured, to catch my 6 a.m. return flight to New York. I woke up at 10 a.m., feeling scorched from the inside out, my clothes still in the closet and the bureau, my shoes in the bathroom, my body still in Kentucky. Instead of setting my alarm, I had typed "430" into my Notes app.

Nine hundred dollars got me a new one-way ticket home, on an afternoon flight.

That night I smoked a little weed and had one beer, and in the morning, I texted my old *Wine Spectator* buddy Rob, once a chemically dependent alcoholic who had gotten clean in a hospital detox and was now two years sober. I asked him for help, worried that he would try to talk me out of it, that he would tell me that I didn't have a real problem, but he sent me a schedule of Manhattan 12-step meetings happening that day, and suggested I find one for beginners.

The first meeting on Rob's list began at 1 p.m., in a grubby room on the third floor of a midtown building, directly across the street from a Scientology church. I got there at 12:55 p.m. There were several rows of chairs, facing a small table with one chair behind it. I sat toward the back of the room and watched it quickly fill up.

A young woman called the meeting to order at exactly 1 p.m. A man told a story involving drinking and drugs, violence, jail time, relapses, estrangements, regrets. I listened hard, cried about my own feelings and did not raise my hand or say anything. I put two dollars in the basket when it was passed to me. I clapped when other people clapped. I mumbled the words of the serenity prayer, which I knew from that one Sinead O'Connor song. I didn't think I was supposed to be there, but I also knew that I had to be there. I went home and I didn't tell anyone that I had gone.

The next day I went to another meeting, this time in a church basement on the east side of Manhattan. The crowd skewed elderly, many of them in visibly rough shape, and there was a very famous person there whom no one but me seemed to recognize. Afterward, I called Alex at work and told him that I thought I might be an alcoholic, and that I had just been to a meeting. He seemed surprised but was supportive. "Whatever you need to do," he said. "Should *I* stop drinking?"

"No, I don't think you really have a problem like I do," I said. I was grateful for this offer of solidarity but didn't want to make getting sober a group activity. Whether or not he was aware, there was already so much distance between us; getting sober together somehow felt too intimate, especially if it was going to require so much honesty, as I'd already heard repeatedly in my two meetings.

The next day I went back to the midtown meeting, and the day after that I went to a meeting in Queens. I kept going, not every day but most days, crying before and during and after each meeting. I kept completely quiet at first, and eventually shared a few things, and tried not to visibly cringe at the applause that followed every day count I shared.

"I have ten days."

"I have fourteen days and I have no idea what to do with myself. I miss the chaos of getting drunk all the time."

"I have nineteen days. Yesterday I told my eight-year-old son that I stopped drinking and he said, 'That's good, because you used to get *wasted*.' I'm mortified. I didn't think he ever noticed."

"I have twenty-five days since my last drink, and I'm not sure if I'm even supposed to be here. It's hard for me to say that I am an alcoholic. I still have my job and my kid, but I don't think I can drink anymore."

"Hi, I'm Laurie, I'm an alcoholic. I have thirty-seven days. I'm going home for Easter soon and I'm afraid to tell my mom that I stopped drinking. She's in a wheelchair and can't go out much, and drinking is pretty much the only fun thing we can do together. I think she's gonna be so disappointed."

I listened to the words of the readings and the prayers, and I listened to other people tell their stories of what their lives were like when they were drinking. I put a few bucks in the basket when it was passed to me. I was no longer drinking, and I felt like all turtle, no shell.

chapter 26

Jaffna

After seventy-five days without a drink, I went with Tony and a handful of crew members to Sri Lanka.

I was slowly learning how to live as a non-drinker in New York, but I didn't know what it was to travel without drinking, as in, what was the point of it? At my last 12-step meeting before the trip, I shared my concerns about staying sober on the road.

"There are meetings literally all over the world," someone said. "Get yourself to a meeting, any chance you get. And stay in touch with your sponsor."

I didn't have a sponsor, which was another person who had been in recovery for at least a year, who acted as an accountability partner and sounding board.

After a recent meeting, I'd been approached by a woman with bright red hair and pale skin who looked about half my age. She gave me a mini version of *The Big Book* and told me that her name was Ellie, and asked if I was looking for a sponsor. She made me put her number in my phone, and I gave her mine, but I didn't call her, and I didn't pick up when she called me a few days later. I wasn't ready to be held accountable. In a room full of strangers or in therapy with Joan, I could say out loud what I knew to be true about my addictive behavior, but the complete surrender of committing to a sponsor, which meant committing to a lifetime of real sobriety—I wasn't there yet. Whenever someone read the opening statement about how the program works, the phrases "half-measures availed us nothing" and "we thought we could find an easier, softer way, but we could not" felt squarely aimed at me. I was not ready for "rigorous honesty," and was still dependent on smoking weed as a way to change the channel when I felt anxious or sad.

Some days I felt like a complete mess, and I knew I'd have to get fully sober to start feeling better. Other days, the notion of myself an out-of-control addict felt like a charade, my appetite for self-destruction just something I'd exaggerated to seem interesting. Some days, all the self-examination of sobriety seemed incredibly fucking boring.

My first night in Sri Lanka, I joined the crew for dinner on the grand marble patio at the Galle Face Hotel, in Colombo. The wind was steady and hot, nearly as wet as the Indian Ocean, roiling a few yards away. The humidity and the jet lag and the utter newness of the place made it feel, to me, like drinking weather.

A waiter wearing a white linen jacket, white dress shirt, and a black necktie took our orders. Tony, seated across the table from me, squinted and said, *"Diet Coke?"*

"Yeah, I, uh, I quit drinking," I said. "It was time. I had enough."

His face looked deeply skeptical. "Huh. Really? I never thought you had an issue. I just hope you're not getting involved with AA," he said. "From what I've heard, those motherfuckers are like a cult. They'll blame you for all your problems, and they never stop calling."

"Yeah, we'll see," I said. There was no point in arguing with him.

Our waiter returned with a tray of drinks. The hotel bar really played up the whole old Ceylon thing, and Tony and everyone else got these huge, gorgeous gin and tonics, the classic colonial cocktail. That murky herbal scent carried straight to my brainpan, just killing me. I wanted that woozy, punch-in-the-face feeling that a cold slug of gin had always so reliably delivered.

I sipped my Diet Coke through a straw from the glass bottle, no face-punch, no ice, listening to the crew sketch out a rough plan for the morning market tour, and then I went to bed.

We were in Colombo for four days, during which time I hardly saw Tony and the crew. I had an assignment from *Saveur* to write a recipe feature about Sri Lankan home cooking. While they shot in restaurants and theaters and on beaches around town, I spent my days in home kitchens, sweatily taking notes alongside mostly women and a few men as they grated fresh coconuts, roughly tore fresh curry and pandan leaves, sliced onions and shallots, soaked and squeezed tamarind paste and goraka, pounded together piles of cardamom pods, slivers of fresh ginger, cloves of garlic, planks of cinnamon bark, fresh hot chiles. After all the prep, the fish, mutton, chicken and cashew curries they made came together quickly, in pans of screaming hot oil, where showers of mustard seeds exploded on contact. The final flavors were complex, surprising, and wild.

In the evenings, I was alone. Absent drinking, I didn't quite know what pleasure meant to me anymore, but I tried to find it in food: gloriously messy chili crabs from a stall on the beach, crisp, savory lentil doughnuts at the train station, jackfruit curry from room service. One evening, in pursuit of odiyal kool, I took a tuk tuk to Palmyrah, a restaurant specializing in cuisine from the northern city of Jaffna, which had been ravaged by the twenty-eight-year civil war. Odiyal kool is a stew of local river and lagoon crabs, prawns, and mullet, thickened with flour made from a root vegetable called odiyal or palmyra, soured with tamarind and seasoned with roasted fenugreek and fennel, turmeric, and plenty of hot chilis. With its combination of warmth and herbal earthiness, sweetness, salinity, and acidity, odiyal kool felt like a distant cousin to the fennel-intensive bouillabaisse that Tony included in the *Les Halles Cookbook*, served with fragrant shallot-studded rice in lieu of toasted baguette. I drank about two gallons of water in a futile attempt to mitigate the spice and nearly peed my pants on the bumpy tuk tuk ride back to the hotel.

On our fifth day in Sri Lanka, we all boarded a 6 a.m. train from Colombo to go see Jaffna up close. Two camera operators filmed Tony traversing the station, taking his seat, and, later, leaning out the window, wearing sunglasses and looking approximately as miserable as he said he was, thanks to a case of the nauseated shits that had circulated among the crew. It was a hot, slow ten-hour ride, with dozens of stops. Tony waved away all the men selling samosas and chips and nuts up and down the aisle, but sent a PA running out of the train at one brief stop to buy him a small personal pie from the Pizza Hut kiosk on the platform. For the last few hours of the journey, Sam, the network photographer, told me stories about his wild southern childhood and the years he spent shooting for newspapers in DC. Sam was sober the same way Jack was sober: as an adolescent, he'd looked around at the drunks in his family and community, and decided it wasn't for him to even start.

When we got to Jaffna, our local fixer, Mr. L, was waiting at the station with two drivers and two large vans to take us to the Jetwing Hotel, which was new and clean and beautiful, though Tony gave the director Tom a lot of shit about it anyway, because it was adjacent to a crematorium and a large open pit of stagnant water, origin unknown.

The next day was a shoot at a temple a few kilometers out of town, where the annual Madai Festival was ramping up. It's a day in which devout Hindus balance their spiritual ledger through fasting and dramatic acts of physical suffering, called *kavadis*, or "the burden debts."

Every religion has some form of this, right? But this isn't like getting a Filet-O-Fish on a Friday because it's Lent and you can't eat meat. This isn't one day of fasting on Yom Kippur, followed by a sundown bagel brunch. People fast for a month before the Madai Festival, and that's just a precursor to the real suffering.

Young women walk a mile or more, wearing shoes with nails hammered into the insoles, business side up, or carrying metal pots of something flammable that is actively on fire. Young men, meanwhile, have heavy-gauge hooks driven through the flesh of their backs, which are then are attached to ropes, which are then yanked around by other men, or used to suspend the hooked men from cranes, festooned with fruits and flower garlands, bouncing slowly along the rutted parade route, while crowds of other men play drums and chant and dance in clear religious ecstasy.

Tony didn't have to show up until 4 p.m., but the crew had been on the temple grounds all day, in the hot sun, trying to respectfully, artfully capture preparations for these spectacles of devotion and pain, which would intensify as the sun set, and would last all night.

Mr. L. had assured the crew that there would be plenty of food available, but some vital detail of timing, or quantity, or maybe a mutually agreed-upon definition of the word *food*, had gotten fucked up somewhere, and there had only been a few handfuls of cooked rice and some candy passed around among the camera and sound operators, producers, assistants, and Sam the sober photographer.

Working hungry and hot may have given the crew empathy for the fasting devotees, but it did little to improve morale, which had already been battered by their GI sickness in Colombo. Was it the ice in the cocktails? The crabs from the unregulated beach vendors? Did someone eat the raw fruit on the hotel breakfast buffet? Unclear, but everyone was grumpy, down a few pounds, and their teeth had a bubblegum pink sheen, leftover from crunching dry Pepto tablets, after they ran out of Imodium.

I rode with Tony from the hotel to the festival in a chauffeur-driven SUV. We arrived at the dusty temple grounds just as the parade of piety was beginning. He got out, expertly conducted his thirty-minute interview with a local coconut farmer, and was then filmed observing the procession. As usual, I stayed out of the way, lest a camera pick up a stray shot of the one American woman at the festival, with heavy black-framed eyeglasses and blonde hair, freely sweating through her ill-chosen black denim jeans.

Once the sound guy disengaged Tony from his mic pack, Tom hustled us back into the car. The parade eddied around us, while the driver inched us forward like an ancient tortoise through the crowd, and we could see everything—the devotion, the pain, the delirium, the dancing, the drumming—close-up, through tinted glass. I sat riveted for several minutes, feeling grateful for the opportunity, the anonymity, and the air conditioning.

I looked over at Tony, expecting to see him taking in the sacred spectacle with the same level of enthusiasm, but he was slightly hunched over, with a portable Wi-Fi transponder in his lap, his face close to his phone, in a rapid-fire text exchange with his girlfriend. He might as well have been stuck in JFK-bound traffic on the Grand Central Parkway. It made me sad, his indifference to the extraordinary thing happening just outside the car. He'd been doing this, traveling for television, for a long time.

He sighed, looked up.

"Let's figure out if there's KFC in Jaffna. I was thinking we get some chicken, a bottle of good scotch, get everyone to hang out on the hotel roof," he said, and I knew that this meant "manifest this for me, please." It was on me to bring in the food and beverages, and to make sure that a critical mass of exhausted and queasy crew members showed up, so that it would feel like, if not a party, then at least like fun. I was done with my *Saveur* reporting, and had nothing to do in Jaffna, so I was pleased that he'd given me a task.

I used my phone to find a KFC near the hotel, and a liquor store just a few blocks away. I sent gently persuasive texts to each crew member, imploring them to please make an appearance on the roof, despite their exhaustion, their need to call home, and/or their need to prepare for the next day's shoot.

Back at the hotel, Tony took the elevator up to his room, and I put on my backpack and headed out on my mission. The street smelled more than a little of sewage and was half-dark, streetlights being rare, many shops closing or having just closed. I passed an emaciated cow, hunkered down among dozens of parked motor bikes. I held my breath while skittering through the damp, unlit underpass that led to the liquor store. I should have checked whether the hotel bar would sell us a bottle of whiskey.

The store was a just a window through which money and booze were exchanged. I asked the young man in charge for a bottle of Johnnie Walker Black Label and handed him my Amex, which he swiped through his machine. After a disheartening series of beeps and retro modem noises, he looked up at me and said, not unkindly, "Declined."

I handed him my Mastercard, which elicited a shorter and altogether more promising series of beeps. "OK," he said, ripping off and handing me a paper receipt and a pen with which to sign it.

"Where you are from?" he asked.

"New York City," I said.

"I love it. I visit New York. I love it," he said.

"Thank you," I said.

I put the bottle into my backpack, zipped it up, and walked to the KFC, which was in a shopping mall. Most of the stores on the first floor were shuttered, but I could see the illuminated red signage, smell the warm, spicy fryer oil, and hear the muted buzz of fast food commerce coming from the level above. I boarded the elevator behind a young man who looked to be in his early twenties. He was taller than me, slender, wearing white pants and a pink dress shirt, untucked.

As the door slid closed, he said, "Where you are from?"

"The United States," I said, keeping my voice friendly, but my eyes down.

"I will join you."

My stomach fluttered slightly. What did he mean?

"I'm sorry. I'm not staying here to eat," I said, as the door slid open and there was the KFC counter and about a dozen tables and chairs arranged nearby, most of them occupied by families with children, or couples, reaching into their buckets of chicken, drinking sodas through straws. I took my place a short line to make my order, and the young man joined a different line. While waiting, I noticed a layer of dead flies inside the base of the illuminated KFC sign.

I ordered a twelve-piece bucket and an eight-piece bucket, and took the sweaty straps of my backpack off my sweaty shoulders to extract my wallet. As I opened it, I realized with a flush of exasperation that I'd left my Mastercard with the man at the liquor store. *Fuck.*

I paid for the chicken in cash.

"Your chicken is ready in twenty minutes," said the cashier, handing me a receipt.

I hustled into the elevator, out the door and back onto the fetid street, and standing there was the young man in the pink shirt who'd asked to join me. I turned in the direction of the liquor store and he started walking next to me.

"You are beautiful," he said, and I laughed without thinking. "I go with you to your hotel."

"I'm married," I said, walking faster, holding up my left hand, waving my ring.

"I go with you," he said. "I have a big penis. I put in your mouth."

I laughed again, at the absurdity and my own fear. A few nights prior, a Sri Lankan man told me that every woman walking alone at night is assumed to be a prostitute, whether or not she has dirty hair in a messy bun or is wearing Western clothes or tells you she's married.

I crossed the street, and he crossed with me. "Go away, leave me alone," I said. He kept walking with me. I knew I was very close to the liquor store, but there was still that dark overpass to get through, and I didn't want to lead him there. I just wanted to get my credit card back, pick up the fucking chicken, and make a nice little rooftop party for my lonely boss and his crew.

I crossed over again, to a wide median that split the road, where four tuk tuk drivers were gathered. I wasn't sure whether I just wanted to be in company, or whether I should hire one to take me the rest of the pitifully short distance to the liquor store.

"That man is following me," I said, pointing to the guy in the pink shirt, who had stopped walking, and stood smiling at me from across the street. I felt like a fucking idiot, for being out alone at night, for leaving my card at the store, for not knowing if it was rude to presume that the drivers would understand me. "Will you take me to the liquor store?" I held out my phone to the men, who exchanged blank looks with me, with each other. I pointed to the store on the map.

"Is one hundred meters only," said one driver. "Not a ride."

"Please," I said. "I'll pay double. The liquor store, and then Jet-wing hotel." There was an exchange of a few words of Tamil among them, and the same driver who had initially refused said, "OK."

I climbed in, untethered myself from my backpack, and enjoyed a minute or so of relatively cooling breeze while he motored us the short distance to the liquor store. When I looked back, the guy in the pink shirt was still standing there, having not yet given up on the chance to introduce my mouth to his dick.

"I'll be right back," I said to the driver. As a show of good faith, I left my backpack on the seat, then hopped out and up to the window, where the clerk smiled slightly and handed me my card before I could ask for it.

"You left," he said.

"Yes," I said. We smiled at each other for a beat too long, neither of us having any further observations to share. As I turned away, I heard the tuk tuk driver drop the motor into gear. He maneuvered in a tight circle and sped off and away toward that dark overpass, with my backpack—containing my phone, wallet, hotel key, passport, the whiskey, all the notes for the *Saveur* story I'd been reporting in Co-lombo and my eyeglasses—bouncing in the back seat.

I yelled, "Hey, what the fuck?!" The tuk tuk kept going, up the street and out of sight. A couple of hot tears leaked out around my crackly disposable contact lenses. I was the world's biggest fucking idiot, watching my shit disappear into the hot Jaffna night. I still had to pick up the chicken, and my receipt was in the backpack, too.

The liquor store guy hustled out from behind the service window to the sidewalk, where he mounted a small motorbike parked on the curb.

"Come with me," he said, motioning to the sliver of seat behind him, then turning a small key to start the engine. "We find the tuk tuk."

I was paralyzed with a surreal kind of indecision. This was fucking ridiculous. What might *this* guy do to me? Were all these dudes fucking working together? How many men would I have to deal with, just to buy some goddamn chicken and whiskey for some other men?

I threw my leg over the back of the bike and sat down gingerly, awkwardly, wondering if the liquor store guy thought I was a prostitute, and whether I could balance on the bike without touching him, just as the tuk tuk came roaring back toward us, with my bag still on the seat.

I dismounted the bike. "Thank you," I said to the liquor store guy. I was still crying.

I climbed into the back of the tuk tuk, and asked the driver to please take me to the Jetwing Hotel. I wanted to ask him *why* and *what the fuck*? but I kept quiet and I clutched my stupid backpack as we approached the hotel, and then kept going right past it. I looked out at the culvert and the gravel and wondered how many and which bones I'd break if I jumped.

The driver slowed down and made a huge, arcing U-turn in the middle of the empty road, gracefully turning left into the hotel parking lot and up to the front door.

"Two hundred rupees," he said, turned halfway toward me in his seat, and smiling placidly. I opened my wallet and fished out three hundred, handed him the bills with two hands, like I'd been taught was polite in Japan, uncertain whether the gesture translated to anyplace else in Asia. I didn't know whether he was under- or overcharging me, whether he took pity on me or wanted to fuck with me, whether he'd intended to steal my things or just had a habit of making excessively wide U-turns, whether either of us understood a single thing that the other wanted or needed. He counted the bills.

"You want tuk tuk tomorrow?" he asked.

"Maybe," I said. "If I need you, I'll find you." I got out, unzipped the top of my backpack, and put my hand around the top of the whiskey bottle. It would feel great, I thought, to take a long fiery slug, right off the top, just burn down my brain and body, and go eat chicken with Tony and the crew and make a funny story out of what had just happened.

The hotel doors slid open as I approached. Sober Sam was on his way out, he said, to buy a Mountain Dew and a candy bar. Dude was a sugar addict. I told him my story while he walked me back to KFC. The chicken was ready, and still hot.

Up on the hotel roof, Tony and Tom and the rest of the guys had pulled some rattan chairs and stools together around a low table in a corner and were drinking Carlsberg beers and smoking cigarettes. I put the food and the whiskey on the table, then went to the bar and ordered a Diet Coke.

A visibly drunk young British man approached our group. His T-shirt was too tight across his belly. He held a can of Lion Lager in his paw and took a big pull as his eyes scanned our faces.

"Heyyyy, you lot are *Americans!*" he said. He didn't seem to recognize Tony, who had gone very still, staring into middle distance.

"What you doing in this shithole, then?" the Brit asked.

"We're working," said Tom, not unkindly, holding his gaze. There was a long beat.

"All right," said the Brit. He turned back to the bar. Tony was safe.

I ate a wing and listened to them all tell stories about other shoots, involving a hapless Romanian honey trap, a hooker in Peru, a horny lesbian in Greece who'd seduced a young male PA. These were all stories I'd heard before.

chapter 27

Threat

In 2018, Mario Batali's flagship restaurant Babbo would mark its twentieth anniversary. It's no small thing to keep a business thriving for so long in the ruthless New York real estate landscape, where the expiration of a ten-year lease typically means a massive rent hike for the next ten years. Knowing this, Mario and his partner Joe had shrewdly purchased the building, investing in the restaurant's long-term future. To celebrate and capitalize on twenty years of expansively successful survival, he and his team were now working on a new Babbo cookbook.

In September 2017, I was pleased and surprised to get an email from one of Mario's three assistants, inviting me, as a "friend of the house," to write a short essay about Babbo, to be included in the book. I was also invited to come drink wine and eat some signature dishes, with some other "friends," for a photo shoot. I eagerly said yes to both, though it had been six months since I quit drinking, so I'd have to fake the wine part.

Before leaving the apartment on photo day, I took two red Sudafed pills, for energy and appetite control, and smoked most of a big joint, a kind of discount speedball I used to psych myself up and numb myself out before important events.

I took my place in the Babbo dining room alongside Bill Buford, the author of *Heat*, and Patrick, the novelist with the good coke, for whom I'd long-ago cooked a dinner party. I picked at the corner of a beef cheek raviolo and pretended to drink from a glass of Sangiovese, sliding it back and forth in front of my plate while the photographer moved gracefully around the table. Bill and Patrick drained their glasses again and again, jovially sharing literary gossip and comparing notes on their recent travels. I spoke only when spoken to, which is to say, I barely spoke. After the plates were cleared, the chef, Frank, came out with a few desserts.

"Mario sends his regrets," he said. "He got caught up in meetings and isn't gonna make it." This was fine with me; I was dying to get out of there, away from the demon carbs and the smell of the wine.

The next morning, I sat at my dining room table and wrote my essay for the new Babbo book:

After college, in the mid 90s, most of my friends went on to law school, or medical school, or pursued PhDs in the arts or sciences. I went to cooking school, then spent nearly four years working as Mario Batali's assistant, in the dining room, kitchen, and basement of his flagship restaurant, Babbo, where I received at least as good and thorough and useful an education as my friends, at a fraction of the cost.

I learned how to write a recipe, how to talk to important people (and people who believed themselves to be important, against prevailing evidence), how to slice prosciutto, and how to negotiate for half-price seats on the Concorde. I scratched a number of youthful itches, and learned that it's better, actually, to conduct one's love life outside the confines of the restaurant business. I learned a little Italian, a little Spanish, a little HTML; how to check two hundred coats into a space built for fifty, how to properly dress and season a salad, how to drink grappa, and subsequently how to mine the first aid kit for hangover cures. For these lessons and countless others, I am

forever grateful to Mario, and to the cooks, and the waiters,
bartenders, food runners, busboys, customers, vendors,
friends, and neighbors who made up the faculty, staff, and
student body at Babbo, my most beloved alma mater.

I sent it off to Mario's office, along with a note of thanks for having included me.

Eli's school had its annual PTA Halloween party that afternoon, and I went to help out. It was a cold and overcast day with a stiff breeze blowing off the East River and across the blacktop, where hundreds of costumed kids played games and gobbled junk and sort of danced to "Despacito" and "Monster Mash" and "It's Raining Tacos" and "What Does the Fox Say?"

I wanted to be fully present for Eli in this ephemeral moment of his rapidly blossoming life. He was a funny, openhearted eight-year-old, dressed as a professional soccer player and jacked up on Skittles, racing around with his friends and frequently stopping in to ask me for more game tickets or to hand me a wadded-up candy wrapper or napkin so I could throw it away. I set my phone to "do not disturb," but after five minutes, I put it back on "disturb," worried that I'd miss some urgent request from Tony. Whether stoned or half-asleep, at dinner or on the subway or reading a book to Eli, I could never forget that at any minute Tony might need me to do or arrange or buy or inquire after something. Today was one of those increasingly rare days when he was actually in New York, having just returned from Newfoundland, and soon to depart for Armenia. A Tony in New York day often held surprises; I had to stay vigilant. The defining element of my job was making his life easier and providing him exactly what he asked for, as quickly as possible.

I stood over a rented cotton candy machine, spinning hot blue sugar into sticky clouds for a little fireman, a Dora, and a bad guy who'd been played by Willem Dafoe in some very boring superhero movie I'd recently suffered through with Eli. My phone vibrated in my coat pocket, and as soon as I had a free hand, I checked the voicemail, which was from my friend Chris, a reliable source of restaurant industry gossip.

"You might want to rethink doing that Babbo cookbook thing you told me about," he said. "You should know that there are some really serious allegations of sexual harassment and assault about Mario Batali being investigated by the *Washington Post*."

Woof. I was well acquainted with Mario's capacity to harass, but the term *assault* came as a shock. The costumed kids and the party faded into the background.

Did *assault* mean ass grabbing and forced hugs or something worse? How bad had it gotten in the many years since I'd been within grabbing distance? I wondered if anyone I knew had been talking to the press, and what stories they were sharing. What would the fallout be for people willing to talk and for the people in Mario's orbit? Being credibly accused of sexual assault would put him at the center of a supernova-level explosion that would at least singe everyone aligned with him, including his good old pal Tony Bourdain.

Mario and Tony enjoyed the kind of public-facing friendship that Tony had with a number of fellow celebs, in which they frequently appeared on each other's TV shows and made hyperbolic displays of mutual admiration, sometimes bordering on awe. They didn't necessarily know each other's kids' or spouse's names, had never been and would probably never be inside each other's homes, but in the times they spent together, there was a genuine-seeming camaraderie. Until this current #MeToo moment, there had been no call for Tony to interrogate how friends like Mario conducted themselves around others.

I sat down on a bench, as far away as possible from the Halloween chaos, and shared the news with Tony, who seemed genuinely surprised to hear that Mario was capable of hurting anyone.

"I've seen him drunk and maybe over-affectionate, but I never saw him make a woman feel visibly uncomfortable or awkward," he said. "How wrong am I?"

Very fucking wrong, I thought.

"So, I don't know exactly what's being alleged," I said, which was true. I knew what I had personally seen and experienced all those years prior, but I didn't yet know just how many more female employees Mario had humiliated by talking about the fuckability of their bodies, right in front of them, to groups of men. I didn't know that he had groped so many dozens of women's breasts and asses, forced his tongue into so many unwilling women's ears and mouths. I didn't yet know that he had openly grabbed a manager's vulva in a dining room full of diners. I didn't yet know that he also occasionally groped male employees, as a way to dominate and humiliate. I didn't yet know about the hostess who had gone to the hospital early one morning, believing he'd assaulted her while she was blacked out, only she was too scared of him to file a police report, which was the only way to have her rape kit tested.

"Tell me what you do know," Tony said.

"Well, I always knew that Mario was an ass-grabber," I said, "and even that 'over-affectionate' thing that you saw, that shit makes women uncomfortable, whether or not they show it. And I'm sure you understand that there are reasons to not show it, in the moment, especially if they're at work."

I told him about the relentless lascivious behavior and the few disturbing stories I'd heard about Mario over the years.

"It's not a big deal, but he grabbed my ass once, too, when I worked for him," I said. "I told him right away never to do it again, and he didn't. I mean, I'm old enough to know that things were different then. If you wanted to be in that world, you just kind of took it. I don't know that any of it rose to the level of a crime, but I guess in retrospect it was pretty gross."

"This is horrifying," said Tony.

"I know. I'm sorry," I said, and I *was* sorry, for having shattered his illusions about his good-time friend, and for causing him distress.

Tony's girlfriend Asia had recently gone on record in the *New Yorker* about having been assaulted by Harvey Weinstein. Tony was very much caught up in it, using every platform he had to proclaim his support for victims of abuse and harassment, and railing against those whom he saw as complicit.

He said, "If you know anyone who'd want to talk to a journalist, on the record or off, I can help. I have good contacts now. I think you should talk, too. You may not think your own story is a big deal, but the more people who talk, the more willing others might be. Safety in numbers."

"Yeah, I don't know," I said. "I kind of just want to stay out of it."

I was afraid of crossing Mario, and I really didn't think this had anything to do with me. Wouldn't it be hypocritical to call myself a "victim" now, when I had never truly felt like one, and had benefited from years of access and association? Sure, I'd cried when Mario grabbed my ass, and felt sickened by his behavior, but hadn't I also gotten drunk with him, laughed at his jokes, and made plenty of my own? Who was I to throw stones, when I was currently behaving pretty badly in my own life?

The next day, while I sat on a cold metal bleacher watching Eli play Little League baseball, Tony texted me the name and phone number for Jason Horowitz, the Rome bureau chief for the *New York Times*, who was Asia's closest contact at the paper. "Call this guy and tell him what you told me. Let's get the *Times* on this story," he wrote.

I didn't want to call Horowitz, but apart from refusing to try jiu jitsu, I had never said no to Tony. I wondered whether he was using the Mario situation, and me, to perform his allyship and secure a place in Asia's increasingly fickle heart. He was one thousand percent in obsessive love with this woman, as he would tell anyone who'd listen, but their relationship was volatile, prone to dramatic breakups and reconciliations, plans canceled at the last minute, wild highs and lows. It seemed he would do anything to please or impress her, in order to keep her.

That afternoon, I dug into my file cabinet and pulled out the journals I'd kept while working for Mario. On the lined and dated pages, I found my own handwritten accounts of the things I remembered: him grabbing my ass, and that time he'd grazed that one young woman's crotch, and how he'd made me straddle him on the flight to Melbourne in order to get in and out of my seat. There were also a few things I'd forgotten: the time he hugged me too long and close, and stuck his tongue in my ear, after a drunken dinner. The time he grabbed a pastry cook in a humpy bear hug that she clearly didn't want but had no power to refuse, while making eye contact with me. That happened minutes before he did a cooking demo for a charity in the Babbo dining room. About this incident, I wrote:

> *I felt on Saturday, in the coffee/wait station before the benefit, that he was trying to establish the fact that he'd sexually harass everyone, because he could. I felt sick and angry, but then I thought, you knew what you were getting into. Don't make a fuss.*

Fuck. How could I have just forgotten that? And what was the difference between humor and harassment? It came down to power, and from what I could see, Mario was the only one who had any.

I called Jason Horowitz to share, strictly on background, the few things I knew firsthand. Tony had said that Horowitz was expecting my call, but when I introduced myself and said why I was calling, he seemed confused. This wasn't really his beat, he said, and he didn't know why Tony had put us in touch, or why we thought there was a story to be told. I ended the call feeling foolish and exposed, and tried to put it out of my mind.

A few days later, Maura Judkis, a *Washington Post* reporter, reached out to me, and a few days after that, I heard from Kitty Greenwald, who was working on a piece for Eater. They both knew I'd worked for Mario, and wondered if I had anything to add to their reporting. At first I spoke with them on background but eventually, both reporters convinced me to detail my own story on the record, which I did, albeit anonymously.

Then, another *Times* reporter, Julia Moskin, called to ask if I knew anything about Ken Friedman, Mario's business partner at the Spotted Pig, an extremely popular restaurant in the West Village. I didn't; I'd never even met Ken, and didn't personally know anyone who'd worked for him. Off the record, we talked a bit about Mario. I told her that I had mixed feelings about what was coming for him, that I knew he'd treated women badly and abused his power, but that I still had some vestigial loyalty and gratitude toward him.

She said that kind of ambivalence was common among her sources, probably because restaurant employees often see their coworkers as family. "It seems to be like knowing that your uncle is kind of a creep, but you also find him funny and you want him to like you, because sometimes he gives everyone a hundred-dollar bill for Christmas."

Weeks passed while the journalists continued to quietly do their reporting, and Tony got impatient when the stories didn't materialize fast enough for his taste. He dropped big, obvious hints on social media, and asked me whether he ought to sic an unhinged celebrity friend of Asia's on the situation, to have her just blow the whole thing open on Twitter and force the papers' hands.

I advised patience, and he advised me that I would need to protect myself once the stories broke, because my knowing that Mario had a pattern of bad behavior would make me seem complicit.

"You need a plan," he said, "and 'no comment' ain't gonna work. Get a statement ready to go, specifically saying whether or not you saw anything untoward during your time with him, and what you think of any allegations. If you're fast and firm and decisive, you'll be OK."

The whole situation felt like lunacy, and I resented Tony's implication that I was in any way responsible for Mario's behavior. *Was* I? What could I possibly have done to stop him? I smoked cigarettes in the courtyard of my building, took and made long phone calls with reporters and potential sources as I paced back and forth in the cold autumn air, keeping my voice low, and avoiding eye contact with my neighbors.

Then, a few days before Thanksgiving, I got an email from Mario, subject line "Threat," that stopped my heart.

Hey woolie i just got a crazy email about a story in the washington post from someone I've never met. Are you involved in an article ?

Spaghetti is love

mb

What the fuck was happening? I texted Tony, who'd also just heard from Mario. An anonymous "concerned friend" had emailed him, claiming to have evidence that Tony and Asia were forcing me to dig up dirt on Mario, in order to "increase the fame and glory they'd gained through alignment with the metoo movement." Mario had forwarded Tony the email, asking him if it was true, and Tony denied it all.

Tony told me that there were specific details in the message that could only have been gleaned by someone who'd hacked into his email, or mine. Because his girlfriend was a Weinstein accuser, he already believed that his web activity was being monitored by one or more of the black ops investigative firms that Weinstein's attorneys had hired to surveil victims and their associates.

"It's an intimidation strategy, meant to sow chaos and disruption in the lives of people who've spoken up," said Tony. He was a lifelong student of espionage, the author of three crime novels, and this kind of spy shit was something he'd always been fascinated by. Now that it was disrupting his own life, it was unnerving, and he felt awful, he said, that it had bled into my life, too.

I replied to Mario's email, saying that I had no idea what he was talking about, that I wasn't involved in any article about him. He wrote back and complimented my recent Sri Lanka story in *Saveur*, and said how much he enjoyed my Instagram feed. I wished him and his family a happy Thanksgiving, and he wrote back, "Gobble gobble!"

After that, Tony and I limited our communications to an encrypted messaging app, and I used a VPN whenever I went online. I was paranoid, anxious, and full of regret at having ever gotten involved.

When I talked about it in therapy, Joan said, "You didn't start this thing, and you couldn't have stopped it even if you wanted to."

A few weeks later, when several stories about Mario and his business partner Ken Friedman finally broke over the course of two days, I didn't feel relief, only more sorrow, fear, and anxiety. I was sickened by reading all the details I hadn't known, and further sickened by Mario's breezy apology statement that somehow, incredibly, ended with a fucking pizza dough cinnamon roll recipe. He was fired from his TV show, banned from his restaurants. The new Babbo cookbook was shitcanned forever.

chapter 28

Asia

"I just don't know that you're capable of seeing the beauty in simple things," said Jack one afternoon, when I asked if he thought we might be together in a more substantial way, if I got divorced. "You're so negative. You hate the show *Friends*, and I love the show *Friends*, and I just don't think I can really be with someone who doesn't love *Friends*."

I couldn't tell if he was joking. "Gaslighting" was just starting to enter the cultural conversation. Was I being gaslit? If I asked Jack, he'd probably tell me that gaslighting wasn't even a real thing. I was becoming increasingly obsessed with the unpredictable emotional switchbacks of this man, who said he wanted me in his life, kissed me and called me a "good girl," while also insisting with theatrical regret that I wasn't qualified to be his true romantic partner. I felt insane for putting up with his ever-shifting goalposts, keeping me on the hook while pushing me away, but I couldn't stop. I thought there must be a code I hadn't cracked yet that would make him want to be my real boyfriend.

Hi attention, when he deigned to give it, was intoxicating, flooding my system with endorphins every time he put his hand in my hair or talked about the truth and rarity of This Thing of Ours, as he liked to call it.

"We have a genuine connection, and I value it very much," he said. "But I cannot be the bridge out of your marriage. You're going to have to find someone else to do that for you. It's a good thing that you're pretty, because there are few worse things than a plain-faced, loveless woman."

For this, I was still deceiving sweet, loyal Alex. Simmering with confusion and self-loathing, I shuffled around in a mild stupor, trying to work out the impossible mechanics of wriggling free from my marriage without having to disclose anything about my behavior.

Months after the publisher had approved the idea, Tony and I were still waiting on the contract for our new travel book, but I got started on the research anyway, taking a trip to Tokyo and staying in my friend Emily's guest bedroom.

Emily and I had been fellow overwhelmed new mothers, hauling our infants around our neighborhood, eating cookies, and comparing anxieties. She was smart and funny and fearless, and had great stories from her time in the Peace Corps and various New York media jobs. Emily now worked as a Foreign Service officer, and lived in a capacious embassy-owned apartment in Roppongi with her husband, three kids, and a dog. Together, we checked out some of Tony's Tokyo favorites: Tsukiji Market, Robot Restaurant, Yakitori Toriki, and the Albatross Bar, where I drank a Diet Coke and confessed to her my numerous marital sins. She listened, and gently encouraged me to find a way out.

"Alex deserves the chance to find someone who's right for him," she said, and of course I agreed, if only I could figure out a way to skip over the part where I had to take responsibility for my own shit.

One afternoon, we all got into the family minivan and drove to a suburban mall for a lunch of conveyor belt sushi, followed by a walk on a nearby beach. It was a sweet afternoon outing, but I felt like clawing off my skin. I missed Eli, and Jack, and I missed smoking weed. The last time I'd been in Tokyo, I drank my way through each waking hour and fooled around with a stranger at the Park Hyatt. Now I was eating shrimp tempura off a plastic boat and listening to children bicker over an iPad.

Later, I attended a 12-step meeting in the basement of a Lutheran church near Emily's apartment. The room was full of American, British, and Australian ex-pats. We read aloud from the familiar literature, shared and listened in the same way I knew from New York meetings.

One person said, "Sometimes I think that I am both the most important person in the world, and a complete piece of shit." When it was my turn, I said, "I spent all this money to come here and get away from my real life at home, and I'm not having any fun, because I don't know how to have fun without drinking."

Toward the end of my time in Tokyo, I Googled my way to a website operated by a collective of men specializing in "erotic massage therapy for women," and arranged for one such man to meet me at a Ginza district business hotel. Prostitution is illegal in Japan, but only when narrowly defined as the exchange of money for penis-and-vagina contact; everything else that consenting adults might like to do, such as hand stuff, slips through a loophole.

"Your therapist will meet you at 6 p.m. in front of the hotel, wearing a white shirt and blue pants," said the email. I went outside at 5:55 p.m. At exactly 6 p.m., a young man in the aforementioned outfit, pleasingly young and fit, came around the corner. He smiled shyly and said, "Hello."

He then pulled his phone out of his pocket, fiddled with it a bit, spoke a few phrases into it, and held it up so that I could read the words on his screen.

My name is Itsuki. I am sorry that I don't speak English. Shall we go inside?

Itsuki was a skilled and efficient therapist, and he smelled clean in an entirely neutral way. With his help, I finally found some straightforward pleasure, both in the act itself and the transgressive and transactional nature of the encounter. Later that night, I sent Jack a text, hinting at what I had arranged for myself ("I had a professional visitor to my room this evening"), and when he replied, "I'm extremely jealous. It should have been me," I felt happy, powerful, and alive.

Back in New York, my job responsibilities became ever-more oriented toward helping Tony revolve like a planet around his girlfriend, the blinding sun. I fiercely guarded his schedule, fighting off any little incursions that would keep him from visiting her in Rome or hosting her in New York. Anything involving Asia was great; anything that kept him away from her was a miserable distraction, evidence of the cruel world conspiring to thwart their beautiful and perfect love.

He had me frequently ship gifts to her home, the first of which was a large box of vinyl records, hand-selected from various record stores around town, a sweet and geeky gesture of love. Unfortunately, I hadn't anticipated the very steep import duties to be paid on such a gift, nor the multiple copies of forms she was required to print and complete, before FedEx Italia would release the package into her hands. She told Tony with frank annoyance that it was all too big a hassle, and had the box returned to him.

"Find another way to get them to her," said Tony, who didn't have to curse or yell for me to know that he was deeply disappointed by my fuckup.

After that, I always hired Sara, who lived in Rome and had been a fixer on a few episodes of his shows, to receive packages, pay the fees, and deliver them to Asia's home.

Whenever Tony and Asia were together in New York, I was on high alert, because I never knew when a big idea might occur to him. At any moment, he could ask for anything: a reservation at Masa within the hour, tickets and a car service to a movie that started in twenty minutes, a next-day appointment with a famous tattoo artist. He was reminding me more and more of my old billionaire bosses, the Smiths, who believed that everything was possible if you could pay for it.

Even when Tony was in Rome, staying in a luxury hotel with a twenty-four-hour, English-speaking concierge service, I remained super-vigilant, because he would often text me a request for a cab or a restaurant reservation. It was absurd, but he was Tony, the best boss I'd ever had. I made a good salary, had great health insurance, and would receive a generous fee to work on the travel book, so where, exactly, was my leverage to set a boundary now?

My value was in my willingness to do anything at any time. It scared me to even think about upsetting him. I just wanted him to get what he wanted, as soon as he wanted it.

In January 2018, I joined Tony and the *Parts Unknown* crew on a shoot in Hong Kong. When Mike, the episode's original director, needed emergency gallbladder surgery, Tony hired Asia to replace him.

My first night in town, Tony asked me to join them at the bar of the Peninsula Hotel. I got there first, and fifteen minutes after our scheduled meeting time, they showed up drunk from dinner and kept drinking. I had only ever known Tony to be pathologically early, and the natural center of attention; it was stunning to watch him arrive late, hold his tongue, smile and nod as she interrupted, contradicted, and talked over him for nearly two hours.

Wary of the on-set chaos I'd heard about from veteran producers Helen and Jared, I didn't go to a single shoot for the Hong Kong episode. I spent my time making my way through the night markets and cha chaan tengs, crisscrossing Victoria Harbour between Kowloon and Hong Kong Island on the Star Ferry, eating dumplings and rice rolls, fish balls, tripe stew, pineapple buns, lobster with salted egg yolk, almond milk puddings, and juicy roasted duck.

One evening, about halfway through the shoot week, I met up with Helen and Jared in a bar near their hotel. They were tense and miserable, and told me how frustrating and absurd it had been so far, trying to make a television show around Tony's utter thrall to Asia.

She had a chaotic directing style that put her at odds with all the plans that had been carefully set for the shoot, and also at odds with meticulous veteran cameraman Zach. She was volatile, defensive, and mean, they said, which seemed like an attempt to deflect from that fact that she was disorganized and out of her depth. Adding to the bedlam was the sustained presence of the legendary cinematographer Christopher Doyle, an idol of Tony's who had been slated for a single brief interview but decided to stick around for the entire shoot. The only constant, they said, was the on-set consumption of huge quantities of beer and white wine from the nearest 7-Eleven.

Jared's phone was face-up on the bar table when it rang; the screen said "TONY." He answered and quickly went out in the street, away from the considerable din of international drunks and American Top 40 hits.

When he returned a few minutes later, he was pale and sweating. "Asia told Tony to send Zach home, or else she's quitting," he said. "He's making me fucking fire Zach."

This was chilling: if Tony was willing to trash one of his most fruitful and protected professional relationships because *his girlfriend told him to*, what chance did any of us have at keeping our jobs, unless we unquestioningly supported his slavish devotion to his relationship? Asia was the captain now.

Before going to Hong Kong, I had wrangled two assignments to write about chefs and restaurants there, but back in New York, I found it difficult to focus on anything, apart from meeting Tony's needs, keeping my family fed, and chasing attention from Jack, who would send me a series of just-right filthy texts or a long and beautifully written email, full of vulnerability and desire, then go maddeningly silent for a few days, kicking off a spiral of despair and rage that melted into euphoria the second he finally connected with me again. At a 12-step meeting, while listening to a woman share her story of romantic turmoil fueled by drinking, I was hit with the obvious truth that my relationship with Jack was itself a form of addiction.

I would frequently ask myself, *What's going to happen? This can't be my life. What would Tony do?* Only I didn't mean the successful, driven, ambitious Tony who had run kitchens, kicked hard drugs, written books, made TV. I meant the obsessive romantic who was willing to burn down his whole life for love.

In discussing it with Joan, I decided to initiate a gentle series of conversations with Alex about our relationship, eventually introducing the suggestion of separating, perhaps with the guidance of a couples therapist. Best case scenario, I'd back out slowly, like an oversized truck in a cul de sac, without doing any damage—beep, beep, beep—and once I got safely to the main road, I'd haul ass to a divorce lawyer's office, then live the rest of my life in total honesty.

Joan suggested that I write it all down, as a way of understanding and assessing my situation. I sat and puked out a bunch of words one morning:

> *Am I doing this for the story? I'm seeking out all of these experiences to feel something, to have them, to feel entertained. For maximum distraction. I have been collecting these stories for years. It is not so much the sex as the experience. I am doing it for the story, but who am I telling this story to?*
>
> *I have this old idea, left over from adolescence, of creating value for myself by amassing sexual experiences. The inverse of slut shaming. The more sex I have, the more powerful I am. The more I transgress, the more powerful I am. The more I fuck strangers, the more I feel I am worth something.*
>
> *I don't know what happiness feels like when it doesn't involve some measure of shame. My happiest moments of the last several years have involved illicit sex acts in strange places, blind drunkenness and loud music, the first twenty*

*minutes of being very stoned for the first time in a day, and
rewatching certain scenes from* Aqua Teen Hunger Force.

*There are days when I tell myself that I am a better spouse,
happier and more engaged at home, when I am cheating. It's
some real Esther Perel shit, only wishful thinking, because I
think that approach is for people who are really invested in
staying in their marriages, and I am not.*

*My desire to do bad things keeps burning through the
layers of tissue paper I wrap around the hot coal that is true
nature of me: I am a piece of shit.*

*But: is unchecked excess always the road to ruin? Is there
any story in which someone who indulges with no limits ends
up happy, successful, healthy, loved?*

*I just feel miserably trapped in this situation of my own
making. I have so many secrets that I am scared to even start
talking to my husband honestly. And I am in love with J,
whom I fear doesn't love me, and sometimes doesn't even seem
to like or respect me.*

And then I hit "save" and closed it up and went on with my daily
life: Eli's Friday-evening Little League game, a pizza for dinner.
On Saturday, the three of us visited friends who'd just moved from
Queens to East Orange, New Jersey, and on Sunday, another baseball
game, followed by big beefy bowls of pho at the Vietnamese place by
the subway station. Monday morning, it was back to school and work
for everyone. Monday night, I went to bed at eleven. Alex was still up,
on a phone call with one of his old his school buddies, pacing in the
courtyard. I waved to him from the bedroom before pulling the shade
and turning off the light.

I'd been asleep about two hours when Alex noisily opened our
bedroom door and switched on the overhead light. I sat up, deeply
annoyed, and confused. Was he drunk?

"What the fuck is going on?" I said.

"Why don't you tell *me* what the *fuck* is going on," he said.

"OK. What do you mean? What's wrong?"

"I was looking for a document on the server on Friday night, and I found your little *essay*, about how you've been fucking strangers, right? And that you're in love with someone whose name starts with fucking *J*? So, yeah, you tell me what the *fuck* is going on."

His rage sucked all the oxygen from the room, from my lungs. Alex had never spoken to me like this. I was fascinated, relieved, terrified. I shrank down in the bed, pulling my limbs in toward my middle, trying to understand. He'd read my thing on Friday night, but waited till one o'clock on Tuesday morning to confront me? I couldn't make sense of it.

"OK," I said, picking up my glasses from the side table, sliding them onto my face, getting out of bed. "Let's go talk in the living room." I was trying to project a calm I didn't feel. "I don't want Eli to wake up and hear us."

For a second I was reminded of the revolting scene in *Ratatouille*, everyone's favorite food movie, in the French countryside, when hundreds of rats finally burst forth from the ceiling of the old woman's decrepit home. I was the ceiling, and the rats.

chapter 29
Family Emergency

During that terrible middle of the night confrontation, and several times again over the next few weeks, Alex told me that I was a monster, a slut, a parasite, evil. He said that the person he thought he knew was dead, and I was just some shitty ghost. He told me that when he first read my inadvertent confessional, he wanted to die. He said that he hated the fact that I was his son's mother. He said that despite all my striving and pretensions, I was just upstate trash.

I woke up on the couch that first morning desperate to get Joan's perspective, some reassurance, some sense of how to proceed with our son, how to survive until one of us moved out, and what to do after that. I was supposed to have a therapy session that afternoon, but when I checked my email, I saw that Joan had sent a message at 1:19 a.m., around the time that Alex had confronted me.

"I must cancel our session due to a family emergency," Joan wrote, which was something she'd never done in our eighteen years of working together. I wrote back, expressing my hope that everything was OK, and asked whether she had a backup doctor to recommend.

"I'm so sorry to bother you, but I am in profound crisis," I wrote.

"Alex confronted me about my infidelities, and I told him that I didn't want to be married anymore."

"I'm also in the midst of a crisis, but I want to be there for you," Joan wrote back. "I'll call you tomorrow at 9:30 a.m."

When she called, I was sitting at the dining table. Alex had left for work at some ungodly early hour, to get away from me, and Eli was at school. It was a beautiful sunny morning, not too hot, the new leaves dark green and making lush dancing shadows on the dusty windows and brick walls of our building. May was my favorite time to be in New York.

"Hi, Joan, how are you?" I asked. "Is everything OK?"

"I, uh . . . I guess you haven't seen the *Times*?" she said.

"No, I haven't looked at it this morning." The newspaper sat unread and still folded on the table.

"Well, my husband was murdered in our home on Monday," she said. "The story's in the front section, on page twenty-one."

I opened the paper and there it was: a relatively brief account of a horrific crime, perpetrated by a stranger who'd been found and arrested in Joan's basement, covered in Joan's husband's blood.

"Oh, my god. I'm so sorry. We don't have to talk right now, I mean—"

"No, it's OK at the moment. I'm actually glad to have something else to focus on for a bit. But there are police all over my house right now, so I'm not sure how long I'll be able to stay on," she said.

Feeling like an asshole, I nonetheless told Joan about the confrontation with Alex, and how I was feeling, which was a combination of shock, shame, giddy relief, abject terror, and some sliver of hope for a less complicated future. She listened and asked a few questions and then she told me that she had to go and talk to a detective.

I sat on a bench in the courtyard of our building, chain smoking and rereading the *Times* report about Joan's husband, this time on my phone, trying to make sense of the horror of it, the cruel destruction of a life, perpetrated by a stranger who had entered a random home, by chance, who found an unlocked door and an unsuspecting man, and murdered him with a hammer. Jesus *fuck*.

I sent a quick message to Tony, in whom I'd impulsively confided my marital doubts many months prior. I let him know that the shit had hit the fan for me, and that while I wasn't at my best, I was committed to staying on top of my work. He replied:

"I hope and expect that as terrible as things are right now, it's kind of a relief and a liberation. There's a reason cops always see a suspect who falls asleep after arrest as a probable guilty party: the sense of relief that the worst has finally happened. It's universal. It will seem like a long dark night, but it gets better. It really does. You deserve freedom and happiness, and I am sure you will have it. Don't worry about money. Don't get a shitty apartment because you think you can't afford something better. If you need help, I can help you. I've got your back."

Tony and I had a joint checking account that contained a huge amount of his money, which I used to pay his cleaning lady and tip his building staff in cash. He gave me permission to include this asset in my application for a two-bedroom apartment that was just a block away from the home I'd shared with Alex and Eli for the past nine years.

In those few weeks between the confrontation and my moving out, Alex and I had three meetings with a divorce and custody mediator, who helped us make a parenting plan, with an even split of time and responsibility. I forfeited any financial claim to our apartment, because to do so would have put Eli's home in precarity, and because I felt that I deserved no financial reward for having destroyed my family.

I smoked a lot of weed and cigarettes, ate Twizzlers, and chewed nicotine gum when it was impossible to smoke.

Alex's fury and grief seemed to flare up in irregular waves. There were calm moments when we could have almost-normal conversations about logistical matters, and terrible, chaotic times when he would pelt me with curt expressions of disgust and rage, to which I would reply, "OK," and "I know." I stopped saying, "I'm sorry" when he told me that it was meaningless to him.

I tiptoed around him, tried to make myself scarce and small, slept on the couch. I took a previously scheduled five-day book research trip to Oaxaca, during which he texted me furious questions about whether I'd exposed him to STDs and whether I cared about how much of his life I'd wasted. We kept a placid front around Eli, who had never seemed more content and well adjusted than in the hours before we broke the bad news to him. In the first few awful moments of that conversation, we had to work hard to convince him that we weren't joking.

I was paralyzed with dread about telling my sister and my parents. They loved Alex, and I'd never mentioned my dissatisfaction, because I couldn't stand to share with them a problem for which I had no solution. Now I couldn't bear the idea of admitting to them what I'd done. Every time I thought about such a conversation, I envisioned a high-pressure fire hose of vomit emerging from my mouth. I wanted Joan's advice on dealing with this part of the process, but Joan wouldn't be available for at least a month.

"You'd better not be fucking writing about all this," Alex spat in passing one morning, and I said that I wasn't, while knowing that it was just a matter of time before I did.

I moved out of the old apartment with a few boxes of clothes and books and housewares at a time, piled into a granny cart that I'd bought from the dollar store. I hired a man with a van to transport one bureau and our wooden sleigh bed, which Tony had bought in Vietnam on one of his earliest TV outings, and then handed down to me in 2014, when he bought all new furniture for his new apartment. Alex said the presence of a bed that I'd slept in now made him feel sick.

There was a small, bright moment in all of this, carting my stuff between my old and new homes in the clear and direct sunshine, when I felt a brief wave of relief and optimism about what my life could be when the dust settled.

I did it, I thought. *I may be a selfish, terrible monster, but now I can get what I want, do anything I want. I have my own apartment, I have a job, I have Eli, and I have another book to write with Tony.*

Jack met me for dinner at L'Amico on a Wednesday, shortly after I'd finished moving into the new apartment. It was a warm, windy evening, the kind of night that had once encouraged reckless outdoor drinking. We approached the host stand, just inside the open front door, where a slender man in tailored shorts, a short-sleeve dress shirt, and work boots, with a grimy gray backpack on one shoulder, stood with his back to us, arguing with the young hostess.

"I'm just gonna get a drink," he said, gesturing to the empty tables and chairs in front of the restaurant. There was a crackling menace to his voice and his stance. I took a step back from him.

"I'm sorry, sir, but as I said, those tables are being held for people with dinner reservations," she said to him. "Do you have a reservation?"

"I don't got a reservation," he said, "but I'm gonna sit there anyway." He turned away from her and yanked out a chair from a nearby outdoor table while we all three watched him. The host rolled her eyes and smiled knowingly at us, looked up Jack's reservation on her iPad, picked up two menus, and motioned for us to follow her to our table. She led us directly past the unhinged man, who abruptly stood up when I passed next to him, swiveled his neck, and unleashed a gob of spit in my face. It landed wetly on my right cheek, close to my eye.

"Are you fucking kidding me?!" I said without thinking.

"Fuck you. You're a fucking *cunt*," he said, his face a snarl as he grabbed his backpack off the ground and pushed past us, up the block and around the corner, out of sight.

The hostess grabbed a linen napkin from an empty table and handed it to me, trilling a flurry of apologies.

"Go wash off your face with soap and very hot water," Jack murmured. I walked back to the bathroom, where I scrubbed my entire face and neck and both hands, using one of the plush white hand towels stacked in a basket on the white marble countertop. I had red blotches on my cheeks and mascara melting under my eyes.

There was a strange relief in being spat on by an angry, unwell stranger. I wanted to tell Alex about it; it might give him some satisfaction. I wondered for a second whether he might have actually arranged it, if he'd hacked my texts and emails and knew that I'd be at L'Amico with Jack, open-faced and vulnerable.

I took several deep breaths in front of the mirror before returning to the table.

"Thank you for not making a scene," Jack said. "I'm quite hungry, and it's really not worth creating a fuss. It certainly wasn't personal. Let's order the ricotta, shall we?"

couldn't really say to Alex what I wanted to say out loud, so I tried to explain myself to him in a long, tortured email.

I know I have behaved terribly and in a deeply selfish and cowardly fashion, for a long time, and that the depth of the betrayal is profoundly hurtful. I can't undo that damage. I can't really blame drinking, though my behaviors have an addictive component.

There were many consecutive years when I didn't look outside our marriage for fulfillment, when I thought it was possible to make it work and find what I needed there, from before we were married until Eli was a few years old. Then I succumbed again to the things I wanted, even though I knew that would put distance between us and erode our marriage. The more I did it, the more I was able to normalize and rationalize it to myself, despite feeling guilt and shame.

Since I quit drinking, I have been thinking about what I really want and how to get it. Everything keeps coming down to trying to live more honestly. I tried to figure out how to start the conversation with you, what a separation would look like, how it would be achieved with the least amount of damage. I knew that once I opened the box, there would be no closing it, so I wanted to take my time and be very sure of my motivations.

Disclosing my transgressions would have caused damage that I hoped to spare you. I knew that just saying how unhappy

I was, and that I thought we should try being apart, would be hard enough. My infidelity, as I see it, was a symptom of my unhappiness.

I'm not leaving because I want to be with a specific someone else. It's because I'm not the right person for you. I may well not be the right person for anyone, ever. I don't know.

I am quite ashamed of myself and, having hidden for so long, I still find it hard to speak specifically about times, places, and people. And anyway, I'm not sure that having more specifics will be useful to you, though I understand your desire to know everything.

I'd like you to know that, despite whatever satisfaction I couldn't find between us as a romantic married couple, I love you and I know how lucky I am to have had as many good times as we did together. I've learned a lot from you. I think you're smart and funny and an incredible father. You're patient and kind and gentle, supremely competent and, despite my protests to the contrary, a very good driver. Your commitment to our family's security and comfort is absolute.

I know that you wanted me to be happy, and that I made it very difficult for you to know me. I took advantage of your trust, and I violated the promises we made to each other. I have avoided saying 'I'm sorry' too much, because you told me it doesn't mean anything to you. I know it sounds empty and doesn't change anything, but I am very sorry about this mess I've made for us. I appreciate how well you've been handling it, and I want to acknowledge your deep pain, anger and sadness, and the burdens you will continue to bear because of my dishonesty.

His response was brief and raw, did not engage with any of my points, and ended thus:

"I can never forgive you. Ever. Fuck you."

And, yeah, well, I could see his point.

got an "Anthony Bourdain" Google alert email every morning. On the first Monday in June, in among the pieces about the heavily promoted *Parts Unknown* Hong Kong episode was a link to a story in the UK *Daily Mail*. I clicked on it. It was about Asia Argento, identified up front as Tony's girlfriend, having been spotted kissing and dancing with and holding hands all over Rome with a handsome young French journalist. I quickly scanned the photo evidence. A few hours later, an editor from the *National Enquirer* contacted me by email and phone. They planned to publish a story using the same photos, and were seeking comment from Tony.

I was confused. Was the story a fakery, maybe some new bit of subterfuge being perpetuated by Harvey Weinstein's operatives? Asia was about to be announced as a judge on Italian *X Factor*; maybe this was some weird strategy designed to draw attention to her, and therefore the show? The most obvious answer, that she was carrying on a public romance with someone other than Tony, didn't square with my understanding of their relationship, and I didn't want it to be true.

Tony was on a *Parts Unknown* shoot in Alsace. When I asked him what he'd like me to do about the *Enquirer*, he said, "Ignore it, and ignore any similar queries from other pubs. But let me know when the *Enquirer* piece drops. They work directly for Weinstein. It's gonna be bad."

I had a few brief conversations about it later that day, with Kim, Tony's agent, and Helen, the producer who had been in Hong Kong; she was my friend, and Tony's friend, too. Helen had heard that things were apparently tense on set in France, and everyone was walking the tightrope, trying to give him both the emotional support he seemed to need and the space to process his pain with a measure of private dignity.

The next day, he asked me to schedule a number of things for him—a lunch, a haircut, a doctor appointment, a private session with his jiu-jitsu trainer—for the week after his return to New York.

"I hope you're doing OK," I texted to him, and when he responded,

"I'll live, and we'll survive," I assumed that the "we" meant him and Asia, their complicated relationship.

That night, I walked around my still rather empty apartment, on a phone call with my friend Jessica, who was now a happy newlywed, expecting a baby. The place smelled strongly of the pale yellow paint that had been freshly applied to the bedrooms, hallway, and living room walls. I'd ordered some discount rugs, which had arrived by UPS but were still rolled up in their heavy plastic wrappers. Eli was there, watching videos on his iPad, on his oddly sized new IKEA bed. We had dishes, a microwave, and window air-conditioning units.

"Things are settling down a little bit. I'm starting to eat more normally," I told Jessica. "I'm not gripped with panic every second."

At 4:25 the next morning, my phone vibrated on the windowsill next to my bed, waking me from a light sleep. It was Kim, Tony's agent. When I answered the call, she said, "Tony has taken his life."

chapter 30
I'll Live

It took me a few seconds to process the meaning of what Kim had just said: "Tony has taken his life."

I thought, *We can fix this.* I'd spent the last nine years, and Kim much longer than that, helping Tony meet his obligations, get where he needed to be. We were his occasional sounding boards, editors, fixers, friends. *We can fix this.*

We'd helped him arrange all of his situations and obligations exactly to his liking, and helped him gracefully get out of things that no longer suited him. We could, we *had to*, help him un-fuck the mess he made when he *fucking hung himself in his hotel room,* just like he had glibly threatened to do a million times, in the face of something as minor as a bad hamburger or a delayed flight.

"I'm gonna find a strong beam and throw a rope over it," he'd often say, in mock agony, for a laugh.

We can fix this.

"In the last year or so," Kim said, "whenever I asked him what he was looking forward to in life, what his goals were, and what would make him happy, it was all about Asia—figuring out a way to integrate her into his entire life. I think, when he saw it falling apart, he didn't know what else he was living for." She had somehow already crafted an answer to the impossible question of what the fuck was happening.

With every word she spoke, it became harder to hold on to the slippery notion that this was something we could fix, because Tony was dead, for real, forever. He had made the colossally stupid but somehow wholly plausible decision to die of a broken heart. He'd ignored all that he still had, which was more than almost anyone alive, but it didn't matter to him, because he was a romantic, an obsessive, an addict, and he was apparently more unwell than anyone had realized. How could we not have realized?

It was 4:35 a.m., still dark, though the sun would be up soon; it was less than two weeks from the summer solstice. Kim told me that CNN had agreed to hold off on announcing Tony's death for a few hours, until his family, close colleagues, and friends could be informed. She asked me for three people's phone numbers: his brother Chris, his ex-wife Nancy, and Asia.

"Once this gets out, you're gonna get a lot of calls from the press," said Kim. "My advice is, don't even answer them. There's absolutely nothing to be gained by commenting to anyone."

I had a few hours to live with the news before it became real to the rest of the world. Knowing that Eli was a very heavy sleeper, I left the apartment and went outside to smoke and walk and try to absorb the shock. I only got as far as my old building, Alex's building. I used my key to let myself into the gated courtyard, sat down on the steps that led to the back of the building, and pulled up my last texts from Tony.

"I'll live. And we'll survive."

Goddammit, I thought. *I should have dug in deeper, made sure that he was really OK. I should have known that he would do this.*

Alex had said he'd wanted to die when he discovered my infidelities, and I'd just spent the last month witnessing his rage, pain, and sadness up close. How could I not have seen that Tony was in danger?

I should have done something. I should have known. The thought of him alone, in unbearable pain, acting on the worst impulse imaginable, made me feel sick with regret.

I opened my email and sent a quick note to the company through which I'd just chartered a yacht for Tony and Asia. They had a plan to sail among the islands of the Tuscan archipelago for ten days in August.

"I'm sorry to say that Tony has had a change of plans," I wrote. "Per our contract, I trust that you will return the deposit to the checking account from which it was drawn." There was a strange comfort in acting as if Tony were still alive. I scrolled through my email, to see if there was any other business I could plausibly handle before the news broke, but found nothing.

At 6:30 a.m. I texted Alex about Tony. The impulse to share important news with him was a muscle memory, and I wondered whether this development might slightly soften his stance against me.

Within a few minutes, he wrote back. "I don't know why you're telling me this," the text said. "Tell it to your boyfriend."

Jack wasn't my boyfriend, but I emailed the news to him anyway, then walked back to my own apartment, woke Eli up, and toasted him a waffle without letting on that anything was wrong. At 7:28 a.m., I said goodbye to him at the bus stop, and at 7:30 a.m., CNN broke the news.

Within five minutes, I got calls from TMZ, *People*, the *New York Times*, *Entertainment Weekly*, *Variety*, and my sister, which was the only one I picked up. She was sobbing.

"What is *happening* to your *life*?" she wailed. I'd only just told her about splitting with Alex a few days prior.

"Yeah, it's fucking awful, I don't know," I said.

"Are you OK? What are you going to do today?"

"I don't know," I repeated. "Probably talk to people who knew him. Unpack my stuff. Take a nap. I don't really know what to do."

I didn't yet have a couch, but I had Wi-Fi. I sat on my bed and hit the weed pen till it ran dry, scrolling and refreshing and watching the online world react. I got dozens of sympathetic emails and texts from friends and associates. Alec Baldwin, Donald Trump, and Barack Obama tweeted about Tony's death within an hour of each other. A WWE wrestler whom Tony had recently met at Madison Square Garden texted to say that Tony's family would have free WrestleMania tickets for life. I turned off my phone and took a nap.

Later in the day, my friend and neighbor and onetime drinking buddy Alison offered to meet Eli at the school bus drop-off and keep him at her place after school for a few hours. When I went to pick him up around dinnertime, her two boys and Eli and a handful of others were playing a running game in the courtyard. Alison handed me a cold can of seltzer and we went into her apartment, on the ground floor, where we could still see the kids through the dining room window.

My eyes felt like burnt holes in a blanket. I sat at Alison's table while she beat together two eggs with a fork. She melted a generous knob of salted butter in a pan, poured in the eggs, seasoned them with salt, and stirred them carefully with a wooden spatula until they were cooked into silky curds. It was the best thing I'd eaten in a long time. She ordered pizza for our boys, and they ate it outside, standing up, between laps around the picnic tables and benches.

As Eli and I walked home later, I told him that Tony had died, and when he asked how it happened, I told him the truth, that he had hung himself. He looked scared and said, "Holy shit," which made me laugh for a second. I hadn't been great about policing my own use of language around him.

"What about your job? What are you gonna do now?" he said.

"I'm not sure yet, but don't worry, I'll be OK," I said, and although I felt entirely unmoored, I also knew that I would, eventually, be OK.

The next day, Eli went to Alex's, where he would stay for the next five days, and I went to Brooklyn, to cinematographer Todd's house, for a gathering of the shattered crew members who had just returned from France, along with a number of others who lived in New York and hadn't been on the shoot. There was a lot of drinking and smoking, some crying, some extremely dark jokes, the telling and retelling to each other what had happened in the lead-up to Tony's death, and immediately after, and what it felt like to learn and know that he was dead. Todd's elderly dog, Stella, wandered around all these strangers in her home, barking and snuffling up crumbs off the floor. I ate a sesame bagel with cream cheese, smoked my vape on the balcony, and left when the abandoned glass of whiskey next to me started to smell too good.

The subsequent few days were long and awful and increasingly empty of the busyness that had given my life structure. I lost hours scrolling through the online swirl of speculation and rumor and vitriol and grief, the endless variations on "I only met him once but . . ." stories, the endless "my selfie with Tony" photos.

Everyone was suddenly an expert on depression, addiction, burnout, jealousy, and Tony's personal life. I got DMs and Twitter mentions from people convinced he had been killed by Clinton operatives, or that he'd auto-erotic asphyxiated himself. An actress friend of Asia's wrote and distributed a cynically performative press release calling for a "national conversation about mental health" while insisting that Asia and Tony had had an open relationship, and urging his fans not to blame Asia for Tony's death.

As angry as I felt about the way that her behavior had humiliated and devastated Tony, I could also see the essential truth: Asia may have been the catalyst, but she was not the cause. She didn't kill Tony.

The cause of Tony's death was Tony, a human, mortal, grown man who loved and suffered so deeply that it killed him. He was lonely and stubborn and delusional, and despite all his intellect and world-weariness, he was a bone-deep believer in romantic old-school fucking Romeo and Juliet–style love. He'd survived heroin addiction and all kinds of dangerous and terrifying shit all over the world, but in a specific moment in his extraordinary life, he didn't have the resilience to survive the cruel and brutal end of his last great love affair.

Within a few days of his death, Tony was canonized by his public into Saint Tony, which, OK, I get it: when something so unfathomable happens, people need to categorize the person, to try to organize the chaos of early grief. Tony was the first to say that he was far from a perfect person, that he was vain, impatient, self-absorbed, impulsive—but I guess when you're a beloved public figure, even your unlovable traits get polished up and used to bolster your hero status.

It was all quite a lot: the T-shirts, the candles, the posters, the bake sales and cookouts and negroni specials to raise money for suicide prevention work. The restaurant that created Bourdain Fries topped with escargot, Pernod, absinthe, butter, and shredded Gruyère? I could almost hear Tony groaning and speculating about the tensile strength of the overhead beams, using his comedy voice.

chapter 31

Life Insurance

Tony was dead, but he was still getting mail at the production office, so one Thursday afternoon in August I got stoned and took the train into Manhattan to sort through it all.

I went straight to the office manager's desk, where the mail was collected, hoping not to run into anyone from the *Parts Unknown* crew. I didn't feel like talking. What was there to say? That first white-hot, shocking blast of Tony's suicide had worn off, and now there was just grief, in increasingly intense and longer-lasting waves. When any well-meaning person said to me, "I'm sorry for your loss," as many people did, my immediate impulse was to shake it off. I felt my privacy being intolerably invaded by their assumptions about how close I'd been to Tony. I felt undeserving of their sympathy, because if I'd been close enough to be shattered by his suicide, I should have been close enough to prevent it from happening in the first place.

Within a week of his death, things got very quiet on my phone and in my email inbox. Tony's family and attorneys had taken over all his business; I had no more role to play, apart from getting back to work on the travel book, which I wasn't yet willing to do. I was jealous of the camaraderie among the *Parts Unknown* crew, their continued shared purpose as they worked on the few final episodes, finished without Tony's voice-over, because he had died before recording it.

The office manager, Ruby, was a sweet and welcoming older woman, a much-needed soft and maternal presence in a company full of jittery young and young-ish creative types. She hugged me and we made a few minutes' worth of small talk, then she handed me a shopping bag full of envelopes and papers of all sizes. I sat down at a small desk in the corner and began sorting. Among the handwritten letters and cards, the advance copies of new books and the advertising circulars and postcards, there was a large padded envelope with the name of a PR firm stamped on the outside. The postage label was dated 06/11/18, three days after Tony's death. When I punctured the top seam with Ruby's silver letter opener, the room abruptly filled with a sickening smell. Inside the envelope was a heavy-duty piece of paper printed with a press release about a new brand of vodka, and it was wet from having absorbed the squelchy remains of a putrefying potato.

This was a truly terrible idea that one professional adult had suggested and at least one other adult had approved: sealing individual raw potatoes into plastic-lined envelopes and mailing them out on the cusp of summertime to a list of influential people including Tony, a famously dead man, in order to market a new brand of booze.

I started laughing. It was so fucking stupid. I thought about how Tony might have reacted to this clusterfuck of a publicity stunt, and to the terrible smell, which was like a hundred rotten dead mice braised with durian, simmering in a well-trafficked porta-john. I rolled the envelope tightly around the potato and stuffed it in the bottom of the office's kitchen trash, and went home, smoked more weed, and lay down on my shitty couch and scanned Twitter for mentions of Tony and his death until I nodded off. I woke up an hour later. My back was sore. I didn't have Eli with me that night, so I popped some popcorn and cut up an apple for dinner, and ate it while watching the *Real Housewives of New York* cast succumb to a South American strain of *E. coli* and shit themselves on a boat off the coast of Cartagena.

I had a five-day stretch with Eli that started late the next afternoon, when I picked him up from baseball day camp at the nearby Catholic high school. He handed me his backpack and we walked home slowly in the heat while he told me about the drills they'd run, the hits and catches he'd made and almost made. Back in the air-conditioned cool of our apartment, he took off his T-shirt and lay on the couch, watching back-to-back episodes of *Futurama*. In our new galley kitchen, with its mismatched cabinets and cheap countertops, I arranged for him a stack of potato chips, some rolled-up deli ham, a slice of cheese pizza scavenged from the freezer and crisped in the toaster oven, and three Oreos in a package, which I'd picked up in a bodega the day before. This is how I fed him most nights, with a no-cook snack sampler that bypassed the challenge of vegetables and left me more time to scroll social media, looking at the conspiracy theories and general long tail of reaction to Tony's death.

I set the plate down on the coffee table next to Eli, and went to retrieve a tray table from the kitchen. When I came back, he was squirming in a way that instantly telegraphed to me his discomfort, his shoulders around his ears as he shifted from side to side, his mouth twisted.

"What's the matter?" I said.

"I just . . . I want . . . can you start making me, like, real dinner food again?"

I went back into the kitchen and put on a pot of water for spaghetti, which I cooked and served to him hot, with butter and diced deli ham.

L ower East Side," the final episode of *Parts Unknown*, had its premiere screening at the Angel Orensanz Foundation, a decommissioned nineteenth-century synagogue on Norfolk Street, in the heart of the neighborhood. The screening was part of the Food Film Festival, and had been programmed months before Tony's death.

I showed up stoned, as usual, and soon found the cacophonic energy inside the venue nearly unbearable. There was something both too cheerful and incredibly dark about this first Tony-centric public event since his death. It had the feeling of a heavily sponsored funeral, with a CNN-branded step and repeat, lots of garish liquor branding, substantial passed appetizers, and rented ballroom chairs packed tightly into the screening space.

In an early scene of the episode, there's a candid moment in which Tony stands on the corner of Avenue B and East Third Street, reminiscing about the nearby storefronts where he'd habitually scored heroin in the 80s. Romanticizing his own addiction to narcotics had been a cornerstone of Tony's origin story since long before *Kitchen Confidential*, but it had never seemed so pathetic as it did in that scene. One of the last shots in the segment lingers on his face much longer than he would have allowed, were he still alive for the editing process. With four months' hindsight, I could see exhaustion and pain in his face, and I wondered how we all could have missed that pain, and what, if anything, we could have done about it, if he'd lived.

As a condition of my divorce agreement with Alex, I had to get a life insurance policy. When I met with a broker in my neighborhood, the morning after the *Parts Unknown* screening party, he asked, "Do you drink alcohol?"

"No, I quit about a year and a half ago," I said.

"Do you smoke?" he asked.

"I smoke weed, but I quit cigarettes last month," I said. I hadn't yet gotten high that day.

"You should stop," he said. "A life insurance policy will cost you about three times as much money every month if you're a smoker of anything. You have to have a physical, and there's a blood test, and they don't differentiate between evidence of nicotine and THC."

"Huh," I said.

"Take two weeks off smoking before you get the physical," he said.

I followed his suggestions, and that was it: this helpful young insurance broker, working out of a dusty, cluttered office on Roosevelt Avenue, under the roaring tracks of the 7 train, had given me a sufficient motivation to surrender. I gave away the duffel bag full of weed, asked a sober person I knew to be my 12-step sponsor, and re-started my day count at one.

chapter 32
Emotional Sobriety

I thought I had been using weed to manage my anxiety, but it turned out that I'd been using weed to manage the *anticipation* of my anxiety, which would then reliably manifest the second I got high. Being completely sober for the first time in decades, I quickly found myself far less tortured by the minutiae of daily living in an imperfect world, and also far more aware of the wonderful ordinariness all around me. I learned the name of the pink and white and blue flowering bushes (hydrangeas) that were all over my neighborhood, which I'd never before noticed, despite their being extraordinarily common. I (discreetly) scanned the faces and outfits and shoes of the people I saw in the grocery store and on the train. I suddenly had the attention span to read the newspaper. I patiently helped Eli put together his Halloween costume ("injured zombie Mets player"), using white makeup and blood gel and a fake ninja star from the dollar store that we attached to his face with spirit gum, to look as if it were half-embedded there.

The first Christmas Eve after our split, when I had about sixty days sober, Alex took Eli to his parents' house in New Jersey. This was what we had agreed on when devising our parenting plan, and I'd brought Eli to my parents' house for Thanksgiving, but being away from him at Christmas still felt sad and punitive, like an indictment of my fitness as a mother.

Before Alex and Eli left town, I baked them a pan of magic bars, which are a combination of sweetened shredded coconut, gobs of chocolate chunks, butterscotch chips, and pecans, all suspended in a matrix of thick, glistening condensed milk, atop a buttery crushed graham cracker crust. Eli didn't even like magic bars—he was an ice cream kid—but they were Alex's favorite Christmas cookie, and I'd been making them for years, using the reliable recipe from the side of the Eagle condensed milk can. I wanted to show him and his parents that I could be a thoughtful person, a generous person, that I wasn't a complete monster. I wrapped the still-warm bars in foil, put them into a plastic grocery bag, and hung them on the door of his apartment. I sent a text, to let him know they were there. He didn't respond.

Really looking forward to our Christmas together," Jack texted to me on Christmas Eve morning. Reading this simple sentiment made me feel high and hopeful. We hadn't fooled around in a long time; he'd been in and out of town for much of the fall, and then his beloved cat Pedro died, which had made him morose and withdrawn for several weeks. Spending Christmas together felt like an opportunity to reset our physical connection.

Jack had made us a reservation at a blandly beautiful restaurant on the ground floor of a blue-glass apartment tower with a view of the East River. After a technically great but largely forgettable tasting menu, we took a cab back to his apartment. I presented him with his Christmas gift, which was a batch of Rice Krispies treats cut into perfect three-inch-diameter circles, topped with a thick layer of chewy caramel jam, enrobed in tempered milk chocolate and garnished with flaky sea salt.

They were his favorite thing from Bouchon Bakery, where they'd been individually wrapped in fine gold foil and sold under the name "Fuhgeddaboudits," until their recent, inexplicable discontinuation. I found the recipe online, lifted by a blogger from *Bouchon Bakery* (the cookbook), and created a reasonably good dupe, using high-quality milk chocolate pastilles from the Michel Cluizel shop on Madison Avenue and Lyle's Golden Syrup from Kalustyan's for the fussy caramel jam. I arranged the treats in a Veuve Clicquot box I'd been holding on to for years.

"This is a fantastic gift, exactly what I wanted, thank you so much," Jack said, kissing me drily on the forehead. "I'm exhausted. Let's watch this new Sandra Bullock film."

The film was *Bird Box*, a brightly lit horror story about hysteria and mass suicide. Jack fell asleep after twenty minutes. I stayed awake for the whole thing, then slept very badly through the night, while dreaming that I ate a fine-dining meal alone in a dimly lit restaurant. The menu had no prices, but the waiter dropped a check for $373 plus gratuity. I handed him my Amex, then insisted upon cleaning the restaurant's bathroom. I scrubbed the sink and toilet with Clorox spray, in the process ruining my gray cashmere dress with bleach stains. When I finished cleaning and went to my job at a video rental store, I had an awful realization that the large, friendly dog who hung out under the counter was actually a mentally ill man in a dog suit.

Jack and I spent Christmas morning and afternoon eating Fuhgeddaboudits and watching beautifully shot, extremely violent Korean films. I put my hands in his hair, on the back of his neck; I caught his eye and put my hands on various parts of my own body.

"No," he said quietly, though it landed like a hard slap, and I turned my head so he wouldn't see the few hot tears of humiliation and sadness that slid from my eyes.

We had an early dinner reservation at Quality Eats, a pleases-everyone New American joint. There were lots of families with dressed-up young children; the dining room was too loud, and everyone seemed drunk. The only option was a prix-fixe menu of fancy

Chinese-ish dishes. Over pork dumplings doused with a slightly sugary chili oil, I said to Jack, "Do you even like me?"

"What are you talking about?"

"Why did you invite me to spend Christmas with you if you don't even want to touch me?"

"I care a great deal for you."

"You sound like you're talking to a dementia patient."

"Do we have to get into all of this? We've had a lovely Christmas together." I felt like the room was tilted, that I was watching him slowly slide away from me.

"Why can't you ever talk about anything? Why are you always so fucking obtuse?"

"I think I may be coming down with a cold," he said. "I need to be alone tonight."

I'd planned on staying at least one more night with Jack—it would be a few more days before Eli came to my place—but instead I went home on the subway, because he sent me home, and when I came up the stairs from the train tracks underground, I had an email from him, subject line:

BEING DIRECT

Since you asked, I do actually like you, and I think you know that, but I don't feel we were meant to be in a romantic relationship because, fundamentally, I can't trust you; you were cheating on your husband for years. While you were married, I found your situation and your conduct rather tawdry.

I've been sending out signals to you for a long time now that I didn't want to be more than close friends. I should have been more clear, but you've had a nightmarish several months in which the major moorings of your life became unpegged. Further, I'm British and therefore passive/non-confrontational; you're prone to agonizing about things that are much slighter than you read them to be, and with the death of Pedro, I've been at my emotional limit.

It's difficult for me to be direct with you because you are so sensitive, so prone to feelings of rejection and self-loathing. Even now, I imagine you curling up and retracting like an oyster hit with a squirt of lemon juice.

I think we ought to take a clean break from each other for a little while, then see how we do as friends. xx

For a few crushing hours between Christmas and Boxing Day, horribly lonely and now confronted by a truth I hadn't wanted to hear, there wasn't enough candy or sleep or trashy TV in the world to distract me from the pain of Jack's overt rejection. I felt a little closer to understanding Tony's last decision, though there's a yawning gulf between suicidal ideation and suicidal action, and it was never more than a thought experiment. I wanted to live.

One of the first suggestions my sponsor made, when I told her how hollowed out I felt about the end of the road with Jack, was to stay single for a year. She said I should sit with those feelings of sadness and longing, and know that I could survive through them.

"Develop your emotional sobriety," she said.

Fuck that, I thought, instead almost immediately taking up with a funny, charming, and down-to-earth chef with whom I'd been trading flirtatious Instagram DMs for months. He ran the flagship steakhouse of a small restaurant group. He was, like me, the divorced parent of an adolescent, and was free some evenings and every other weekend.

Being with the chef was such a lovely contrast to being with Jack, that inconsistent slot machine of a man. He was warm, honest, and straightforward, totally into monogamy, and eager to cook for me: porcini risotto made the same way he'd done it as a line cook at Daniel; crunchy, feathery eggplant Parmesan, layered with ricotta, taught to him by a friend's Italian grandma; tender, garlicky pernil with arroz con gandules (pigeon peas and rice) the way his uncle made it the Bronx. We had an easy chemistry and made each other laugh, and for the first several months, it seemed that we were exceptionally compatible.

When his company tapped him to open a new restaurant, he began working much longer hours, mornings into late nights with no days off. He didn't have much time to see me, or to even speak on the phone or think about anything but the menu, hiring cooks, setting up the walk-in, training new dishwashers. On the rare occasions that we connected by phone, he'd complain about work for a few minutes, then beg off so that he could get back to it. We were mutually frustrated with each other—he with my need for more attention, me with his workaholic tunnel vision—and I figured we wouldn't make it through the first six months of the new restaurant, which was open only six weeks when COVID rolled through the world and shut it down.

The chef fled New York City for the Catskills, a few hours' drive north, and we limped through a year as a long-distance couple, seeing each other, almost always on his turf, about once a month.

He came to visit me one time, for one night. Just before he arrived, I went to Zabar's and loaded up on belly lox, sturgeon, whitefish salad, bagels, cream cheese, chocolate babka, and black and white cookies. I made homemade sofrito, spiked it with a packet of Goya Sazón, and mixed it into my first attempt at arroz con gandules.

"Very 'white girl,' but not bad for a first try," he said, mixing a second packet of Sazón into the peas. He didn't want to talk much, just wanted to watch movies, so that's what we did. He chose *No Country for Old Men*, the brilliant, super-violent Coen brothers western, which we both loved, then it was my turn.

"This is one of my favorites," I said, pressing play on *Phantom Thread*, Paul Thomas Anderson's portrait of a fastidious, withholding dressmaker and his frustrated younger muse, which the chef hated and proceeded to roast mercilessly. "What's she *whining* about? Look at how nice their house is. She should just cook the asparagus the way he likes it."

When he broke up with me over the phone a few weeks later, telling me, "I don't feel the same way about you anymore," I had a physical pain in my chest and a humiliated rage that made me want to drink a bottle of wine and burn the world down. I hung up on him and logged on to a Zoom 12-step meeting and told a bunch of sober strangers about my pain.

I didn't drink wine or anything else, both because I had no booze in my home and because I had learned, over my few years of sobriety, that as bad as I felt about the breakup, drinking would only create new problems. The practice of tracking my accumulated sober time was an effective guardrail, as it would have been humiliating to reset my day count. Still, every second I was awake, I yearned to change the channel on this latest misery, to feel less awful about getting dumped from afar.

My sponsor once again suggested remaining single for a while, to work on my "emotional sobriety." I weakly protested that I didn't really know what that meant, that the term wasn't anywhere in the 12-step literature, and it sounded like it might be some woo-woo bullshit. She texted me an article from *Scientific American*, which summarized the research conducted on the topic at Stanford:

> *The idea is that alcoholics and other addicts hoping to stay sober over the long haul must learn to regulate the negative feelings that can lead to discomfort, craving and—ultimately—relapse. Doing so is a lifelong project and requires cultivating a whole new way of thinking about life's travails.*

OK, cool, very helpful, I texted back, but the minute I passed the two-week waiting period after the new COVID vaccine, I set up an online dating profile.

That summer, while I spent all of my time and energy on the ego balm of no-strings dalliances, my mother's fragile health began to collapse in a series of infections, seizures, and bizarre personality shifts, necessitating multiple hospital and rehab stays. "Circling the drain" was a phrase I'd heard her use when describing the decline of various older relatives; now, when she was lucid enough to speak about her condition, my mother turned it on herself.

I called her one early fall afternoon, on the landline telephone next to her bed, in the nursing facility where she'd just been settled. Her caretaking needs were now beyond what my father could safely manage at home. Open beds were hard to come by, because of COVID restrictions, and the institution she'd landed in was not great by any metric, but it was the only place in three counties that had room after her latest hospital discharge.

"This place is awful," she said. "They don't have enough people working here, and the girls that're here suck *shit*. They dress really slutty and they're on their phones when they change the bedpan, if they even bother to come in at all. The other night a couple of them set off the fire alarm because they were smoking so much weed in the hallway. I'm lying in my own piss all night. I'm ready to die, if this is my life."

"*Mom.*"

"Do me a favor: no obituary. No funeral. Just scatter my ashes at Nicky Doodles."

This was a dark joke; Nicky Doodles is an ice cream stand, where you can get a soft-serve cone, about twenty-five flavors of hard-packed Hershey's, various sundaes and shakes, plus burgers and fries and hot ham sandwiches.

About a week after that, a bed opened up in a much better facility, and my dad arranged for her transport there, by ambulance. Still, she'd be dead within six weeks of that conversation, shortly after Nicky Doodles closed down for the winter. Her ashes are buried in the same cemetery where the bodies of the rest of her side of the family are or will someday be.

In those last six weeks, my mother's eyesight became unreliable, and for days at a time, she couldn't read a book or watch jarringly full-volume Facebook videos on her iPad. Her fingers stopped working to the point that she could no longer operate her Jitterbug phone or the

TV remote. When she could no longer hold a utensil to feed herself, I think she stopped trying to live.

One early November afternoon, the last time I saw my mom sitting up, wearing lipstick and earrings, an aide who might have been all of twenty-five years old came into the room, pushing a tray on a cart.

"I'm here to give you lunch!" she chirped, and it was clear that she meant to feed my mother like a baby. I held my breath.

"I'm not hungry," said my mother, and I could see the lights inside her blinking off.

The aide retreated with the tray, and my mother asked me about my new boyfriend, for whom I had just deleted the dating app from my phone. She seemed satisfied when I said that he was nice, and that I was happy. Just before I left, she asked me to kiss her cheek, and I did, though I felt embarrassed for both of us by the intimacy of the gesture. She had never asked for it before. We were not affectionate people.

The last thing she said to me before she died two weeks later was "I don't have a bra on." She'd been moved to a private alcove next to the nurses' station, and was indeed not wearing a bra, only a hospital gown, lying under layers of flannel and cotton blankets, eyes closed, metabolizing alarming quantities of morphine and Ativan. The drugs made her hallucinate and shake and mumble mostly nonsense. Why was the (imaginary) dog eating her food? When was the last time my nephew washed his hair? Why was there peanut butter in the Advil? She'd occasionally stop talking to take a little juice or water from a sponge that one of us held up her mouth. From the CD player in the corner came languid instrumental versions of "Send in the Clowns" and "Yankee Doodle Dandy" and some deep cuts from the *Annie* soundtrack. *This is some real last-rites shit*, I thought, only I didn't actually believe it was the end, because she had weirdly impressive grip strength. One of us was always holding her hand, and when it was me, I thought, *There's no way she's dying right now.*

A few hours into the maybe-vigil, an aide wheeled in a cart with a pitcher of coffee, juice boxes, packets of Oreos, Lorna Doones, Fig Newtons, and Cheez-Its, and that's when I knew my mother's death was imminent. You didn't get these snacks if your loved one was just having a bad day. Still, when I left that evening, I told her, "I'll be back for Thanksgiving. See you next week." She was quiet then, and she died two days later, while I was back in New York. When my sister called to tell me the news, I was unsurprised and hugely relieved. I walked to the grocery store and bought all the things I needed to make a batch of macaroni and cheese for me and Eli, who would be home from school soon.

Epilogue
Jujubes and Diamonds

As I write this, I have six years of total sobriety, and, recently, I've taken the suggestion of fellow alcoholics, to engage in prayer. It's not a regular practice; it's more something I do when I'm feeling splenetic and catch myself muttering one of my decades-old mantras (usually "fuck you" or "kill me") on the inhale and the exhale. That's when I'll sometimes remember to say, or think, "Thank you, god, for keeping me sober today."

For me, an agnostic, prayer feels like "fake it till you make it" behavior, but so far it's the closest I've come to a meditation practice (which is another thing that 12-steppers swear by). Those few words are a quiet little reset, and reminder of how far I have come since my years of blackout drinking and getting stoned and lying all the time, trying to fill a hole in a life (mine) that was actually already quite full. It's an acknowledgment that a terrible sober day is almost always better than my dim memory of a great loaded one. And it's a reminder that I got sober, and I stay sober, with the help of others. For me, the word *god* is shorthand for a higher power of my understanding: the entropy-defying human inclination to work together, caring for and about each other.

I used to think that the only way to do things was to ruinous excess, and for a while after I quit drinking, I thought that my relatively mild rock-bottom moment—just some alcoholic shaky hands and a missed flight—was sort of weak bullshit. I couldn't see then how lucky I was to have pulled out of the nosedive long before the ground became visible (though I did plenty of damage, to my doomed marriage and my mental health, on my way down). "Thank you, god, for keeping me sober today" reminds me to be grateful that I didn't have to lose it all before I found another way to live. It is a privilege to be upright, happy, and alive.

Here are some of the guidelines I've learned from 12-step meetings, the associated literature, and conversations with people in recovery: be honest, acknowledge your part in any situation, keep perspective, let go of self-centered thinking, help others, don't drink. So far, the only one I've been able to do without fail is "don't drink," but by bearing the rest in mind, I've calmed down, stayed sober, and cobbled together a career as a writer.

Being "just" a writer used to seem financially impossible to me, and in lean times it still does, though I am lucky to have a few people in my life who can lend me money when I need it. I clean my own (rented) home, rarely buy new clothes, never get takeout, and do not own a car. All my streaming services are the cheap versions, with ads, which is how I know that every new pharmacist-dispensed drug has a stupid fucking name with multiple unlikely combinations of consonants, and will snuff out your eczema, at the cost of diarrhea and organ failure.

When my bank balance dips below a particularly anemic number, I think about a scene in the classic 1987 film *Dirty Dancing*, right before working-class dance instructor Johnny Castle (Patrick Swayze) and upper-middle-class teenager Francis "Baby" Houseman (Jennifer Grey) submit to their long-smoldering sex tension. Johnny describes his poverty to Baby, whom he is about to deflower:

"You don't understand the way it is, I mean for somebody like me. Last month, I'm eating jujubes to keep alive, and this month, women are stuffing diamonds in my pocket. I'm balancing on shit as quick as that [snaps his fingers] I could be down there again."

Shortly after Tony Bourdain died, while contemplating an all-jujube diet in a haze of grief and confusion, I was lucky enough to have a diamond stuffed into my pocket, in the form of a contract for *Bourdain: The Definitive Oral Biography*, which, in concert with the advance from *World Travel: An Irreverent Guide*, already in progress, was enough to keep me and my kid in store-brand peanut butter and shitty health insurance for about three years. The financial cushion from those two books gave me the space to process Tony's death as I dived into his whole story, getting to better understand him through talking to, and writing about, the people who helped define his singular life.

If Tony were still alive, I'd almost certainly still be working for him, maybe collaborating on a new book, instead of having written this one. If Mario Batali hadn't been outed as a predator, I wouldn't have felt safe writing about my experiences working for him. If my mother were still alive, I wouldn't have written all these truths about myself, because I spent my whole life as her daughter trying to protect her from knowing who I really was, and what motivated me, though she may have known but was too polite to say. This is the hand I've been dealt, and how I chose to play it.

E ven after the great #MeToo reckoning that began in 2017, and COVID, and after so many years in and around it, participating and observing, I don't know how much the hospitality industry has changed since 1998, the year I graduated from culinary school. Are restaurants any more or less "toxic" than the worlds of politics, media, education, healthcare, manufacturing, the arts, religion, finance, or law? These are all institutions, made up of people, many of them good-natured, a few not so much. The conditions improve or deteriorate, through some combination of global and local politics, big decisions, shifts in the weather, trifles of fate. Everything moves in cycles, the pendulum swings, the think piece goes viral. People sometimes screw up and get caught, and then there are consequences, or sometimes there aren't consequences. We'll all continue to make mistakes, because some things can't be litigated out of human nature: hunger, thirst, our need for validation, our sex drive, our stubbornness, our pride, our base desire to be distracted from the certainty of death.

People are imperfect; sometimes we hurt each other, a little or a lot, accidentally or with full intent. I know now that all we can do is try to learn from the fallout, do a little better the next time, and continue to take care of each other as best we know how.

Acknowledgments

I am extremely grateful to Jessica Troy, Alison Tozzi Liu, Kim Reed, Ben Arthur, Nat Ives, Javier Romero, Christine Bastoni, Owen Dugan, and Julie Lauck, my smart and generous friends who acted as early readers, and whose feedback made this book much better.

Thank you to my editor, Gabriella Doob, who is patient and encouraging, asks all the right questions, and makes me feel like a real writer. Thank you to Kim Witherspoon and Jessica Mileo for looking out for me. Thank you to Helen Atsma, Sonya Cheuse, Miriam Parker, Meghan Deans, Allison Saltzman, David Koral, TJ Calhoun, and everyone at Ecco and HarperCollins who work hard and believe in the power of books.

Many thanks to the following people who weighed in on the details, offered advice, showed me something new, and/or made it possible to have so many stories to tell: Jared Andrukanis, Vidya Balachander, Nancy Bourdain, Margaret Braun, Maria Bustillos, Helen Cho, Christen Clifford, Jennifer Cohan, Mitchell Davis, Lisa Donovan, Charlotte Druckman, Forty-Sixth Street Clubhouse, Jennifer Gross, Johanna Gutlerner, Anya Hoffman, Tracy Jones, Samarra Khaja, Yasmin Khan, Ivy Knight, Adam Koppels, the Kornblum family, Stefanie Koseff, Kate Krader, Cory Leadbeater,

Sarah Lefton, Youngmi Mayer, Wade Moises, Erika Mooney, Antonio Mora, New Phoenix, Andy Nusser, Patty Nusser, Tamara Reynolds, Naz Riahi, Blythe Roberson, Rebecca Scott, Robert Taylor, Chris Thornton, Alicia Anne Tobin, Seth Unger, and Emily Zeeberg.

Thank you to Joan, who helped me figure myself out, on a generous sliding scale.

Tony Bourdain is gone but I'll thank him anyway, for modeling what it is to be a good boss, a curious person, and a man who used his power to lift others up.

Thank you Café Bustelo, Lucky Charms, and Zoloft.

A huge loving thank-you to my mom and dad, my sister, my son, Mark, and Rooster.